Manufacturing Mennonites
Work and Religion in Post-War Manitoba

Manufacturing Mennonites examines the efforts of Mennonite intellectuals and business leaders to redefine the group's ethno-religious identity in response to changing economic and social conditions after 1945. As the industrial workplace was one of the most significant venues in which competing identity claims were contested during this period, Janis Thiessen explores how Mennonite workers responded to such redefinitions and how they affected class relations.

Through unprecedented access to extensive private company records, Thiessen provides an innovative comparison of three businesses founded, owned, and originally staffed by Mennonites: the printing firm Friesens Corporation, the window manufacturer Loewen, and the furniture manufacturer Palliser. Complemented with interviews with workers, managers, and business owners, *Manufacturing Mennonites* pioneers two important new trajectories for scholarship – how religion can affect business history, and how class relations have influenced religious history.

JANIS THIESSEN is an assistant professor in the Department of History at the University of Winnipeg.

Manufacturing Mennonites

Work and Religion in Post-War Manitoba

Janis Thiessen

UNIVERSITY OF TORONTO PRESS
Toronto Buffalo London

© University of Toronto Press 2013
Toronto Buffalo London
www.utppublishing.com
Printed in Canada

ISBN 978-1-4426-4213-3 (cloth)
ISBN 978-1-4426-1113-9 (paper)

Printed on acid-free, 100% post-consumer recycled paper with
vegetable-based inks

Library and Archives Canada Cataloguing in Publication

Thiessen, Janis, 1971–
Manufacturing Mennonites : work and religion in post-war
Manitoba / Janis Thiessen.

Includes bibliographical references and index.
ISBN 978-1-4426-4213-3 (bound)   ISBN 978-1-4426-1113-9 (pbk.)

1. Mennonites – Manitoba – History – 20th century.   2. Work – Religious aspects –
Mennonites.   3. Economics – Religious aspects – Mennonites.
4. Christian sociology – Mennonites.   I. Title.

BX8128.E36T55 2013   289.7'7127   C2012-907219-2

University of Toronto Press acknowledges the financial assistance to its publishing program of the Canada Council for the Arts and the Ontario Arts Council.

 Canada Council **Conseil des Arts**
for the Arts **du Canada**

ONTARIO ARTS COUNCIL
CONSEIL DES ARTS DE L'ONTARIO
50 YEARS OF ONTARIO GOVERNMENT SUPPORT OF THE ARTS
50 ANS DE SOUTIEN DU GOUVERNEMENT DE L'ONTARIO AUX ARTS

University of Toronto Press acknowledges the financial support of the Government of Canada through the Canada Book Fund for its publishing activities.

This book has been published with the help of a grant from the Canadian Federation for the Humanities and Social Sciences, through the Awards to Scholarly Publications Program, using funds provided by the Social Sciences and Humanities Research Council.

For 'the Folks'

and especially
Frank James Thiessen
1925–2005

Contents

Acknowledgments

This project would have been impossible without the patience and generosity of the factory workers who were so willing to share their stories. My heartfelt thanks to them for their hospitality and willing participation. A study of privately held companies would be challenging indeed without the cooperation of their owners. I am grateful to David Glenn Friesen and Ted Friesen of Friesens Corporation, Charles Loewen and Clyde Loewen of Loewen, and Art DeFehr of Palliser Furniture for their openness to my research. They exercised no editorial control over the final product.

Others played a significant supporting role in this project. My former employer (Westgate Mennonite Collegiate) generously granted me two leaves of absence: the first, to conduct the research as a doctoral student; the second, to revise the manuscript while simultaneously commencing a new research project as a postdoctoral fellow. Much welcome financial support was provided by the Social Sciences and Humanities Research Council of Canada (for both doctoral and postdoctoral fellowships) and by the University of New Brunswick, Fredericton. The staff of a number of organizations provided much-needed aid in locating source material: the Library and Archives Canada; the University of Manitoba Archives; the Provincial Archives of Manitoba; the Mennonite Heritage Centre Archives; the Legislative Library of Manitoba; the Manitoba Companies Office; Manitoba Labour and Immigration, Workplace Safety and Health Division; Mennonite Central Committee (Manitoba); Mennonite Economic Development Associates; the Harriet Irving Library of the University of New Brunswick (Fredericton); the Elizabeth Dafoe Library of the University of Manitoba; the Jake Epp Library in Steinbach, Manitoba; and the Altona and District Heritage Research Centre in Altona, Manitoba.

This study owes its origins to Kathryn Young, who encouraged my first ventures into Mennonite labour history while I was a student at the University of Manitoba. As the supervisor of my MA thesis, Gerald Friesen introduced me to business history and the rigours of graduate study. The research and writing of this project were further developed under the tutelage of the Winnipeg Immigration History Research Group, led by Metropolis Project researchers Royden Loewen and Gerald Friesen. My doctoral dissertation, supervised by Gregory Kealey with input from Margaret Conrad and Gary Waite, was an earlier and considerably different version of this book. The ad hoc dissertation discussion group at the University of New Brunswick offered moral support and valuable comments on draft chapters of that dissertation. I was blessed to receive the advice and critique of a number of academics, colleagues, mentors, and friends, including Marlene Epp, Nolan Reilly, Bruno Dyck, and the late Roy Vogt. Suggestions by Kirk Niergarth, Alexander Freund, and Mark Gabbert shaped my analysis in key chapters and challenged my interpretation. Doug Durksen proposed the book's title. Royden Loewen kindly read multiple drafts and participated in innumerable conversations during various stages of the writing. The manuscript in its current form was improved greatly by his editorial advice, as well as that of Bob Hummelt, Gerald Friesen, and the anonymous reviewers of University of Toronto Press. I am indebted as well to Len Husband and the editorial team at UTP.

Finally, I am grateful to my parents, Frank and Margret Thiessen, who functioned as a sounding board and newspaper-clipping service for many years. This book is dedicated to my father, Frank James Thiessen, who believed in the importance of integrating one's identity as a Mennonite and as a worker without compromising either.

Manufacturing Mennonites
Work and Religion in Post-War Manitoba

Introduction

A few ethnic and religious groups, not including the Mennonites, dominate the literature in Canadian labour history. The traditions of labour radicalism within the Jewish, Finnish, and Ukrainian communities, for example, are examined in numerous publications, as are the work narratives of Italian immigrants.[1] But Mennonites, if they are thought of at all, are connected with Old Order barn raising or with images of farming without the benefit of rubber-tired tractors. By contrast, the agrarian and entrepreneurial roles of Mennonites in Canada and the United States have been addressed in survey works by sociologist Calvin Redekop and historians Frank Epp, Ted Regehr, and Royden Loewen.[2] The history of Mennonites as industrial workers within twentieth-century North American capitalism remains largely unexplored.

Mennonites' behaviour often has not conformed to traditional understandings of labour struggle and resistance. Mennonites may have been the 'left wing of the Reformation' in the words of historian Roland Bainton, but they were certainly not known in the twentieth century as radicals of the labour movement.[3] Union records, which remain important primary sources in labour history, are virtually useless when studying North American Mennonite workers in this century, as these workers tended to be non-unionized.[4] If this kind of traditional labour history is not an option, how does one study Mennonite labour? Is there even a Mennonite working class to be studied?

What little statistical information is available reveals that this neglected group constituted a significant portion of the North American

Table I.1. North American Mennonite occupations (%)

Occupation	1972	1989
Professional	16	28
Business proprietor/manager	5	9
Sales/clerical workers	7	11
Craftspeople	5	5
Machine operators	5	4
Service workers	4	4
Farmers	11	7
Labourers	2	1
Housewives/husbands	32	25
Students	14	6

Source: Kauffman and Driedger, The Mennonite Mosaic, 38.

Mennonite population in the late twentieth century. Counting only those who are baptized members of Mennonite and Brethren in Christ churches,[5] there were more than 1.3 million Mennonites worldwide in 2003; the third largest national group was Canadian Mennonites, numbering 127,851.[6] Within Canada, Manitoba had more Mennonites in 2001 than any other province (51,540), and Winnipeg had the highest urban concentration of Mennonites in the world (18,240).[7] A survey of North American Mennonite church members in 1972 by Kauffman and Harder showed that some 23 per cent of Mennonites at that time were working class (which they defined to include sales/clerical workers, craftspeople, machine operators, service workers, and labourers). A 1989 survey by Kauffman and Driedger found that 25 per cent of North American Mennonites were working class (see table I.1). Another survey was conducted by the now defunct *Mennonite Reporter* in Winnipeg in 1980; researcher Elfrieda Rempel found that 27 per cent of Winnipeg Mennonites were blue-collar workers.[8]

It is surprising then that so little has been written, even by Mennonites, about a group that comprises roughly one-quarter of all Mennonites in North America. Not only is the Mennonite working class itself neglected, but 'practically no discussion [of work] exists' in Anabaptist-Mennonite history and theology,[9] declares Calvin Redekop in *The Global Anabaptist Mennonite Encyclopedia*. A perusal of the index for *Mennonite Quarterly Review*, the oldest North American academic journal of Mennonite history, supports this view. Since its founding in 1927, only two articles were published on the topic of 'industrial relations' – the first in 1939 and the second sixty years later.[10]

Readers may have difficulty categorizing this study as it attempts to address some gaps in the literature. It is simultaneously a labour history, a business history, a history of 'lived religion,'[11] an intellectual history in so far as it examines theology – and, above all, it is a social history. While conversations between some of these fields have occurred, too often it is religion that continues to be omitted from the debate. Specialists in any one of these fields may feel that their area of expertise receives inadequate emphasis, but that is the risk of the approach taken here.

Business history is a comparatively new field in the discipline of history. Fogel and Engerman's *The Redefinition of American Economic History* ushered in cliometrics (the mathematical analysis of history) in 1971 and led to the division of economic history into a statistics-focused economic history and an institution-focused business history.[12] Alfred Chandler's publication of *The Visible Hand* in 1977 dominated the field of business history for decades, turning the focus from the role of entrepreneurs to that of management in the success of large-scale industries.[13]

Social history has been successfully – though insufficiently – integrated into the study of business history. Scholars have incorporated the roles of state intervention, small business, family firms, ethnicity, gender, and culture.[14] The organization and management of a business, management scholar Gordon Redding asserts, are culturally dependent in that they 'do not consist of making or moving tangible objects, but of manipulating symbols which have meaning to the people who are managed or organized.'[15] His is a view shared by business historian Pamela Walker Laird, who notes that 'business decisions are not always about business, narrowly speaking. Instead, they are often complicated by social and cultural considerations, including social capital's blend of cultural values and social mechanisms.'[16] Redding invokes anthropologist Clifford Geertz's notion of 'thick description,' arguing that international business theory needs to draw on history, culture, and geography in a more systematic manner.[17] Social historian John Walton agrees that business history remains too wedded to Chandler, and its engagement with other fields of history is unsatisfactory.[18] Indeed, he asserts that some of the 'liveliest' business historians are not, in fact, business historians: he cites Patrick Joyce's work on paternalism as an example.[19]

Despite these calls for, and examples of, the integration of social history and business history, 'lived religion' and business history remain independent fields of study. Much as labour history has expanded beyond the bounds of institutions and organizations to explore the social history of the working class, so too has the study of religion; the focus has shifted from denominational studies to investigations of religion as lived in people's everyday lives. While race, ethnicity, and gender have been incorporated into the study of religious history, class (and thus labour history and business history) remains largely ignored.[20] Historian Patrick Pasture notes the limited attention religion has received from labour historians, and suggests they need to become more 'open and reflective' towards religious history.[21] Another related problem is the neglect of the twentieth century in the study of lived religion; historians have embraced the secularization thesis and fail to see the continued relevance of religious beliefs for many in the modern world.[22] This study of Mennonite-owned businesses in Manitoba, then, is a step towards addressing these absences and integrating these disparate fields. My exploration of Mennonite religious identity in the workplace attempts to answer Laurence Moore's challenge that historians 'should investigate how religion, among other sorts of institutions, operates within particular societies to reify particular structures of inequality.'[23]

The study of lived religion entails risks, however. Robert Orsi, an oral historian and scholar of lived religion, observes that the researcher's 'most deeply held existential orientations and moral values are on display with an obviousness not found in earlier ethnographic or, especially, historical accounts.'[24] Nor are the dangers confined to the researcher. Interview participants can be 'hesitant or unable to talk about their beliefs ... There may be generational or denominational differences in the narrator's comfort level when talking about religion, with younger people and those in groups that emphasize testifying more able to verbalize their inner experience.'[25] Awareness of one's own biases and respect for interview participants' views can be complicated by a common religious background. Participants may make assumptions about the researcher, ascribing a shared philosophy that may or may not exist. The researcher may make assumptions about the meanings behind a participant's words, interpreting from her own experience rather than that of her informant. 'The challenge of a lived religion approach is to balance carefully and self-reflectively on the border between familiarity and difference, strangeness and recognizability, whether in relation to people in the past or in another cultural world.'[26] Such challenges are not limited to the work of oral historians, though, as the work of postmodern theorists has made all historians more aware of the problems of discourse analysis.

Even discounting these recent trends in the fields of business, oral, and religious history, the secondary literature on business in Manitoba is limited at best. There are few studies of industry in Manitoba that are not corporate commissioned histories, and even fewer that are comparative social histories rather than single industry studies. The Manitoba Trucking Association, for example, commissioned the writing of *Trucking in Manitoba: A History*, which focuses on legislation and, to a lesser extent, economics and its effects on the trucking industry.[27] A history of market gardening in the province is a notable exception, with consideration given to Aboriginal and (im)migrant farmers and farm workers, marketing cooperatives, government legislation regulating farm workers, and international trade agreements.[28] Henry Klassen's *A Business History of Alberta* similarly focuses on federal and provincial government regulations, corporate structures, and biographies of entrepreneurs; there is no similar comprehensive, scholarly overview of the history of business in Manitoba.[29]

As for studies incorporating Mennonites, businesses and their founders have received far more scholarly attention than workers and their relations with their employers. Calvin Redekop's assertion that business is 'one of the most underrated, ignored, and misunderstood topics in Mennonite life' is no longer tenable, though it is an argument with a curious persistence, which in itself says something about class relations within the North American Mennonite community. A variety of works recount the personal histories of individual Mennonite business owners. Some are privately published memoirs.[30] Other works attempt to find commonalities in the experiences of Mennonite entrepreneurs in Canada and the United States.[31]

Economist Roy Vogt was among the first to criticize the tendency to promote triumphalist entrepreneurialism over labour history.[32] Vogt deplores the focus on the relationship of Mennonite entrepreneurs to their church congregations at the expense of the arguably far more

significant shop-floor relationships. 'The modern business organization is a highly inter-dependent social organism in which the dreams
and aspirations of hundreds and more persons are played out. This is
the community in which most entrepreneurs spend by far the largest
portion of their time. What does it mean to foster community values
in such a setting? This question is not even asked in these studies.'[33]
Further, the role of the entrepreneur in the Mennonite church is open
to different interpretations. When employers and employees worship
in the same congregation, is this indeed evidence of employer-worker
solidarity? Or does the cartoon drawn by a worker at one Mennonite
business, depicting the employer praying in front of his workers with
his folded hands clasped tightly around the neck of a worker, convey a
more accurate truth?[34] Vogt warned that work in this field would remain
'suspect and parochial' unless and until academics ask more challenging questions and examine the history of Mennonites from a more critical standpoint.[35]

A valuable counterpoint to the entrepreneurial and business histories
Vogt critiques are the very small number of works that present the oral
histories of employees.[36] In some instances, the perspective of workers
differs greatly from that of their employers with respect to labour relations and the attempted integration of religious identity and economic
practice.[37] A few studies examine the gendered and ethnically divided
labour process, noting that Mennonite religious commitments were not
always sufficient to overcome shop-floor tensions.[38]

In addition to these rare worker histories, there are a limited number
of studies in the fields of economics and sociology.[39] Vogt contributes
one of the few explicit academic examinations of Mennonite workers
with his investigation of the effects of class position on religious beliefs
among North American Mennonites.[40] He makes use of unpublished
data from the 1972 Church Membership Profile, which assessed Mennonites' degree of adherence to Anabaptist principles, pacifism, and
fundamentalism; their attitudes towards ecumenism, political participation, relations with other races, and the role of women; their degree
of social and religious prejudice; and their stance regarding organized
labour and communism.

Vogt uses the 1972 data to compare the responses of professionals,
business people, farmers, and blue-collar workers. The 1972 profile had
divided the Canadian and American respondents into four socio-eco-

Table I.2. Beliefs of North American Mennonites, differentiated by class, 1972. Workers who scored 'high' on issue (%)

Type of issue	Professional	Business	Farmer	Blue collar
Anabaptism	48	34	55	48
Pacifism	45	25	34	21
Fundamentalism	18	39	52	47
Political participation	64	50	57	41
Race relations (favourable)	53	28	20	24
Social prejudice	6	24	34	24
Ecumenism	30	21	15	17
Role of women (favourable)	43	23	15	17
Religious prejudice (against Jews, Catholics)	13	26	28	24
Anti-labour	16	21	30	25
Anti-communism	12	27	25	28

Source: Vogt, 'Impact of Economic and Social Class,' 145.

nomic groups on the basis of their education, occupation, and income, which blurred distinctions between business people and professionals. Vogt re-examines the raw data to take into consideration such differences (see table I.2).

Four of the scales in this table require further clarification. The Anabaptism scale included questions that tested adherence to the 'Anabaptist Vision.'[41] The pacifism scale included questions regarding opposition to war and militarism and support of peacemaking. The fundamentalism scale questioned whether respondents believed in the virgin birth of Jesus, the Great Flood, the inerrancy of the Bible, Christ as Saviour from eternal punishment, and the literal interpretation of Genesis. The anti-labour scale investigated attitudes towards and involvement in labour unions.

The data reveals that in the 1970s North American Mennonite blue-collar workers[42] were more opposed to union membership than most other Mennonites. They were less committed to gender equity and pacifism and less interested in political involvement than Mennonites in other occupations. Vogt explains these responses in terms of the degree of Mennonites' involvement in the class struggle. He maintains that one of the attractions of the white-collar professions for many Mennonites is that these occupations permit them to be commentators on, though not participants in, class struggle.[43] The Mennonite worker, by contrast, cannot withdraw from class struggle, and subsequently 'becomes conservative and inner-directed in his religion and selectively uses Anabaptist principles to thwart those forces in his immediate environment which most threaten him. Such principles are dropped, however, when world problems are considered.'[44] Vogt concludes that neither professionals nor blue-collar workers 'really [want] to be involved in urban society. The professional withdraws and then pretends that he is involved. The nonprofessional is really involved, but pretends that he isn't.'[45]

The historical experience of Mennonites is important in understanding their adaptation to the industrial work experience. Mennonites arrived in Manitoba from Russia in 1874 and settled south of Winnipeg on two reserves of land set aside for them by the Canadian government. Farmers constituted the first immigrant group. The arrival of more educated and urbanized Russian Mennonites in the 1920s and the decline of the small family farm resulted in Mennonites moving to Winnipeg to establish or find work in businesses, a process that accelerated dramatically after the Second World War. In 1941, 87 per cent of Canadian Mennonites lived in rural areas; by 1971, that figure had dropped to 53 per cent.[46] This rural-to-urban migration necessitated a re-examination and recreation of Mennonite religious identity.

Historically, Mennonites have made use of traditions, experiences, and influences external to themselves to shape their identity. Sociologist Calvin Redekop observes that persecution, pietism, humanism, nationalism, religious fundamentalism, and education all have influenced Mennonites' understanding of themselves. By the end of the twentieth century, the pace, scope, and quantity of change was so great that integration of broader cultural phenomena with Mennonite identity became difficult.[47]

The subsequent diversity of definitions of Mennonite identity has resulted in efforts to reduce Mennonitism to either religious or ethnic traits.[48] Sociologist Daphne Naomi Winland has argued that both religious and ethnic components are necessary to the definition of Mennonite identity and that the integration of these components is continually renegotiated.[49] Accordingly, Mennonite identity is not a static set of religious and ethnic attributes, but is historically conditioned and subject to ongoing transformation.[50]

This century was not the first in which Mennonites examined the interplay between their religious beliefs and their economic circumstances. From their beginnings in the sixteenth century, Mennonites have been interested in economic questions from a religious perspective. No division was made by the sixteenth-century Anabaptists between the realms of the secular and the sacred.[51] Indeed, for the Anabaptists, the validity of one's spiritual beliefs was revealed by their application in the material world.[52] A key New Testament passage was the last half of chapter 2 of the Letter of James, culminating in the words: 'faith without works is dead.'[53] According to Mennonite economist Roy Vogt, the influence of these early Anabaptist examinations of the connection between faith and economics lingers today in such Mennonite principles as the rejection of the use of force in labour relations, the importance of a simple lifestyle, the refusal to exploit labour, and the treatment of all property as common though such property is privately owned.[54] The practical operation (or absence) of these religious principles in Mennonite-owned businesses, though, has rarely been studied.[55]

Nor was the twentieth century the first time in which changing economic and social conditions resulted in redefinition of ethno-religious identity by Mennonites. The acculturation of Dutch Mennonites in seventeenth-century 'Golden Age' Netherlands presents some parallels to this study of twentieth-century Canadian Mennonites. With the transition to capitalism in the Low Countries, many Mennonites became wealthy business owners, merchants, and shippers. They questioned how to apply Mennonite religious principles to their business activities.[56] As early as 1649, Dutch Mennonites were publishing books on business ethics which critiqued capitalism and consumption.[57] At the same time, these writings justified capital accumulation provided that profits benefited the community rather than the individual; thus 'Mennonites could go about their businesses without guilt.'[58] In practice, many of these Dutch Mennonites gave generously to the poor while simultaneously indulging in conspicuous consumption. They rationalized such contradictory behaviour by convincing themselves that 're-structuring society was not on their agenda, for God had created the rich and the poor.'[59]

Three centuries later and a continent away, twentieth-century North American Mennonites continued the debate regarding how to reconcile their religious beliefs with the capitalist system in which they were immersed. This interaction of religion and economics raises a variety of questions. How have ethno-religious groups redefined their identity in response to changing economic and social conditions? Conversely, how have they attempted to use their ethno-religious identity to shape those material circumstances themselves? Have these processes transformed the unity of ethno-religious communities over time? These are questions that can best be answered through comparative micro-histories of businesses and workforces, using an approach that acknowledges the interaction of ethno-religious identity, corporate structure, and the labour process. This book explores these questions in the context of the post-war Mennonite community in Manitoba.

Three major Canadian businesses, founded, owned, and originally staffed by Mennonites, are the geographic focus of this study. These three companies, all based in Manitoba, are Friesen Printers, Loewen Windows, and Palliser Furniture.[60] These companies were chosen to provide a representative sample of Mennonite manufacturing in Manitoba. All three are national leaders in their fields. In addition, they were situated in three different but well-established Mennonite communities in Manitoba.

Friesen Printers is located in Altona, a town in Manitoba's Mennonite West Reserve. One of Canada's largest printers, it had more than six hundred employees in 2003. The company was established in 1933 when David K. Friesen, a descendant of Russian Mennonite immigrants of the 1870s, bought a Gordon press. He operated this press for two years in the basement of the confectionery store of his father, David W. Friesen, and then bought a second press and rented his own building. Originally incorporated as D.W. Friesen & Sons in 1951, the business was renamed Friesens Corporation in 1995. While the company was involved briefly in publishing, in the early twenty-first century it specialized in printing full-colour art books, producing school yearbooks, and manufacturing Birks blue boxes.[61]

Loewen Windows was founded in 1905 by C.T. Loewen, a descendant of Russian Mennonite immigrants of the 1870s. Originally named C.T. Loewen & Sons, the business began as a lumber planing mill in Steinbach, a town in Manitoba's Mennonite East Reserve. The company began making windows in 1917. In 1972, the business was renamed Loewen Millwork, became Loewen Windows in 1985, and was christened Loewen in 2001. Loewen became Canada's largest wood window manufacturer, with more than one thousand employees in 2003.[62]

Palliser Furniture was founded by Abram A. DeFehr, a Russian Mennonite who immigrated to Canada via Mexico in 1924. Abram formed the A.A. DeFehr Furniture Manufacturing Company in the basement of his suburban Winnipeg home in 1944, making occasional tables and clothes-drying racks. Within two years, he had moved the operation into a factory in the same Winnipeg suburb of North Kildonan, an area heavily populated by Mennonites. Renamed Palliser Furniture, the company became Manitoba's second largest employer and Canada's largest manufacturer of wood and leather furniture. In 2003, the business employed more than five thousand workers.[63]

The research for this work incorporates the techniques and perspectives of labour, ethnic, gender, religious, and oral history, as well as theology. Interviews conducted with Mennonite workers as well as Mennonite business owners and managers are a major source for this study.[64] Oral narratives are no longer dismissed by historians as subjective, anecdotal accounts.[65] Historians, thanks in large part to the work of Alessandro Portelli, are aware that how an individual remembers an event is an important part of the event itself, and that individual memory is shaped by collective memory.[66] 'How people view their past is always grounded in their experience, but how they frame their remembrances depends on the social context.'[67] Thus individuals repress, reinterpret, and recall various experiences in accordance with their need to be part of a community and the community's need to create a mythic identity.[68] Marlene Epp, in her study of immigrant women's narratives of war and relocation, for example, observes that collective memory is particularly significant for a religious community – such as the Mennonites – that 'imbues history with religious significance and for whom, as has been said about the Jews, the memory of history is a religious duty.'[69] History thus is not the dry recollection of facts: it is the emotion-laden memories of historical actors.[70]

Interviews for this study were conducted under the auspices of the University of Manitoba's Faculty of Arts Ethics Review Committee and the University of New Brunswick's Research Ethics Board. Five interviews were conducted with workers and managers at Friesen Printers in 1995 as part of the research for a Master of Arts in history at the University of Manitoba. Thirty-one interviews were arranged with workers and managers at various Manitoba Mennonite businesses from 1996 to 1999 while I was employed as a research associate with the Winnipeg Immigration History Research Group, under the direction of Gerald Friesen and Royden Loewen and affiliated with the Prairie Centre of Excellence for Research on Immigration and Integration (the Metropolis Project). Interviews with an additional thirty workers and managers at Loewen Windows were held in 2003 while I was a doctoral student at the University of New Brunswick.

Potential interviewees were identified primarily by use of snowball sampling. At my request, the president of Friesen Printers also provided me with the names and home phone numbers of a number of long-term employees as potential interview participants. Some interviews with employees and managers at Loewen Windows were arranged by office staff at that company. The majority of interviews were conducted in the homes of the participants; two were conducted in coffee shops, one was conducted in my own home, and the interviews arranged by Loewen were conducted in an office at the factory.

Efforts were made to interview a representative sample of workers and managers at the three firms. Key informants included (where possible) founders and owners, the first employees of the firms, as well as long-term employees. The history of these businesses meant that there was some overlap in the categories of worker and manager. In the early decades of these companies, it was not unusual for the earliest employees to migrate from shop-floor to supervisory positions. Such individuals thus were able to discuss their experiences both as workers and as managers; in some cases, they personally identified more with one role than with the other. The overwhelming majority of those contacted accepted my request for an interview, which typically lasted from one to two hours. In a few cases, follow-up interviews were conducted. Recorded interviews were taped with the participant's approval and transcribed before archival deposit; otherwise, detailed notes were written during the course of the interview.

Participants were given the choice of remaining anonymous: most participants chose to allow the use of their real name. For those who preferred to retain their anonymity, I have used pseudonyms in the text that follows. In some cases, the nature of a participant's responses to questions led to my decision to use a pseudonym despite his or her desire to be named.

An interview guide was prepared prior to contacting interviewees. Topics addressed included immigration history, settlement experiences, educational background, career aspirations, the labour process, social relations with co-workers and employers, strategies to address job stress, ethno-religious identity, and self-determination. Participants were explicitly asked to make value judgments on their work experiences and (if they were immigrants) to compare their experiences in the host country of Canada with their country or countries of origin. The interviews were semi-structured, which allowed participants to direct the conversation to a degree, thereby permitting the introduction of questions and themes not anticipated by the researcher. Unscripted follow-up questions often were used during the course of the interview to draw out further details from an interviewee's response to a question, or to invite participants to compare their experiences against that of other (unnamed) participants.

In addition to interviews, other sources used in this study include government documents, union records, newspaper and magazine articles, private company records, letters, speeches, and company promotional material (print, videos, and websites). Scholars in the field of business history are dependent to a great extent on the good will of the businesses themselves for primary materials since these resources are generally not available in archives if the business is privately held. Most business owners are reluctant to reveal their innermost actions and transactions to the broader public. Some do not preserve the minutes, private correspondence, and other minutiae that provide a glimpse into the social history of their corporation, preferring to focus their attention on the day-to-day operations of their business. Those companies whose owners do choose to preserve these details of their past, and are willing to share them with outsiders, are therefore comparatively rare. This book has benefited from the openness and generosity of several business executives, particularly Ted and David Friesen of Friesen Printers, Charles Loewen of Loewen Windows, and Art DeFehr of Palliser Furniture.

Ted Friesen was for years the president of the Mennonite Historical Society of Canada; his interest in history has meant that an extensive range of private records have been preserved at Friesen Printers. Since conducting my research at this company, some of these documents have been deposited at the Altona Heritage Centre Archives in Altona, Manitoba. Fewer records are extant at Palliser Furniture, due to a number of plant relocations and a major fire. Private records at Loewen Windows are also limited; as a privately owned, family-run company, minutes of board meetings were not always kept in the earlier years. I was fortunate to have full access to records at both Friesen Printers and Loewen Windows and circumscribed access at Palliser Furniture.[71]

The argument made here is that ethnic identity and religious identity have shaped and been shaped by class relations and that the business and labour history of non-unionized Mennonites is best understood via an approach that incorporates the techniques of business history, social history of the working class, 'lived religion,' theology, and oral history. This argument is developed over six chapters.

Chapter 1 examines the definition of Mennonite religious identity by the Mennonite intellectual elite in the last half of the twentieth century. An overview of the histories and structures of the three factories central to this study in chapter 2 is followed by an examination of Mennonite corporate mythology in chapter 3. Chapter 4 is an exploration of the work experience of the Mennonite employees at these factories, including the labour process and corporate ideology within the plants. The broader North American Mennonite community's theological responses to industrial capitalism, as well as Mennonites' reactions to the election of the New Democratic Party to power for the first time in Manitoba, is examined in chapter 5. Chapter 6 addresses workers' efforts to unionize these Mennonite-owned factories and the subsequent responses of management. A brief personal epilogue gives readers insight into my own interest in this history. The conclusion posits that twentieth-century North American Mennonites, unlike E.P. Thompson's eighteenth-century British religious dissenters, have largely chosen not to use their religious tradition to either question or develop alternatives to the existing economic order.[72]

Historian Kenneth Lipartito asserts that business history that ignores culture 'creates an untenable abstraction of human action.'[73] The reconstruction of Mennonite identity within the workplace as a consequence of late twentieth century industrial and global capitalism is the focus of this book. Given its growing importance in North American Mennonite society after 1945, the industrial workplace was one of the most significant venues in which competing identity claims were contested. The interests of the Mennonite intellectual elite (academics, theologians, historians, and pastors), the Mennonite corporate elite, and the Mennonite working class were not always in accord. The consequence by the end of the twentieth century, however, was the upholding of the capitalist status quo with respect to labour relations among Manitoban Mennonites.

1

The Mennonite Intellectual Elite: Yieldedness, Non-resistance, and Neighbourly Love

During the second half of the twentieth century Mennonite workers and employers in Canada alike received a simplified version of a religious identity in their churches and Bible colleges – a version promoted by the Mennonite intellectual elite. The two most significant intellectuals in this process in Canada were two non-Canadians, U.S. historian Harold S. Bender and theologian John Howard Yoder. Even though these two men had significant influence in Canadian churches and colleges, Mennonite employers in particular did not accept this ideological construction of their identity without reservation. Indeed, Mennonite employers resisted the intellectual elites' construction as put to them in the churches and colleges and strove to create an alternative Mennonite identity, one which corresponded with the ideological requirements of quite a different world, as will be seen in later chapters. The business-men in this study countered the Mennonite intellectuals' version of Mennonite identity just as the workers seemed to accept that identity. For Mennonite workers and their employers, the workplace was filled with religious meaning.

The historical study of religion has undergone a renaissance in the last thirty years, though investigation of the intersection of labour and religion in the twentieth century remains limited. Certainly some of the credit for the transformation of the field may be placed with E.P. Thompson's *The Making of the English Working Class*. Thompson's eloquent presentation of the significance of Methodism for industrializing English workers challenged the traditional Marxist rejection of religion and, by extension, religious history.[1] Historians interested in the intersection of religion and labour in the Western world have tended to focus on the eighteenth- and nineteenth-century industrializing class rather than the twentieth-century industrialized class, much as Thompson did.[2] And some studies that do consider the twentieth century still have a tendency to focus on old categories of analysis, such as politics.[3] Some scholars blame secularization for this state of affairs, whether as an observable trend in North American society or as a explanatory theory (mis)used by religious historians.[4]

The transformation of the field of religious history, though slow, was occasioned by the emergence of social history. The exclusive focus on intellectual history (i.e., theology and doctrine) and on institutional (i.e., church and denominational) history was supplanted by the study of popular religion.[5] More recently, 'lived religion' has become the paradigm of historical studies of religion.[6] Scholars of 'lived religion' recognize that religious identity is not fixed, but is developed in a context of, and in response to, particular historical and material conditions.[7] They argue that an understanding of religious identity cannot be reduced to a study of theological doctrines or religious rituals. Nor can a clear division between elite and lay religious beliefs and practices be made; Robert Orsi notes that historians of 'lived religion' require a diachronic understanding of how religion shapes and is shaped by 'everyday experience' and in 'mutually transforming exchanges' by religious authorities and religious believers.[8] An analysis of power relations between the theological elite and laypeople is thus an essential, albeit a limited, part of understanding religious identity from a 'lived religion' perspective.

A history of a religious group such as the Mennonites is, of necessity, a religious history. This book is an examination of the contested identities of Mennonites in manufacturing in post-war Manitoba. As such, it examines the practices of Mennonite business owners in light of their own religious understandings, including the means by which their particular religious beliefs infused a Mennonite identity that furthered their own ends: what I call a Mennonite 'corporate mythology.' It also examines the religious understandings of Mennonite workers, including their acceptance of – and occasional attempts to challenge – their employers' particular definition of Mennonitism. These two groups were not alone in their attempts to refashion Mennonite religious identity. A third group participated in this debate, one which saw itself as having the voice of authority: Mennonite theologians and historians – the North American Mennonite intellectual elite.

After outlining the significance of the shift to a 'from the ground up' approach to religious history, it may seem odd (and contradictory) to introduce a chapter that is largely an intellectual history of Mennonite theology. The personal and material interests of business owners and managers, not to mention their agency (that is, their ability to make choices and to act on them), would appear to be neglected by such an approach. It is impossible to understand the 'lived religion' of owners, managers, and employees in their workplaces, however, without first understanding the religious worldview that the Mennonite intellectual elite strove to create. This elite disseminated their worldview through Mennonite Sunday school curricula, the sermons of Mennonite seminary-trained pastors, and the courses of Mennonite Bible college instructors. Mennonite owners and workers alike thus were raised in a culture whose authorities attempted to inculcate this worldview in them. Mennonite owners and workers did not accept this worldview unquestioned. As will be argued in subsequent chapters, they instead recreated a Mennonite religious identity that both challenged and incorporated aspects of this elite worldview, yet clearly advanced their own particular ideological perspective.

An analysis of continuity and change in twentieth century Mennonite theology as articulated by this intellectual elite allows for some cautious generalizations. The shifts in emphasis among three theological themes – yieldedness, non-resistance, and neighbourly love – are examined here, with the caveat that what follows is, of necessity, not a comprehensive analysis of Anabaptist-Mennonite theology. These three are only a few of the themes emphasized by Mennonite theologians and historians in twentieth century North America. These three themes are chosen not only because they often have been promoted as definitional of Mennonite religious identity, but because they are particularly problematic for labour. The three themes are connected closely to each other, and their meanings, as well as the degree of emphasis each has received, have changed over time as North American Mennonites experienced the Second World War and urbanization.

Definitions of these three theological emphases therefore are not simple. Non-resistance, for example, at first was equated with pacifism (the rejection of military service), but this definition later came to be supplanted by non-violent resistance. A more complete comprehension of these theological terms necessitates their historicization. Before doing so, both yieldedness and neighbourly love require some initial explanation, as they stem from non-English terms.

The concept of yieldedness stems from the German *Gelassenheit*. *Gelassenheit* stands for a much more elaborate philosophy of thought than the common translation of 'yieldedness' would suggest. It involves not merely the submission to God of individuals, as is commonly preached by evangelical Christians, but also submission of the individual to the faith community.[9] The principle of *Gelassenheit* also has been connected to that of discipleship, or *Nachfolge Christi*, a German expression that more clearly conveys the understanding that discipleship involves modelling one's life after that of Christ.[10]

Robert Friedmann states that there are 'about 15 possible translations, none perfectly fitting' for *Gelassenheit*, including 'self-surrender, resignation in God's will (*Gottergebenheit*), yieldedness to God's will, self-abandonment, the (passive) opening to God's willing, including the readiness to suffer for the sake of God, also peace and calmness of mind.'[11] What is implied is that the precise definition of *Gelassenheit* is hampered by its being a non-English term. The problem is not merely one of translation, however, as such a conclusion elides the insight of literary theory that *all* definitions are historically contingent.

Neighbourly love is the form of love that emphasizes one's relationship with and obligation to one's neighbours. According to the ancient Greeks, there were four types of love: *eros* (romantic), *stergos* (familial), *philos* (brotherly), and *agape*. *Agape*, the highest form of love, was possible for humans only with divine assistance. In the Christian understanding, *agape* is the self-sacrificial love described in 1 Corinthians 13:4–8a: 'Love is patient; love is kind; love is not envious or boastful or arrogant or rude. It does not insist on its own way; it is not irritable or resentful; it does not rejoice in wrongdoing, but rejoices in the truth. It bears all things, believes all things, hopes all things, endures all things. Love never ends.'[12] Sixteenth-century Catholic and Protestant understandings of neighbourly love had been rejected by the Anabaptists as not requiring sufficient application to human relationships. Priests, monks, and nuns were held to high standards, but the laity were not expected to live out the demands of neighbourly love in

the same way.[13] Accordingly, the Anabaptists crafted their own understanding of neighbourly love, connecting it to non-resistance.

At first glance, the implications of these three theological concepts
for Mennonite understandings of labour relations seem obvious – and
somewhat contradictory. The religious community's emphasis on
yieldedness and non-resistance should lead to workers' unquestion-
ing acceptance of authority, whether constituted in the church or the
workplace, and a rejection of groups and organizations that challenged
authority or presented alternative sites of power, such as unions.[14] The
emphasis on non-resistance and neighbourly love, similarly, should
lead to workers' willingness to accept injustice and inequality directed
against oneself in the workplace, whatever the personal cost. Neighbourly love, conversely, could be interpreted as making demands on
employers also – setting limits on mistreatment or exploitation of their
employees. These linkages between Mennonite theology and Mennonite labour relations certainly existed, as will be shown in this study
of three Mennonite-owned workplaces in Manitoba; however, the responses by Mennonite intellectual elites to broader events in the post-
war world led to redefinitions of these theological concepts and their
meanings for Mennonite workplace relations.

The Mennonite theologians and historians whose texts were most
influential for twentieth-century North American Mennonites were employed at colleges and universities in the United States rather than in
Canada.[15] Part of the reason is that the first Mennonite post-secondary
institutions in Canada were created fifty years after those in the United
States. Bethel College was the first Mennonite post-secondary institution in North America, founded in Kansas in 1894; another, Goshen
College, was established in Indiana in 1903.[16] Goshen employed one
of the most significant articulators of a mid-twentieth century Mennonite understanding of yieldedness, non-resistance, and neighbourly
love: Harold S. Bender.

Bender's 'Anabaptist Vision,' a redefinition of Mennonite identity for
the late twentieth century, became normative not only for U.S. Mennonites for two or three decades after the Second World War, but for
Canadian Mennonites as well – and for much longer. The 1943 speech
in which Bender outlined this 'vision' was printed for distribution, and
his interpretation of Anabaptism was disseminated to the broader Mennonite community through the teachings of Mennonite church leaders,

Sunday school curriculum writers, as well as authors and editors of Mennonite periodicals, many of whom studied at Goshen. Mennonite Sunday school curricula used in both Canada and the United States promoted Bender's ideas.[17] Bender's vision was broadcast further by the work of North American Mennonites in post-war relief and service activities in Europe; almost three thousand Mennonite men and women from throughout Canada and the United States volunteered under the auspices of Mennonite Central Committee (the relief, development, and service agency supported by most North American Mennonite churches) from 1945 to 1960. On their return to their hometowns after their term of service, these volunteers were held in high esteem by their local communities and their new Benderian understanding of what it meant to be a Mennonite was given credence.[18]

In Manitoba, Bender's 'Anabaptist Vision' was disseminated not only by these means, but also by the faculty of two Mennonite Bible colleges established in Winnipeg in the 1940s. The first Mennonite Bible college in Canada, Mennonite Brethren Bible College (MBBC), was formed in 1944; the second, Canadian Mennonite Bible College (CMBC), was founded in 1947.[19] The colleges' original purposes were to teach the Mennonite interpretation of the Christian faith, to provide theological education and training for church workers in local congregations, and to promote the German language.[20] Some of the faculty at these Canadian Mennonite institutions had received training in U.S. Mennonite colleges, and it was not unusual for there to be a cross-border exchange in college leadership.[21]

Despite the efforts of Sunday-school-curriculum authors and Bible college faculty, by 1990 commitment to Anabaptism as defined by Bender's 'Vision' was in decline among Mennonites in both Canada and the United States. Such were the findings of two surveys conducted in 1972 and 1989 of the beliefs and practices of members of the five major North American Mennonite denominations: the Mennonite Church, the General Conference Mennonite Church/Conference of Mennonites in Canada, the Mennonite Brethren Church, the Brethren in Christ Church, and the Evangelical Mennonite Church.[22] Though the decline was more rapid in Canada, Canadian Mennonites remained more strongly committed to the 'Vision' than did their American counterparts (see table 1.1).[23] Of the two largest Canadian Mennonite denominations, the Mennonite Brethren were more attracted to

Table 1.1. Mennonites who scored 'upper middle' or 'high' on Anabaptism scale (%)

Denomination	1972	1989	Change
U.S. Mennonite Brethren	50.9	43.0	−7.9
U.S. General Conference Mennonites	55.8	49.4	−6.4
Canadian Mennonite Brethren	80.8	69.1	−11.7
Conference of Mennonites in Canada	74.2	64.2	−10.0

Source: Dueck, 'Canadian Mennonites and the Anabaptist Vision,' 72.

Bender's 'Vision' than were members of the Conference of Mennonites in Canada (the Canadian equivalent of the General Conference Mennonites in the United States). And unlike U.S. Mennonites, the majority of Canadian Mennonites still remained highly supportive of Bender's 'Anabaptist Vision.'

Historian Al Keim provides the historical context for this gradual loss of support for the 'Anabaptist Vision' among the Mennonite population at large, which reflects the weakening of authority of the Mennonite intellectual elite. Keim credits increased enrolment by Mennonites in post-secondary institutions, their shift from agricultural to industrial employment, and their urbanization and suburbanization for the loss of support for the 'Vision.'[24] The authority of the intellectual elite for Mennonites was dissipated further by the emergence of alternate voices in the Mennonite community, such as those of novelists, poets, and artists.[25] The exposure of Mennonites to a larger and more diverse world through overseas service challenged some of the more simplistic assumptions that commitment to Bender's interpretation necessitated. An awareness that it was no longer possible to maintain geographic isolation meant that Mennonites had to confront the question of how and when compromise of religious beliefs was required by the increased complexity of their world.[26]

In addition, U.S. evangelicalism had made significant inroads in Manitoba Mennonite society after the Second World War.[27] The Brunk Brothers from Virginia held revival tent meetings in southern Manitoba in the 1950s, promoting an individualist understanding of Christianity that was at odds with traditional Mennonite stress on the necessity of yieldedness to a community of faith.[28] The message of evangelicalism was further promoted to Manitoba Mennonites by CFAM radio, begun in 1957 by a group of Mennonite businessmen from southern Manitoba.[29] Its religious programming included evangelical programs from the United States, such as 'The Lutheran Hour,' Billy Graham's 'Hour of Decision,' and Theodore H. Epp's 'Back to the Bible.' Epp's broadcast aired daily on CFAM, and attracted more listeners among Manitoba Mennonites than any other radio station.[30] While some programs were broadcast that emphasized Mennonite understandings of non-violence, CFAM avoided giving airtime to programs which advocated a more activist peace position.[31] Though these programming choices undermined Manitoba Mennonites' understandings of yieldedness and non-violence, they did not undercut their acceptance of authority or rejection of labour activism, which evangelicalism's ties to individualism and conservatism served to reinforce rather than challenge.

The thrust of Bender's 'Anabaptist Vision' was his re-evaluation of the traditional Anabaptist-Mennonite stance on non-resistance. Disturbed by U.S. Mennonites' limited engagement with pacifism in both world wars and their drift towards fundamentalist evangelicalism, Bender, editor of *Mennonite Quarterly Review* and professor of history at Goshen College, embarked on a modern-day 'recovery' of the essence of Anabaptism.[32] In doing so, he relied heavily on the Schleitheim Confession as the definitive document for Mennonite self-understanding.[33]

The Schleitheim Confession, one of the earliest known Anabaptist confessions of faith, was drafted by Michael Sattler in Switzerland in 1527.[34] Article 6 of this confession outlined the (Anabaptist) Christian stance with respect to 'the sword,' describing it as 'an ordering of God outside the perfection of Christ.' As to whether Christians may use violence either in self-defence or to achieve noble ends, the response was to follow the peaceful example of Christ. New Testament support for this stance was given, including the description of Christ's gentleness and humility in Matthew 11:29 and his refusal to condemn the woman caught in adultery in John 8:11. The article continued with an admonition to avoid using the courts to settle disputes, citing Christ's refusal to adjudicate a dispute about inheritance in Luke 12:13–14. Further, Anabaptists were to decline to serve as magistrates. Again, reference was made to the example of Christ.[35] Article 6 concluded with a passage that emphasized the connection between Anabaptist non-resistance and separation from the world. 'The rule of the government is according to the flesh, that of the Christians according to the spirit. Their houses and dwelling remain in this world, that of the Christians is in heaven. Their citizenship is in this world, that of the Christians is in heaven (Phil. 3:20). The weapons of their battle and warfare are carnal and only against the flesh, but the weapons of Christians are spiritual, against the fortification of the devil. The worldly are armed with steel and iron, but Christians are armed with the armour of God, with truth, righteousness, peace, faith, salvation, and with the Word of God.'[36] The Anabaptist-Mennonite two-kingdom worldview was established firmly here, with the sword being reserved for 'the world' and the ban (the practice of exclusion) the instrument of discipline within the Christian community.[37]

This separatist ethic of Anabaptist-Mennonites was the topic of the Confession's fourth article, which advocated separation from the world. Cited as support was the New Testament injunction: 'Therefore come out from them, and be separate from them, says the Lord, and touch nothing unclean; then I will welcome you.'[38] Following a listing of activities from which Christians should abstain,[39] the article concluded by returning to the question of violence: 'Thereby shall also fall away from us the diabolical weapons of violence – such as sword, armour, and the like, and all of their use to protect friends or against enemies – by virtue of the word of Christ: "you shall not resist evil" (Mt. 5:39).' Non-resistance thus was a key feature separating the Christian from the world.[40]

Through his ideological use of the sixteenth-century Schleitheim Confession, Bender intended to find a middle ground between the conservative and liberal factions among North American Mennonites in the mid-twentieth century.[41] The increasingly hierarchical nature of North American Mennonite church conferences in the early twentieth century had resulted in deep suspicion of unorthodoxy and limited tolerance for theological debate or differences of spiritual opinion by church authorities.[42] Goshen College was closed by its sponsoring church conference in 1923, ostensibly for financial reasons, but really because the conservative church leadership perceived the college's professors as having a liberal bias in their theology.[43] Bender himself was criticized for his leadership of annual conferences for Mennonite young people during the period 1919–23. Church leaders viewed such gatherings of Goshen College graduates and First World War conscientious objectors as a threat to their authority.[44] Activities such as these resulted in Bender's appointment as a professor of history and sociology – rather than theology – at Goshen.[45]

It was the crisis of the Second World War, however, that saw Bender formulate the clearest articulation of this middle way. Almost half of Mennonite men drafted in the United States did not choose conscientious objector status, a situation which troubled more Mennonites than just Bender.[46] At the 1943 annual convention of the American Society of Church History, of which he was then president, Bender gave a speech titled 'The Anabaptist Vision.' In this address, he sought to remould the theological identity of North American Mennonites, emphasizing Anabaptists' contribution to broader values of modern society and thus the respectability of Mennonites.[47]

Historian Paul Toews emphasizes the significance of Bender's speech, which was distributed widely by North American Mennonite church publishers in 1944.[48] '[It was] a discourse that would reshape the Mennonite historical imagination. For Mennonite scholarship and self-understanding, it was a kairos moment, a moment of breakthrough. No other single event or piece of historical writing has filtered so deeply into Mennonite thinking. The phrase "the Anabaptist Vision" became the identifying incantation of North American Mennonites like no other set of words.'[49]

Bender attempted to infuse North American Mennonites with pride in their religious heritage. Freedom of conscience and modern democracy originated with Anabaptism, he asserted – rhetoric which was part of an effort to secure legitimacy for his interpretation among secularizing North American Mennonites.[50] Anabaptism was depicted as the zenith of the Reformation, as well as the recreation of the New Testament church.[51] Bender declared that the Anabaptists were the 'true' Reformers; Martin Luther and Ulrich Zwingli had compromised their faith for physical safety. Bender identified the key features of Anabaptism as discipleship, voluntarism, and non-resistance.[52]

Discipleship was defined as 'the transformation of the entire way of life of the individual believer and of society so that it should be fashioned after the teachings and example of Christ.'[53] Voluntarism involved not only the independent adult decision for baptism and church membership, but also nonconformity (separation from 'the world').[54] Influenced by the two-kingdom worldview established by the Schleitheim Confession, this separation was to represent 'a judgment on the contemporary social order ... as non-Christian, and [to set] up a line of demarcation between the Christian community and worldly society.'[55] A commitment to non-resistance involved the rejection of war, violence, and the taking of human life.[56] Non-resistance thus shaped the response to the social order, distinguishing Anabaptist Mennonites from Catholics and Protestants alike.

The Anabaptist understanding of the Christian relationship to the world was unique, Bender asserted. Catholics and Calvinists believed in the possibility of redemption of the social order, of its Christianization.[57] Lutherans, disavowing that the world could be redeemed, believed that since Christians had to live within the existing world, they had to make compromises, confident that this compromising was covered by the grace of God.[58] No such compromise was possible for Anabaptists, and by extension, Mennonites. For Bender, a two-kingdom worldview was central to the 'Anabaptist Vision.' The two kingdoms were to remain separate: the kingdom of God (the church) apart from the kingdom of the world (civil society or the social order).[59] Christians were not responsible for the redemptive transformation of the social order, but were to separate themselves from the world. The world would be redeemed only as it voluntarily joined the community of faith.[60]

Bender's ideological use of history to meet perceived theological needs is evident here. Many sixteenth-century Anabaptists in fact *had* sought, at first, to transform the social order. Conrad Grebel, for example, broke with the Protestant leader Ulrich Zwingli over this very issue. Bender, however, preferred the later Anabaptist emphasis on personal rather than societal transformation, which emerged in response to persecution of Anabaptists by both the state and state-supported churches.

Bender's interpretation was a clear departure from the traditional Marxist understanding of the role of the sixteenth-century Anabaptist movement in the resistance to the development of proto-capitalism. Friedrich Engels had declared that, during the German Peasants War, Anabaptists such as Thomas Müntzer were forerunners of a radicalized proletariat.[61] Had Bender incorporated aspects of the Marxist interpretation and thus created a Mennonite mythic identity that emphasized the socially radical nature of early Anabaptism, the history of Mennonite engagement with twentieth-century industrial capitalism may have been very different, as such a theological approach would have been more supportive of unions and other expressions of worker agency. Historian Paul Toews argues that Bender's 'Anabaptist Vision' nonetheless modified the strict separatism that was the two-kingdom theology of the Schleitheim Confession. The 'Anabaptist Vision' was a response to the challenge to geographically isolated Mennonite communities that was presented by modernity, with its concomitant identity crisis.[62] While calling twentieth-century Mennonites to separate from the world, Bender simultaneously 'legitimated an outward missional activity.'[63] 'Anabaptism, as it came to function in American Mennonite life, carried a dual meaning. It offered distinct community but also witness. It promoted particularity but also ecumenicity. It integrated Mennonites into the world but preserved a rhetoric of difference. It brought respect but gave new eloquence to the language of dissent.'[64] As such, Toews rightly asserts that Bender's 'Anabaptist Vision' was not only 'an exceptional exercise in revising history' but also 'the crowning achievement of twentieth-century ideological reconstruction of Mennonite identity.'[65]

The post-war period was not the first time that North American Mennonites were forced to question their theology in light of new social and economic conditions. Guy F. Hershberger, a Mennonite peace theologian and professor of history at Goshen College, had contemplated Mennonite involvement in industrial capitalism already in the 1930s.[66] In the pages of Mennonite periodicals, both academic and popular, he promoted a concept of non-violence that strongly emphasized its connection to neighbourly love and yieldedness. Described by J. Lawrence Burkholder as the 'chief interpreter' of non-resistance in the mid-twentieth century,[67] Hershberger defined non-resistance as the rejection of the use of force in any and all forms. Participation in war, involvement in Gandhian social protests, membership in labour unions, and exploitative business practices were all 'violat[ions of] the greater ethic of love and nonresistance found in the Bible.'[68] Hershberger refused to distinguish in any meaningful way between physical violence and non-violent social protest, asserting that both were immoral uses of coercion.[69] The economic world, Hershberger claimed, brought issues of justice and love, and their interrelationship, into sharp relief. It was in that world that Christians were in greatest danger of 'losing the way of the cross,' which he defined as a willingness to suffer injustice rather than compromise the Christian commitment to self-sacrificial love.[70] Naively, he believed that Mennonite business owners were capable of creating 'islands where ideal relations could exist between boss and worker without struggles for power.'[71] In the absence of such an ideal, workers would have to practice yieldedness, yielding the right to economic justice, refusing to force compliance with labour's demands, because to do so would violate love for the neighbour. Hershberger's passive, rural, isolationist views became increasingly impractical in the post-war urban world in which North American Mennonites found themselves.

The views of Hershberger, as a Swiss Mennonite with the (Old) Mennonite Church, had little influence among Manitoba Mennonites, who were primarily Mennonite Brethren and General Conference Mennonites of Russian background. The implications for labour of Hershberger's very conservative views – an outright rejection of union membership – were provided in this province by another source: memories of the Russian experience itself. Mennonite immigrants from Russia who arrived in Manitoba in the 1920s and 1950s had suffered extreme hardship under the Bolsheviks, anarchists, and Stalinists. Many came to equate any self-assertive activity on the part of labour with the 'godless Communism' they were grateful to have escaped.

There were those within the North American Mennonite intellectual community who offered an alternative perspective, though it was not one which had as much support as Bender's. In the late 1950s, Goshen College theology professor and divinity doctoral candidate J. Lawrence Burkholder challenged what he viewed as the subordination of neighbourly love to the principle of non-resistance in the Hershberger tradition. 'Love itself demands responsible participation in a society for it is in the social realm that the Christian meets the neighbor,' he declared.[72] Burkholder argued that Christians were called to a life of non-violent confrontation with power rather than a meek submission to it.[73] Christian self-sacrifical suffering – the cross of Christ – was to be encountered not through an avoidance of conflict but through the acceptance of the obligation to 'confront the world and try to change it.'[74] Such confrontation and efforts at social transformation necessitated an understanding of yieldedness as a process of mutual discernment rather than as simple acquiescence to authority and a compromise between neighbourly love and non-resistance (which Burkholder viewed as oppositional). Decisions regarding the nature of this compromise were to be made by the faith community as a whole. 'Where to draw the line is the issue,' Burkholder noted. 'Different times, different circumstances, different identities obviously will bring different answers.'[75]

Burkholder had been strongly influenced by his experiences as a service worker dealing with the complexities of suffering and injustice faced by refugees in China.[76] His views were dismissed by other Mennonite intellectuals at the time, fearing, as they did, that the emphasis on compromise would 'reduc[e] the high cost of discipleship as the believer too easily concedes to the ethics of empire' by sacrificing religious commitments (particularly pacifism) for political expediency.[77] Consequently, Burkholder's 1958 Princeton Theological Seminary doctoral dissertation, titled *The Problem of Social Responsibility from the Perspective of the Mennonite Church*, did not find a publisher until more than three decades after its completion.

In his dissertation, Burkholder argued that Mennonites historically had equated non-resistance, yieldedness, and neighbourly love. The essence of Anabaptism had been discipleship, love for the neighbour, and yieldedness practiced to the extreme degree ('the loss of all things for Christ including one's own historical existence, if need be').[78] Over the centuries, love came to be 'almost synonymous' with non-resistance for Anabaptists and Mennonites.[79] In fact, Burkholder asserted, non-resistance was 'applied *agape*.'[80]

This linkage of non-resistance, yieldedness, and neighbourly love resulted in the exclusion of questions of justice and power from Mennonite discourse, Burkholder declared. Love for the neighbour was an inadequate principle for life in the modern world, as it did not address what to do in the face of the competing claims of neighbours. Compromise was the only solution to this dilemma.[81] Compromise would become possible when Mennonites came to terms with their complicity in worldly power struggles, including in the economic realm. 'Mennonites must seek their traditional goals of brotherhood, peace and mutuality under the conditions of compromise. Mennonites must realize that they are a part of the world system and that they share the guilt and responsibility for corporate evil and that their attempts to be obedient to Christ and 'be' the true church must take into consideration the 'ambiguities' of their actual situation. This realistic approach will prevent perfectionistic illusions and despair.'[82] As a consequence, Burkholder redefined non-resistance as non-violent resistance, which would grant Mennonites the theological freedom to work for justice in the world[83] – including the freedom to participate in unions and the labour movement.

Other Mennonite intellectuals were concerned that it was not the community of faith but the secular world that was, in fact, the locus of discernment with respect to how and when to compromise. Burkholder was critiqued for his assumption that the abandonment of passivity necessitated by concern for the neighbour required 'some level of involvement and compromise with the institutions and structures of modern society,' yielding to the demands of the world rather than those of the church.[84] J. Denny Weaver, Mennonite professor of religion at Bluffton College, declared that Burkholder's was a 'neo-Constantinian outlook' in that it subjugated religious beliefs to the demands of government and economy, even as the emperor Constantine had turned religion into a tool of the state.[85] Such a view was anathema to Mennonites, a faith community that came into existence in part because of a belief that sixteenth-century Protestantism had not separated church and state clearly enough. The problem, Weaver explained, was that Burkholder's position assumed that 'Christian social responsibility happens primarily through societal and governmental structures as agents. It assumes that greatest effectiveness occurs through the eventual use of the government's means, namely violence and war, with the criteria for success and relevancy also supplied and defined by those structures.'[86] Of couse, what Weaver fails to note here is that the first corollary need not lead to the second. An emphasis on transformation of social structures (dare one say, even capitalism itself?) need not be predicated on violence and war. The notion that it must be so, of course, restricts the ability of Mennonites to participate in 'societal and governmental structures' like unions and the labour movement in general.

Weaver's critique was shaped by the perspective of John Howard Yoder, the Mennonite professor of theology whose reputation among North American Mennonites began to surpass that of Bender in the 1970s.[87] While Burkholder believed that neighbourly love meant that it was the responsibility of Christians to work within the system for its transformation, Yoder cautioned against the seduction of the system itself.[88] Yoder argued that the Christian was called, like Christ, to reject the assumption that it was a moral duty to exercise social responsibility through these structures and institutions.[89] Thus he rejected the belief of evangelical Christians that the way to change society was through conversion of individuals, 'changing the heart' of those in power, or electing Christians to office. Rather, 'the primary social structure through which the gospel works to change other structures is that of the Christian community.'[90] Christians could not change society; rather, as people identified with Christ and his ecclesial community, practicing yieldedness, society would be transformed. Thus seeking justice and equality through social movements and secular organizations was inappropriate.

Yoder viewed the opposition of neighbourly love and non-resistance established by theologians like Burkholder as artificial. The call to non-resistance of Matthew 5 and the call to obey authority of Romans 13 were not contradictory. The incorrect assumption that they were, he declared, led people to conclude that pacifists were required to subordinate concern for the world to the need to maintain the purity of one's personal ethics, 'preferring Jesus to Paul or eschatology to responsibility.'[91] Rather, Christians were called to respect the work of secular institutions, but not misinterpret their work as that of the Christian church.[92] Those who wished to downplay non-resistance for the sake of social responsibility were deceived in their egoism. Christians were those who, like Christ, renounced the claim to govern history.[93] They were to model in the here and now the kind of peaceful, sacrificial existence that would characterize the future kingdom of God.[94]

Despite his argument that it was not the job of the Christian to redeem the world, Yoder claimed that he was not calling simply for a return to the separatist ethic of Schleitheim (and thus the Benderian religious identity). Paul Toews asserts that Yoder 'offered Mennonites a middle ground' between social marginality and co-option by 'the approved, established order.'[95] Rather than isolation from or acquiescence to the violence of the political world, Christians were called to exhibit the non-violent values of the future sacred kingdom, not as a witness to the world but as a faithful response to the incarnation of Christ. Such special pleading aside, Yoder's argument was equivalent in practice to Bender's rejection of involvement in civil society, in essence a renewed call for a two-kingdom worldview. The target of Yoder's discourse, however, was not only Mennonites but the Christian church as a whole, which Yoder viewed as historically complicit in the violence of the state.

North American Mennonite theological identity underwent a modest shift in the post-war period. From an identity that emphasized yieldedness, submission to the faith community, and the rejection of all forms of force, the Mennonite intellectual elite attempted to recreate Mennonite religious identity, stressing neighbourly love as social responsibility and (to a lesser extent) distinguishing between violence and power. Reflecting this shift, 'non-violence' began to replace the term 'non-resistance' in Mennonite theological discourse. Mennonites' reconsideration of their theological identity was prompted in part by the perceived crisis of their post-war entry into the urban industrial world as well as by the Second World War itself. By the end of the twentieth century, Mennonite theologians were still debating the competing claims of non-violence and neighbourly love. 'The discipleship view of the church has held that just as Jesus died nonviolently in response to the violence done to him, so his disciples are called to respond to sinners in love and forgiveness. The power inherent in this response can transform the lives of sinners. Yet can this power be used strategically to transform the world? On this Mennonites are not agreed.'[96] Bender and Yoder, who argued for maintaining the purity of the peace ethic, seemed willing to abandon the world's downtrodden, as well as the unethical brokers of global power, to their respective fates. Until the second coming of Christ, the disadvantaged and the non-Christian alike could expect only charitable alleviation – rather than transformation – of their social realities, unless and until they yielded to the authority of a community of faith. Burkholder, who advocated an understanding of neighbourly love as compromise, was critiqued for his alleged willingness to believe himself capable of judging who should bear the brunt of socially transformative violence and of keeping that violence in check.[97]

Mennonites in Manitoba were forced to deal with the real-world implications of these theological debates when the New Democratic Party (NDP) was elected to government for the first time in the province in 1969. The election was a watershed for Mennonites, as provincial support for unionization demanded re-examination of their understanding of Mennonite identity in an industrial context. The increased union activity of the 1970s required Mennonites in the province to determine their response to questions of labour involvement that they heretofore had been able largely to ignore. It is unknown how many Mennonites in the province would have read the primary works of the theologians discussed here, though Dueck's study clearly shows that the majority of Canadian Mennonites were familiar with their main ideas.[98] The debates regarding the competing claims of justice and pacifism, of neighbourly love and yieldedness, were encountered by Manitoba Mennonites through church periodicals, sermons, Sunday school curricula, and community contact with Mennonite intellectuals whose religious viewpoint had been shaped by these theological treatises, as well as the faculty at the two Mennonite colleges in Winnipeg. Such publications and encounters were the means by which the North American Mennonite intellectual elite endeavoured to create a specific Mennonite religious identity among all classes of Mennonites.

These efforts to create a religious identity were part of what distinguished Mennonite workers in Manitoba from their non-Mennonite counterparts. In the first half of the twentieth century, Mennonite workers were shaped by a religious ethos that emphasized separation from the world and avoidance of compromising secular commitments. However, Mennonite workers in Manitoba themselves underwent transformation in the late twentieth century. The redefinition of Mennonite religious identity, together with a more radicalized political situation in the province and the transformation of their workplaces, resulted in a change in Mennonite worker identity after 1970. The competing identity constructs of workers and the intellectual elite would not go without contestation by Mennonite employers, who themselves attempted to create a mythic identity for their Mennonite employees, one which suited their own ideological purposes. And one of the prime sites of the struggles between these groups to refashion their identity as Mennonites was the Mennonite workplace.

2

The Mennonite Workplace: Loewen Windows, Friesen Printers, and Palliser Furniture

In post-war Canada, three of the largest companies in wood window manufacturing, full-colour printing, and furniture production were owned and operated by Manitoban Mennonites. They were Loewen Windows, Friesen Printers, and Palliser Furniture. By the late twentieth century, these three businesses – the first two now renamed Loewen and Friesens Corporation respectively – had become the largest employers in their communities; for a time Palliser Furniture was also the largest private employer in Manitoba.[1]

The writing of business history in Canada has evolved slowly over the twentieth century, and its development is impossible to separate from the fields of economic and labour history. The 'Laurentian (or staples) thesis' of political economist Harold Innis was an innovative theoretical approach to the development of the Canadian economy to the nineteenth century, in that it was 'both transcontinental and trans-oceanic.'[2] Innis revised U.S. historian Frederick Jackson Turner's 'frontier thesis,' arguing that rather than expansionism, Canadian economic development was predicated on supplying Britain with staple goods. Until the 1970s, there were few challenges to the staples thesis. Historians focused their attention on the fur trade, the Hudson's Bay Company, the development of railways, the tariff, and the intricacies of Canada-U.S. economic relations. Historian Frederick Armstrong observed in 1972 that, with respect to the history of Canadian manufacturing, 'very little is available, and all too much of the information must be obtained from what might be called "official histories," commissioned by various companies and often far from representative.'[3] Since then, the study of Canadian business history has been reinvigorated by its incorporation of perspectives from the fields of labour, gender, and ethnic history.[4] Nonetheless, historian Desmond Morton notes that by the 1990s, the popularity of business and labour history among academics was in sharp decline.[5]

Business historians categorize the management of twentieth-century North American businesses into two successive approaches. The first is Taylorism, also known as scientific management, with its focus on the detailed analysis and timing of the labour process and on the use of piece rates to control wages. Taylorism was succeeded by welfare capitalism, which provided workers with benefits to cultivate company loyalty and acceptance of corporate ideology.[6] From 1890 through 1940, a form of Taylorism was the preferred approach of many Canadian businesses, both to save money and to 'move effective control of the labour process from the shop floor to the front office.'[7] An influx of immigrant labour in the early twentieth century meant that employers were able to meet employee resistance to the centralization of labour control by firing workers (or threatening to do so) and replacing them with more pliable (or more desperate) employees. A managerial class developed in the process, and developments in mechanization only furthered the subdivision of labour into separate groups.[8] By the 1960s, computerization, the expansion of free trade, and the influence of the United States as a market for Canadian industry further eroded worker control of the labour process.[9]

The leading scholar of North American business in the post-1950 era, and the acknowledged expert on the development of a managerial class, remains business historian Alfred Chandler Jr. His *The Visible Hand: The Managerial Revolution in American Business* examines the internal structure of U.S. businesses and concludes that the largest firms were those where the 'visible hand' of management replaced the 'invisible hand' of the market with respect to production and distribution.[10] Management became increasingly technical and professional, and eventually separate from ownership. Chandler is credited with moving the field of business history beyond 'the robber baron–industrial statesman debate,' which centred around the moral evaluation of industrialists, but he is also criticized for downplaying the role of the workforce.[11]

In Manitoba, labour activism and both federal and provincial politics were at least as important as managerial style and corporate structure in shaping workplace culture after 1945. Trade union membership in Manitoba increased from 38,681 in 1946 to 84,426 in 1970.[12] The expansion of organized labour was enabled at the federal level by 1944's Privy Council Order 1003 (PC 1003), which granted union recognition, recognized collective bargaining, established grievance procedures, and restricted the right to strike. These provisions were incorporated into the 1948 Manitoba Labour Relations Act.

Manitoba's labour history has been a peculiar blend of activism and resistance. The Winnipeg Labour Council was first formed in 1886, and the legacy of the 1919 Winnipeg General Strike is well known.[13] The strike was brutally crushed after six weeks, and it was almost thirty years before the principle of collective bargaining for which the 1919 strikers fought finally was recognized in the Rand Formula.[14] Another legacy of the 1919 strike was the shift of the labour struggle from the arena of unions to politics. In 1961, the New Democratic Party (NDP) was established, a successor to the Cooperative Commonwealth Federation (CCF) that had formed in 1933 with one of the 1919 strike leaders, J.S. Woodsworth, as its leader. The NDP served as the governing party in Manitoba for most of the 1970s and 1980s: their reign from 1969 through 1988 was interrupted briefly by the election of a Progressive Conservative government from 1977 to 1981. While in power, the NDP reformed the Labour Relations Act in 1972 (the first revision since its passage in 1948), and again in 1982, 1984, and 1987.[15] Economist Paul Phillips notes, however, that the 1972 revision 'gave labour little more than was the standard in the other provinces with more sophisticated industrial relations systems.'[16]

Labour militancy peaked in Canada and Manitoba in 1976.[17] Though union membership continued to increase in the province in the 1980s, from 124,000 in 1981 to 153,000 in 1987, so too did opposition to unions in the province.[18] Surveys of Winnipeggers' attitudes towards unions at the end of the 1980s revealed that half of city residents believed unions were too powerful, and only a third believed unions were a necessary counterbalance to employer power.[19]

Manufacturing in Manitoba expanded greatly after the Second World War, increasing by 10 per cent in 1959 alone. In the immediate postwar period, much of the industry in this sector continued to serve the needs of the province's agricultural base.[20] Diversification in the 1960s and 1970s, however, meant that by the 1980s, manufacturing in Manitoba was more varied than in almost any other Canadian province. The exceptions, of course, were Quebec and Ontario, as the nation's manufacturing heartland remained the Quebec-Windsor corridor.[21] Manufacturing in Manitoba was characterized by slower growth than other provinces from the 1950s through the 1970s, but it also was less affected by economic recessions.[22]

The trends in the development of North American business described above existed at the three Manitoba manufacturers that are the focus of this study. The businesses exhibited a paternalist form of welfare capitalism, particularly in their earlier years of operation. As the firms expanded, they developed business structures that relied on the formation of a managerial class. And all three remained non-unionized.

Loewen Windows, a wood window manufacturing firm, was established by a second generation Canadian Mennonite in Steinbach, the largest city in Manitoba's Mennonite East Reserve.[23] Founded by Russian Mennonite farmers in the Mennonite East Reserve in 1874, Steinbach is unusual in that it did not require the presence of a railroad for its development. Historian Royden Loewen credits the existence of a large gap between wealthy and poor Steinbach Mennonites as one of the variables in the growth of the town.[24] The wealthy Mennonites were the business founders in Steinbach; they had run profitable enterprises in Russia prior to emigration. The poorer Steinbach Mennonites served as a readily available labour supply, much as they had in Russia. Businesses that complemented farming activities were established quickly, such as a blacksmith shop and a flour mill.[25] Steinbach's economic base soon diversified beyond the agricultural-support businesses that existed at the turn of the century. By the 1990s, the community had become known as the 'Automobile City,' as more than five thousand vehicles were purchased yearly at the many dealerships that lined Main Street.[26] Trucking firms, funeral homes, and construction-related businesses were major employers by the end of the twentieth century; the city's largest employer, however, was Loewen Windows.

The origin of Loewen Windows can be traced back to 1905, when Cornelius B. Loewen, a *Kanadier* Mennonite[27] and member of the *Kleine Gemeinde* church, operated a sawmill southeast of Steinbach near the Sandilands provincial forest.[28] In 1905, his son Cornelius (C.T.)

Loewen left this business at age twenty-two to establish a road-building and house-moving company with his brother, Jacob T. Loewen. Leaving this business to his brother, C.T. established a lumberyard together with a cousin. The cousin soon left the business, which was then named C.T. Loewen Lumber Yard. C.T. opened an office on Steinbach's Main Street in 1910 in partnership with John R. Toews, an implement dealer.[29] Toews sold his share of the business to C.T. during the First World War; according to corporate advertising, 'true to the traditions of his forefathers [Toews] thought the farm was a better place to raise his growing family.'[30]

Some Mennonite groups rejected business ownership in favour of the ideal of agrarian life. Among the Kleine Gemeinde Mennonites who made up the majority of Steinbach inhabitants, however, business ownership was never frowned upon. The Kleine Gemeinde (literally 'small congregation') were the result of a church schism among Mennonites in nineteenth-century Russia. The group formed in 1812 in response to the perceived permissiveness of the Russian Mennonites. In southern Manitoba, the Kleine Gemeinde church leadership objected not to the formation of businesses so much as to their uncontrolled growth which could lead to unchristian greed and lack of humility.[31]

Indeed, C.T. Loewen's lifestyle was scrutinized by church leadership. He was criticized in *Bruderschaft*[32] meetings for allowing his daughter to play piano and for building a 'large and ostentatious' house.[33] C.T. was reputed to be the first purchaser of a car in Steinbach, a commodity that more conservative Mennonites rejected for its worldliness.[34] C.T.'s daughter, Elvira Loewen Toews, nonetheless suggested that her father had greater latitude in his personal life than other church members because of his financial contributions to the church; the *Bruderschaft* confined themselves to criticism rather than expulsion.[35]

C.T. Loewen began the manufacture of windows in 1917 with the purchase of a three-sided planer and combination woodworker. Brother-in-law Frank Friesen was hired as yardman and millworker; he would later become millwork manager. In 1919, a small factory was built, described as an 'insulated storage shed,' to supply windows and doors to the local market.[36] These were not the ready-to-install units that were marketed in the 1990s, but unassembled sills, jambs, sashes, and frames. Carpenters were needed to put together the windows and doors on site. When, in the winter months, housing construction decreased, the company experimented with a variety of product lines, including apiary supplies, office furniture, hydro pole cross-arms, and church pews.[37]

Expansion occurred in the 1940s. A lumber yard in the nearby town of Rosenort was purchased in 1941.[38] During the Second World War, due to a lumber shortage, the Loewens set up lumber camps at Simonhouse, Manitoba; Hudson Bay Junction, Saskatchewan; and Rock Creek, British Columbia.[39] Many of the Canadian Mennonite men who were granted conscientious objector status in the Second World War were assigned to alternative service work at these lumber camps. The camps provided an opportunity for C.T.'s sons George and Edward to learn management skills. While the Loewens served their religious community by providing Mennonite young men with an alternative to military service, the employment of conscientious objectors also lowered labour costs.[40]

George and Edward joined C.T. in administration of the company in 1946, and the business accordingly was renamed 'C.T. Loewen & Sons Ltd.' The retirement of founder C.T. Loewen in 1951 left management in the hands of his three sons, Edward, George, and C.P. (Cornie) Loewen.[41]

C.T. Loewen & Sons was able to find a market niche with the surge in home construction that followed the Second World War. Historian Veronica Strong-Boag explains that a variety of factors contributed to this housing boom: 'Between 1945 and 1960 nearly continuous prosperity, high employment, the extension of the welfare state, and the presumption of a limitless bank of natural resources generated income and hopes for a better life, and, if possible, the lifestyle of comfortable homes and new products advertised since the 1920s in the continent's popular media.'[42] The securing of 'comfortable homes' was encouraged by the passage in 1944 of the second National Housing Act (NHA) and the creation in 1945 of the Central Mortgage and Housing Corporation (CMHC). The NHA and CMHC were to address the 'large stock of aging and substandard housing, communities that lacked appropriate municipal services, rural areas that lacked electric power, and … substantial number of households living in crowded conditions or paying shelter costs they could ill afford.'[43] The legislation and the institution had the desired effect: 'the number of owner-occupied houses in Canada increased from 57 percent in 1941 to 65 percent in 1951 to 66 percent in 1961.'[44]

In the words of C.T.'s son C.P. Loewen, management at C.T. Loewen & Sons 'recognized that there was a real vacuum created because of the war.' 'Manufacturing plants were busy with war-related projects like airports, army barracks, and schools, and many of them came to us asking if we could supply windows. When the war was over, many of the returning veterans began building new homes, resulting in another big demand for windows.'[45] The millwork factory of C.T. Loewen & Sons began producing ready-to-install windows in 1955, following the lead of Andersen Windows of Minnesota.[46] C.T. Loewen had been producing individual window components (sills and jambs) for on-site assembly for the southeastern Manitoban market since 1917. Sales increased in 1948 when the millwork factory began selling their products through lumberyards in Manitoba and Saskatchewan, and a new planing mill was built in 1952 as a consequence.[47] Production increased again when contracts for building housing for Canadian National Railway workers were obtained in 1951 and 1953.[48]

As a result of the manufacture of prefabricated window units, by 1955 C.T Loewen & Sons was the largest employer in Steinbach.[49] C.P. Loewen explained, 'In 1955, we started to manufacture complete window components. Prior to this, it had just been window frames, so a customer still had to buy the hardware, and arrange for labour and assembly. Since we were one of the first window manufacturers in Western Canada to introduce this new concept and promote a complete window make-up, our sales literally took off.'[50]

The first catalogue advertising Loewen Windows' ready-to-install windows was produced in 1958.[51] Photos of the plant were included, together with descriptions of the manufacturing process. The catalogue explained that Ponderosa pine from British Columbia was kiln-dried on-site, then machined, dipped in a preservative sealant, and assembled. The catalogue advertised that these 'Loewen-Bilt' windows met CMHC specifications.[52] Windows were sent to Toronto for testing to obtain CMHC certification; weather-stripping in particular was checked to see if the windows were watertight.[53]

The catalogue was a key element for the sales staff. Dave Loewen, a cousin of C.P., became the company's first salesman in 1950. Originally hired to work in the millwork plant in 1937, his sales territory was Manitoba and Saskatchewan. By the late 1950s, he was the company's sales manager. Sales strategies in that decade included purchasing and analysing competitors' products. Dave Loewen would also give copies of *The Mennonite Cookbook*[54] to the wives of building supply company managers; 'they have influence, too,' he explained. A significant portion of sales meetings involved reviewing the company's sales catalogue and suggesting changes and improvements.[55]

The company experienced such success as a result of the production of these windows that expansion was necessary in 1960. The millwork factory moved from its location on Main Street to a new 57,000-square-foot operation on the outskirts of Steinbach.[56] The local newspaper described the new facility as 'a well-lit, spacious building which offers the best of working conditions for its employees.'[57] The factory's heating system was cited as an example of amenities that created exemplary working conditions. A dust collector sent waste to the boiler room where it was converted to heat to fire the boilers, which dried the lumber used in manufacturing. This process drew in air from outside, which was warmed as it passed through ducts, thus heating the plant. The newspaper reporter noted as well the provision of a dining room for workers, free coffee, individual lockers, and 'a ladies' lounge "of reasonable privacy," as requested by the Department of Labour but which few firms have.'[58]

The labour process in the plant involved a combination of automated and manual labour. Lumber was loaded onto a flatcar and pushed into the kiln where it was dried for three to ten days. Various machines were then used to transform the wood into window frames. The surfacers smoothed and sanded the wood. Cross-cut saws cut the lumber to length. Moulders and mortisers shaped the wood and ensured that corner joints were tight. The work in the glazing rooms did not rely on equipment, however. These rooms were 'where girls [*sic*] very expertly fasten the glass panes to the window frames and do the glazing' using a special glazing compound to seal the glass in the frame.[59] The few women who worked at the millwork factory were in either the office or the glazing room, where there was less heavy lifting.

In 1971, C.T. Loewen & Sons had become so large that a decision was made to split the lumberyard and millwork factory among the brothers. C.P. Loewen became sole owner of the millwork plant in December, registering the company on 23 May 1972 as 'Loewen Millwork.' Loewen Millwork became known as 'Loewen Windows' on 29 April 1985, and simply as 'Loewen' in 2001.[60] Product sales to western Canada and overseas markets fuelled further growth of Loewen Windows, resulting in numerous plant expansions in Steinbach and the opening of branch offices and showrooms in other provinces. In the early 1990s, taking advantage of the North American Free Trade Agreement, Loewen Windows began sales to the United States. The company also sought markets in Japan. By the end of the millennium, there were more than one thousand Loewen Windows dealers in North America, and more than 60 per cent of the company's production was exported to markets including Central and South America, Europe, and the Middle East.[61]

The manufacturing process at Loewen Windows had changed by the time the company celebrated its seventy-fifth anniversary in 1980. More women were employed on the shop floor, in part because increasing automation had reduced the need for heavy lifting.[62] Many machines continued to perform the same functions, however. Cross-cut saws still were used to cut lumber to length. Finger-jointers saved lumber by 'glue jointing short lengths to usable longer boards.' High-speed moulders still shaped wood, but were now 'enclosed in insulated booths for noise control and employee comfort.' Lumber was now dipped in preservative prior to assembly 'to protect the finished product from moisture and decay.' Double-end tenoners 'precision [cut] both ends of component parts to proper length to insure that the finished product is uniform in size at all times.' Sash assembly involved 'newly designed equipment [that] squares and nails all corners of [the] sash simultaneously.'[63]

Window production was tied to the construction season; few windows were needed during the winter. In the past, management had sought to keep workers busy by producing wood products other than windows, such as church pews and apiary equipment. With the increasing specialization of plant equipment and the abandonment of these sidelines, layoffs could not always be avoided: fifty workers were laid off in October 1977. Job-sharing was introduced from November 1984 to January 1985 in hopes of addressing the problem; employees worked for three days and collected Unemployment Insurance for two days.[64] More recently, cross-training and other job education initiatives have been used to occupy employees during the slow season. During busy times, however, securing and retaining a large enough workforce has been difficult.

The location of Loewen Windows in a small, rural town would appear to be a disadvantage. Basing their operation in Steinbach nonetheless had its benefits. While their competition spread out their manufacturing facilities geographically in their search for cheap labour, Loewen Windows' advantage was that 'everything [was] under one roof.' Admittedly, the limited local labour pool was a challenge, but the knowledge, skill, and work ethic of Steinbach area employees, the company's human resources director asserted, compensated for this difficulty.[65] Sociologist Anthony Winson and social anthropologist Belinda Leach note that rural areas often offer important economic advantages: non-union workforces and lower wages.[66]

Remaining in a small, rural community had other, less obvious advantages. As a town with a dominant industry, the community culture in Steinbach had much in common with single-industry towns.[67] In such communities, in which economic and social life are centred around one key firm, the result is 'a high level of shared knowledge, expectations, and norms.'[68] The fact that the majority of those residing in Steinbach were Mennonite only served to create a more cohesive common culture. Further, as sociologist Rex Lucas observes, 'in any community in which the main work force earns its livelihood in a single industry, and yet must live within the same small community, there can be no meaningful separation of work from non-work.'[69] It is thus much easier to create a paternalist culture of deference in a small, rural community – and in a primarily Mennonite town, it is much easier to reinforce such deference by linking it to religious themes such as yieldedness to authority.

In 2001, Loewen Windows underwent its largest expansion to that date. The decision in the 1990s not to enter the polyvinyl chloride (PVC or plastic) window market but to instead specialize in high-end wood windows was a profitable one for the company.[70] The Steinbach plant gained an additional 157,000 square feet, at a cost of $20 million – a cost borne solely by the company. Loewen Windows announced that it 'proudly draws its workforce from as far away as Lac Du Bonnet, Roseau River, Winnipeg and, of course, from Steinbach. "Our family business has been part of this community for almost 100 years. One of our key values has always been to create jobs that benefit our neighbours," add[ed] [CEO Charles] Loewen.'[71] Of course, Loewen Windows' assertion about corporate values must be balanced by the fact that maintaining the firm's location in a small, rural town guaranteed continued access to a deferential non-union workforce. As the new millennium began, Loewen Windows was transformed from a small business serving the local area with an exclusively Mennonite workforce to a company with a somewhat more ethnically diverse workforce of more than 1100, marketing its upscale products internationally.

Like Loewen Windows, Friesen Printers was founded in a small town by a second-generation Canadian Mennonite.[72] Altona was originally a small village established by Mennonite settlers in the Mennonite West Reserve in 1880; it came to be known as 'Old Altona' to distinguish it from the new town of Altona that was established a half mile to the north with the coming of a Canadian Pacific Railway spur line in 1883.[73] The two towns quickly grew into one. Altona at the end of the twentieth century was primarily a Mennonite agricultural community; many Altona area businesses were established in response to the needs of the surrounding agricultural area.[74] Involvement in business by Mennonites was less tolerated by the Old Colony, Bergthaler, and Sommerfelder Mennonite churches in Altona than by the Kleine Gemeinde Mennonites in Steinbach.[75] The agrarian ideal was upheld by these churches as the only sure way of maintaining the separation from 'the world' necessitated for godly living and spoken of in John 17 and Romans 12.[76]

D.W. Friesen, a *Kanadier* Mennonite and private-school teacher from Lichtfeld, Manitoba, moved to Altona in 1905.[77] After unsuccessfully operating a Massey-Harris implement business bought from John B. Schwartz, he purchased Jacob Schwartz's ten-year-old confectionery store in 1907.[78] In 1923, D.W. purchased a retail bookstore from school inspector G.G. Neufeld. A self-taught man, D.W. also served as Altona's postmaster, operated the local telephone office, and owned the town's general store. These business ventures, in addition to his considerable responsibilities as the only deacon in the Altona Bergthaler Mennonite Church,[79] led his son, Ted, to conclude that D.W. had 'no time for expansion ... he was just busy looking after what he had.'[80]

The most significant act of expansion by D.W. was made in response to his eldest son's desire to move away to a large urban centre. Son D.K. Friesen was eager to follow in the footsteps of his literary hero, Horatio Alger.[81] To curb his son's wanderlust, D.W. bought a car in 1930, which D.K. used to sell school supplies in the surrounding area.[82]

Wanting to establish a more permanent career, D.K. decided to enter the printing business in 1933. The only other printer in town was H.P. Dick, whose shop was often closed due to illness. D.K. bought a small hand-fed Gordon press and operated from the basement of his father's store, hiring his friend David J. Harder to assist with the job printing.[83] In 1935, D.K. purchased a second press, rented the building that had housed the Bergthaler Mennonite Church *Waisenamt* (trust company), and hired his cousin, D.G. ('Doc') Friesen.

Working conditions were challenging in the early years. On early winter mornings, 'Doc' Friesen would start a fire to soften the ink so the presses would be ready to roll by noon. Though employed as a press operator, 'Doc' also would assist with typesetting, as this process was laborious: 'that was all done by hand, taking little characters off of trays to set them together in lines – very primitive.'[84] The printing of one hundred copies of an arithmetic textbook for the local school stood out in his memory as an example of the physical difficulty and repetitive nature of the work in these early years, setting type two pages at a time.

The death of H.P. Dick in 1936 allowed D.K. Friesen to buy his print shop, using money borrowed from a retired farmer. The building was enlarged, and served not only as a print shop but also as living quarters for D.K. and his wife until 1947. More equipment was purchased, including the company's first Linotype.[85] The Linotype was a machine which melted metal to form type, allowing typesetters to set a line of type at a time instead of physically selecting every letter as was the case with hand composition of type.[86] A third employee, Peter Wolfe, was hired in 1939. Together, the men experimented with the unfamiliar equipment. Gregory Kealey's account of nineteenth-century Canadian printers distinguishes between the roles of pressmen and typesetters; at Friesen Printers, during the 1930s, these jobs were combined.[87] Wolfe recalled 'It seemed that every day we had to learn something new. As we had no one to teach us, we learned by working closely with each other. This is how we mastered the first job Mr. [D.K.] Friesen got for us that had to be printed on glossy stock. "Doc" [D.G. Friesen] fed the glossy sheets in at one end of the press, and I was at the other end, putting sheets of newsprint between the glossy sheets, otherwise we would have had a mess of offset.'[88] What they could not teach themselves they learned from their customers. Peter Wolfe recalled that he learned stylistic rules from a University of Manitoba professor for whom the business did some book printing: 'He taught us a lot [about] how book pages had to look. It was from him that we learned that no "widows" would be accepted.'[89]

D.K. began printing and publishing a local newspaper in 1940. The *Altona Echo* was later merged with the *Morris Herald* to become the *Red River Valley Echo*.[90] The first female employee was hired: Elizabeth (Isby) Bergen, a friend of D.K's brother, John.[91] She worked as a 'roving reporter,' visiting people in the community to obtain news. This method resulted in the perception of some that she 'was trying to sell them something, and [she] just wanted news about an anniversary, or a wedding, or whatever.'[92] Others had asked whether it bothered her to be the only woman working among the men. Her response was that she considered them people and it did not matter if they were men or women; she had a job to do and she did it. In fact, she believed her occupation provided her with opportunities that she otherwise might not have had, such as meeting people and travelling across Canada.

The regular production of the newspaper was a daunting task. Press operators like Peter Wolfe, however, found time to assert their independence through horseplay. On one occasion, he decided to 'play a prank on a neighbour' of his, one of the regular advertisers who sold men's clothing. This advertiser, Henry Kreuger, had placed an ad with the tagline 'Prices Low, Quality High.' The press operators printed one copy with the phrasing reversed to read 'Prices High, Quality Low' and had it delivered to Kreuger's store. Wolfe recalled that 'the next morning one of the crew looked out the window and saw [Kreuger] coming down the street, so we were waiting for him. But he didn't come into the print shop.' Instead, Kreuger went straight to D.K. Friesen, who then accompanied him to the composing room. Wolfe explained that Kreuger had the only copy of the newspaper with the faulty advertisement, but Kreuger was not easily convinced. As Kreuger 'was blowing off steam,' Wolfe looked over Kreuger's shoulder to see his employer, D.K. Friesen, wink at him in co-conspiracy.[93]

In 1948, D.K., Ray, and Ted Friesen bought their father's share of the company. The business was incorporated in 1951 as D.W. Friesen & Sons to 'carry on the trade or business of general printers, publishers, newspaper publishers, lithographers, engravers, book binders, book sellers, advertising agents, and the business of embossing, electrotyping, stereotyping, and manufacturing and dealing in stationery supplies of all kinds.'[94] The company name was changed to 'DWFriesen' in 1976 and 'Friesens Corporation' in 1995.[95] The brothers shared management duties: D.K. was responsible for the print shop and was company president, Ted took charge of the wholesale stationery division and served as secretary-treasurer, and Ray expanded the company's sales territory into Saskatchewan and Ontario while functioning as company vice-president.

The brothers sought an area of specialization, believing that 'commercial job printing would not give us the base we required to keep growing.'[96] 'Management foresaw that one could no longer be a general printer that did anything and everything. The thinking at the time had been, like with a general store or restaurant, that if you had the equipment, you could print anything. Management felt they had to pick a product and sell that product rather than sell "printing." People didn't buy printing; they bought a product.'[97] Postcard production was attempted, but colour was poor and the company did not have the equipment needed to coat the cards. The printing of magazines was similarly tried and rejected. Salesman Earl Schmidt suggested that the business expand its production of school yearbooks.[98] As a result of such trial and error, the company had become the third largest yearbook printer in Canada by 1976.[99] 'It was never a conscious decision that we would do "this and nothing else." Instead, it was a matter of trying to find something and exploiting that idea. Most major decisions [with respect to specialization] have been driven by sales staff who identified new areas and products rather than management hiring a consultant or coming up with an idea.'[100]

The adoption of new technology contributed to the success of the business. The switch from letterpress to offset printing began in 1954; a number of Miehle offset presses were purchased in 1959.[101] Former press operator 'Doc' Friesen observed that mastery of this technology was a point of pride for employees. Learning was by trial and error, though an effort was made to minimize errors, since 'that's losing money for the company.' Ultimately, offset printing was, in 'Doc' Friesen's view, 'much easier than the conventional method of hot metal.'[102] Technological innovations were accepted because of the improvements they made to the labour process. Offset printing did not require nearly as much cleaning of equipment as did hot metal printing.[103]

The seasonal nature of yearbook production meant that employees at D.W. Friesen & Sons were as susceptible to layoffs as those at Loewen

Windows had been. A reduction in staff in the late 1960s caused company management to explore other production opportunities. A paperbox manufacturing business was purchased from Scott Hull in 1971 and a 12,000-square-foot addition was built for a box and calendar plant.[104] The company continued to expand through construction of new building and plant additions. The workforce expanded accordingly, the company's growth reflected in the increase of Altona's population.

Management decided in 1976 to specialize in the production of high-quality, full-colour books and began a process of heavy investment in computerized Heidelberg and Komori presses three years later.[105] Mueller binding machines were introduced in 1974, and the bindery became fully automated in 1986 with the addition of casemakers, book-jacketing machines, perfect binders, sewing machines, foil-stamping machines, and embossers.[106] Typesetting was computerized in the early 1980s; authors were advised in 1982 that manuscripts could be submitted either as typescripts or in electronic format.[107] Flatbed scanners, laser scanners, and video cameras allowed all colour work and stripping to be done in-house.[108] Customers were informed in 1994 that 'prepress' is 'a term that is relatively new.' Layout, design, typesetting, proofreading, paste-up, camera work, and stripping had once been separate operations. Now, almost all of these processes could be performed on a desktop computer.[109] The press room was also computerized. Densitometers, which read the density of ink put down on a sheet of paper by the press, were replaced by computerized spectrophotometric devices that allowed inking adjustments to be made automatically and during the press run.[110]

With the closing of Toronto competitor Hunter-Rose in 1985, Friesen Printers took advantage of the opportunity to enter the book market. Several major publishers, including McClelland and Stewart, MacMillan Company of Canada, and Key Porter Books, gave them one book as a test. The trials were successful.[111] Expansion into the United States market occurred, and sales offices were opened in various cities in Canada and the United States. In 1996, Friesen Printers printed four hundred thousand copies of Jean Paré's *Company's Coming for Christmas*, the largest single order of a hardcover book ever printed in Canada, and in 1997, they celebrated the printing of the ten millionth copy of Robert Munch's bestseller, *Love You Forever*.[112]

The third generation of the Friesen family became part of management in the late 1980s. D.K. and Ted Friesen retired in 1986; Ray Friesen retired in 1989. David Glenn Friesen, son of D.K., was made printing division sales manager in 1974 and was assigned responsibility for the marketing of Friesen Printers as a whole. Tim Friesen, son of Ted, and John Victor Friesen, son of Ray, joined David Glenn as directors of Friesen Printers. In 1989, David Glenn became company president.[113] His uncle explained: he was 'the oldest of the three [cousins], the oldest son of the oldest brother, had been in the company the longest, had headed the largest part of the company, and was most capable.'[114]

Like Loewen Windows, Friesen Printers faced the benefits and disadvantages of operating in a small rural centre. The limited labour pool encouraged Friesen Printers to train its own employees through a graphic arts program operated on-site in conjunction with Winnipeg's Red River College. Loewen Windows is located only forty minutes from Manitoba's capital, Winnipeg, and operated its own fleet of delivery trucks. Friesen Printers is located ninety minutes from Winnipeg and also used its own trucking system. Both companies remained non-unionized into the twenty-first century, as did virtually all businesses in the two towns in which they are located. Indeed, the ability to tap into a pool of non-union labour was undoubtedly one of the advantages of remaining in small Mennonite towns rather than transferring production to Winnipeg. And the dependence of these towns on these dominant industries discouraged workplace activism. By 2002, one in seven people in Altona worked for Friesen Printers.[115] Since 1983, Friesen Printers has been among the top one hundred companies in Manitoba in sales; among rural Manitoba companies, Friesen Printers regularly placed in the top ten.[116]

The most successful of the Manitoba businesses founded by Mennonites has been Winnipeg's Palliser Furniture. The company was founded by Abram Albert (A.A.) DeFehr, a *Russlaender* Mennonite, in 1944. Until the privatization of Manitoba Telecom Systems in 1997, Palliser was the largest private employer in the province. Palliser Furniture grew from a handful of employees to become Canada's largest furniture manufacturer, with over three thousand workers by the end of the twentieth century.

The first Mennonites to arrive in Manitoba settled in the two rural ethno-religious reserves on either side of the Red River. The move to urban centres, particularly Winnipeg, began in the early twentieth century and accelerated after the Second World War, eventually turning

Winnipeg into the city with the highest urban concentration of Mennonites in the world. Historian John J. Friesen has attributed the Mennonite rural-to-urban shift to three factors: The establishment of towns on the reserves with railroad service 'broke the isolation of the farm villages as well as provided a haven for Mennonite dissenters.'[117] Immigrant Mennonites from Russia in the 1920s and post-war period were urbanized prior to their arrival in Canada, and so preferred to settle in urban centres. As well, the proximity of the Manitoba Mennonite reserves to Winnipeg facilitated rural-urban migration.

A.A. DeFehr was born in Millerowo, Russia, in 1910 into a wealthy Mennonite family.[118] His father, Abram, operated a mill that produced flour for bakeries in Moscow, St Petersburg, and Poland.[119] In December 1919, fearing that the mill would fall into enemy hands, the Bolshevik government demanded nine train cars of flour and enough equipment to immobilize the factory, threatening death for failure to comply. Abram DeFehr instead loaded the train cars with families wanting to leave the region around Millerowo and bribed station officials to allow the trains to travel south of Moscow to the Kuban. When he heard in 1922 that 'Lenin was reconciling former business owners with their businesses,' he made an unsuccessful effort to reclaim the mill. Informed by communist officials in Millerowo that 'he was not welcome there,' he abandoned his property and made plans to leave Russia.[120]

Religious persecution, the exile of *kulaks* (wealthy farmers), and famine were the reasons many Russian Mennonites wanted to leave the country in the 1920s. Many wished to join their relatives in Canada who had left Russia in the 1870s. Abram DeFehr also wanted to emigrate to Canada, but was unable to do so directly, possibly because of health concerns.[121] Instead, the family emigrated to Mexico in 1924, a country that had a significant Mennonite population due to the emigration of Old Colony Mennonites from Saskatchewan and Manitoba in the 1920s because of the Schools Question.[122] While the DeFehr family's migration to Mexico had some unforeseen advantages ('we got to see Cuba'), they immediately began to make plans for immigration to Canada, in part because the area in which they had settled, Ensenada, had no other Mennonites.[123]

The family was able to obtain the necessary papers for immigration to Canada in 1926. They left Ensenada via Tijuana and arrived in Victoria, British Columbia. Taking the train from Vancouver to Winnipeg, they stopped in Didsbury, Alberta, to spend Christmas with Abram DeFehr's brother-in-law. After a few days, the family continued to Winnipeg, where they had relatives and where a fellow Mennonite and former employee of Abram DeFehr helped them find lodging in the city's north end. Shortly after, the family moved to Lily Street, near the Canadian Pacific Railway station, and took in lodgers. Abram found work in a milling factory at first, and then became a finish carpenter. His son, A.A., found work at a Safeway grocery store. In 1940, A.A. DeFehr married Maria (Mia) Reimer, who was also an immigrant Russian Mennonite.[124] After the wedding, A.A. 'applied for work with Safeway again, and they said they had nothing in Winnipeg, but they had a place in Portage la Prairie [west of Winnipeg]. Well, what could you do? Jobs were not plentiful, so [he] accepted that and rented an upstairs, two rooms.'[125] While working at Safeway, A.A. began making furniture samples, wanting to find work that did not limit opportunities for advancement. Twice he had been promoted to produce manager and then fired and rehired at an entry level position. He said: 'I didn't really like the grocery business that much. I figured I don't want all my life to be a grocery clerk. And so, I was looking around, carpentry was the closest to me, I had learned it from my father, he was ... very accurate [and concerned about] quality ... He had to do everything just right, you know. So then I believe God gave me the idea.'[126]

What happened next is a story that has become a part of Palliser Furniture's corporate mythology, retold at employee orientations. A.A. DeFehr moved to Winnipeg, and on 25 September 1944, he sold his car for five hundred dollars and bought five pieces of woodworking equipment from Ashdown's Hardware and a how-to manual from Eaton's department store.[127] He built a kitchen step stool and took it to Ashdown's. An order for twenty-five step stools was placed. 'I figured, "Well, twenty-five I can't make in just after work, you know; I'll have to quit my job now."'[128] Production began in earnest in the basement of the family home. So began A.A. DeFehr Manufacturing, while later became Palliser Furniture.

A.A. DeFehr's recollection of the origins and development of his business draws on religious terminology and modes of discourse. The decision to go into the furniture business was an inspiration from God, he averred. Recounting the early years of the business in an employee newsletter, he asserted his belief that 'God granted us the grace to lay a good foundation of quality, service, and the ability to work together as a team.'[129] This recitation of corporate history uses the trope of a religious testimony: God inspires, God blesses. No matter the audience – external researcher/interviewer, existing employees, or new hires – the story is told the same way. By casting the early years of the business as a divinely inspired venture, deference and humility on the part of employees and researchers alike (and particularly of those who share his ethno-religious background) is promoted. This discourse was used more prevalently by A.A. DeFehr than either Charles Loewen or David Glenn Friesen, in part because he was from an older generation, but perhaps primarily because he was a member of a more evangelical branch of Mennonitism, one more prone to use religious language in public.[130]

Expansion began in 1945 when DeFehr Manufacturing moved from the basement of the family home to a chicken barn.[131] The first employees were Henry Krahn and George Dyck, who lived with the DeFehrs during the week, Erica Peters, who helped Mia with the children on Friday evenings and worked in the shop on Saturdays, and A.A.'s brother, John.[132] Within three years, the factory needed to be expanded, but residential zoning regulations prevented DeFehr from doing so: though small chicken operations were permitted, other industry was not. DeFehr thought 'maybe I could get away with a double garage, and in the double garage I would paint.' This small expansion was not well received, because of the smell and dust the operation produced. A longer term solution was needed, so A.A. DeFehr serendipitously negotiated a property deal with a man he met on a streetcar. They would trade properties and A.A. would pay to move the man's house and have it connected to hydro. Accordingly, in 1948, the business was moved to a new factory at 400 Edison Avenue in North Kildonan, and a staff of fifteen was hired.

The first products manufactured by the company were unfinished wooden ironing boards, end tables, folding kitchen step stools, ladders, tub stands, and racks for drying clothes.[133] By 1949, A.A. DeFehr had decided to specialize. 'One day I made my first end-table, like a half-moon end-table with three legs; then I took it to Eaton's. There was nothing else they could compare it to … and they became my first customer.'[134] The company stopped the manufacture of household items and focused on furniture production. In the 1950s, the company began producing arborite-topped tables and desks. The first upholstered furniture (gossip benches) was produced in 1963; dinette suites were offered the following year.[135] A new emphasis on style was introduced in the 1970s. Walnut and cherry veneers and the European influence on product design were emphasized in advertisements: 'Cortina occasional tables – our interpretation of Italy' and 'El Greco series occasional tables – featuring the characteristically intense carvings of Spain.' By the 1990s, the product line had expanded to include youth and master bedroom suites, entertainment units, home office furniture in solid oak or laminates, and a wide range of leather furniture.[136] The business was incorporated on 13 December 1955 as A.A. DeFehr Manufacturing Ltd. Its purpose was 'to manufacture, buy, sell, repair, work with and deal in wood, metal and mineral products, lumber, hardware, building materials, furniture, cabinets and accessories, to construct, demolish and repair buildings and to make improvements on both real property and chattels.'[137]

Generational succession became a question by 1960. DeFehr's son Frank had graduated from high school and his son Art was a student at Goshen College. DeFehr asked them, 'Do you want to join the company later in life? ... If you do, I'll plan on buying a new site for further expansion but if you plan to do something else, then this plant is big enough for me.'[138] The sons decided to make the business their career. Frank DeFehr joined the company in 1962, Arthur (Art) joined in 1967 and third son David (Dave) joined in 1972. The family distributed the administrative workload among themselves. A.A. DeFehr was responsible in the 1960s for plant engineering, plant layout, purchasing major equipment, establishing piecework rates, and supervising clerical staff.[139] Frank DeFehr was in charge of financing, personnel administration, purchasing, material supply, costing, and scheduling. Art DeFehr was responsible for product design and pricing, marketing and sales planning, product policy, advertising, shows, catalogues, billing, recruitment, and supervision of salespeople, as well as the finished goods warehouse and transportation fleet.[140]

As at Friesen Printers and Loewen Windows, the labour process and organizational hierarchy at Palliser Furniture were not clearly defined in the first decades after incorporation. A Quebec firm of management consultants hired by the Manitoba government examined Palliser Furniture's operations in 1971 and concluded that 'the plant organization is poorly structured, with too many of the responsibilities being assigned to the Plant Superintendent [Peter Reimer], who should receive more assistance from his staff.'[141] A.A. DeFehr was actively involved in the training of shop-floor workers, leaving much of the office and clerical work in the hands of his personal secretary, Jenny Restall. The result was that 'Miss Restall more or less acts as the office manager, and this seems to have created some friction among the clerical staff.'[142] The design process was criticized. DeFehr's designs were modified copies of other manufacturers' styles; there were no personnel trained in or tasked with product design.[143] Despite these flaws, the company was complimented on its marketing strategy, which was described as 'different but interesting.' A broad product range and a conscious decision not to market to Toronto resulted in a deliberately low profile that avoided challenging larger and more specialized manufacturers from central Canada for market share.[144]

With a master's in business administration from Harvard University, son Art DeFehr had made efforts to introduce modern management practices to the company in the late 1960s. Records were computerized, and production was forecast twelve months into the future on the basis of computer analysis of past orders.[145] These innovations were not sufficient, as the Quebec consultants' 1971 report indicated; founder A.A. DeFehr had not yet transferred full control of the company to the next generation. The recommendations of these consultants were implemented by management at the company. A designer from the United States was hired in 1972.[146] This decision was a marked change from the company's position in 1969, when Art DeFehr stated: 'Our basic approach to producing and selling our furniture is to follow trends once they have established themselves for a number of months. You don't make money on the latest trends ... We find that our furniture, which is mostly of the medium and lower-priced variety, is not affected by the latest styles and innovations.'[147] Wanting to expand their market and produce higher-priced furniture, the business needed to pay more attention to product style.

Expansion of the physical plant was ongoing from the 1960s through 1990s. Seven and a half acres of land were purchased on Vulcan Avenue in East Kildonan[148] in 1963, and a new 45,000-square-foot factory was built to accommodate fifty employees. The plant, including much of the production equipment, was designed primarily by A.A. DeFehr.[149] Upholstered furniture production began in earnest in 1969

Table 2.1. Palliser Furniture corporate divisions and related companies, 1993

Division	Year of inception	Sq. feet of factory	Products
DeFehr	1963	454,000	Casegoods
Towne Hall	1969	86,500	Fabric & leather upholstery
Springfield	1973	N/A	Plastic mirrors, headboards
Comfort	1977	138,000	Fabric & leather upholstery
Fargo	1981	146,640	Leather upholstery
World Trade	1982	17,400	Dinettes, occasional tables
Logic	1986	343,000	Laminate casegoods
Showwood	1988	10,300	Accent wood
Particle Board	1989	66,150	Particle board
Carolina	1989	415,000	Laminate casegoods, leather upholstery

Source: Palliser Furniture employee newsletter 12, no. 5 (Spring 1993).

at a new business in Calgary (which later moved to Airdrie, Alberta) known as Towne Hall Industries. In 1973, Springfield Industries, a urethane and melamine plastic parts plant, was established to provide headboards and mirror trim. Comfort Furniture of Winnipeg was purchased in 1977. A casegoods (wooden furniture) factory was opened in Fargo, North Dakota, in 1981, a particle board furniture plant in Winnipeg in 1986 (the Logic Division), and a World Trade Division in Winnipeg in 1982. In 1982, Rocky View Industries, a casegoods and sleep products factory in Alberta, was combined with Towne Hall Industries.[150] A particle board production facility was purchased and relocated from Germany to Winnipeg in 1989; European particle board technology was well in advance of its North American counterpart.[151] The inability to obtain particle board in the early 1980s due to strikes had convinced the DeFehr family to end their dependency on suppliers in this area.[152] The same year, permanent showrooms and offices were opened in High Point, North Carolina, the furniture capital of North America.[153] In 1991, an upholstery factory was established in Fargo and a casegoods and leather upholstery plant was purchased in Troutman, North Carolina (see table 2.1).[154]

Before 1980, these companies were operated as independent albeit interrelated businesses by A.A. DeFehr and his sons, Frank, Art, and

Dave. They were amalgamated as divisions of Palliser Furniture in January 1980.[155] A.A. DeFehr retired as president, becoming chairman of the board, while his three sons alternated terms as president. All four family members, the family claimed, held 'equal shares in the company and work[ed] with a consensus on all issues.'[156] Until the arrival of Indo-Chinese refugees in 1979–80, Palliser Furniture's workforce remained primarily Mennonite.[157]

The organizational structure changed in 1995 when Art DeFehr left the company after purchasing its leather upholstery divisions. Frank became president of Palliser Furniture.[158] A year later, however, Art became president and majority shareholder of Palliser. Frank left to run the particle board plant 'as a separate entity.' The family's ability to manage the company by consensus had apparently come to an end, though a company news release claimed, 'All family members feel very positive about the outcome of the restructuring.'[159] Palliser Furniture entered the global marketplace in the 1990s with product sales throughout Canada, the United States, Korea, Finland, Turkey, Saudi Arabia, the United Arab Emirates, Scotland, Mexico, Costa Rica, Puerto Rico, Honduras, and Guatemala (see table 2.2). By 2003, such overly aggressive expansion resulted in financial strain, and Art DeFehr sold the DeFehr (solid-wood furniture) Division of Palliser Furniture to his brother, Frank. The former division was renamed DeFehr Furniture and became a separate enterprise employing approximately 550 people.[160]

Art DeFehr has considered the moral implications of this global expansion of Palliser Furniture. In November 1998, he gave a speech at the annual convention of Mennonite Economic Development Associates (MEDA), an association for Mennonite businesspeople and professionals seeking to connect faith and work.[161] He commented that globalization had resulted in the primacy of economics over morality and a disconnection between decision makers and those affected by economic choices. 'What does it mean to be a Christian in a context where the basic economic, political and financial structures are amoral because of this disconnect?' he asked. Morality is only possible in the context of community, he argued, and when business is conducted at great distances, morality is impossible.

The Christian businessperson, DeFehr stated, is condemned to participate in this ethical vacuum in order to compete. DeFehr himself, as chief executive officer of Palliser Furniture, was forced to make morally questionable business decisions, he confessed. He offered as an example a hypothetical decision to cut staff to increase share values. 'A visit to the grocery store would become distinctly unpleasant when we have to look into the eyes of those affected by our arbitrary decisions. But,' he noted, 'Palliser is that arbitrary in Asia.' By hiring contractors to manage overseas production, he said, he insulated himself from the ethical consequences of such business decisions. 'When the value of the currency drops in country A, our contractor will move a product from factory country B to benefit from the lower price. Is that fair? I may never have even visited either factory and will never need to look the affected employees in the eye.'[162] Does the role of the Mennonite businessperson then entail moral responsibility only to the community in which he or she lives? DeFehr asserted that such choices were unavoidable, if regrettable. 'In this larger global world, we stop being accountable to one another, and ethical questions tend to be sacrificed.'[163] Business survival requires the ability to compete on a global scale.

Thus global capitalism was the reason behind Palliser Furniture's decision to open two factories in Saltillo, Mexico, in 1998. DeFehr emphasized that the company's foreign involvement was not that of the typical multinational corporation. For one thing, the DeFehrs had a connection to the country, albeit a tenuous one: 'My father was a shoe shine boy in Mexico during the '20s so the country is not entirely foreign!'[164] Rather than using a contract approach, DeFehr chose to invest directly in the country: he and other Palliser Furniture executives visited Mexico personally, rather than employing a consultant to monitor operations there. Further, DeFehr deliberately avoided establishing a facility in the zone populated with *maquiladoras*.[165] After surveying wages and working conditions in the region, the company 'selected a level [of wages] close to the better employers,' he claimed. DeFehr did not explain why he chose to pay his Mexican employees wages that were 'close to' those of 'the better employers' rather than higher or lower rates. He did this despite his observation that income disparities in North America had increased dramatically, which led him to ask rhetorically, 'Why is there no revolution? Will there be a collapse in the consensus that our society is basically fair? Will there be a collapse in the international consensus about the fairness of the world and its systems?'[166]

There were other aspects of Palliser Furniture's involvement in Mexico that distinguished the company from others operating in the region, DeFehr asserted. 'Our goal is to become part of the Mexican fabric – to get to know our Mexican managers and employees as well as we know their counterparts in Canada … There are many things that we cannot change about Mexico, but we can make choices.'[167] Some of these choices may have had unintended consequences. DeFehr explained that he chose to locate near a city centre 'to make [Palliser's Mexican] factories more appealing to the work force.' Presumably the thinking was that employees would benefit from the products and services available in an urban environment. But did such placement also encourage rural flight? DeFehr noted that he was also involved in the Mexican community by 'encouraging the North American Mennonite agencies to become more active and interventionist' in Canadian-descendent Low German–speaking Mexican Mennonite colonies.[168] 'The real issue is whether the Mexican Mennonites should be pressured to improve their incredibly bad education system and should be encouraged to move to more open leadership.' While DeFehr may have seen such encouragement as a contribution to Mexican Mennonite colony life, the Low German–speaking colonists themselves may have had a different perspective. DeFehr was a member of the Mennonite Brethren Church; the colonists belonged to offshoots of the communitarian Old Colony Mennonite Church. The Mennonite Brethren were arguably among the most evangelical of the Mennonite denominations; the Old Colony placed great importance on ecclesiastical authority and emphasized nonverbalized personal piety (Christian faith as a journey in ecclesial community, with salvation as a hope rather than a certainty) rather than crisis conversion (an individual decision to possess and witness to a personal, salvific relationship with Christ).[169]

Though extolling the virtues of Palliser Furniture's involvement in Mexico, DeFehr did not proffer hope that capitalism's flaws would be readily overcome by such initiatives. Recalling his experiences as a student activist in the 1960s, he regretted his loss of faith in the inevitability of social progress.[170] Individuals were still capable of making the choice to 'operate according to reasonable standards' but these choices were 'largely futile' without a broader change in the social, economic, and political system. 'We can create a few holy corners or at least pretend to. We can be a presence and a testimony and at times clean up the mess created by others. But we should not kid ourselves that we are making the world a better place.' DeFehr warned that the future was 'very ominous.' 'I look in vain for thoughtful and informed voices to present alternatives to the economic currents that are divorcing morality and the marketplace. We need some prophets but there are few in sight.'[171]

Palliser Furniture, Friesen Printers, and Loewen Windows are three Manitoba economic successes. All three were founded by Mennonite men who hired a local Mennonite labour force. All three were able to expand their operations and increase sales to become the largest employers in their communities.[172] In all three cases, the second generation was involved in the family business from an early age. The transition in ownership from the founder-father to the sons was thus comparatively smooth. D.K. Friesen, for example, had worked as the accountant in his father's general store and post office, and later was employed as a stationery salesman. Art DeFehr spent his first years in the business as company sales manager, overseeing everything from product design to shipping. Charles Loewen was responsible for transportation before becoming warehouse manager in Steinbach and branch manager in Edmonton.[173]

Such involvement meant that these companies avoided the 'second-generation decline' characteristic of those firms whose founders relinquished control only at their deaths. Historian Angela Davis observes that, in such cases, the successors' subsequent lack of familiarity with the corporation could result in the death of the business.[174] At all three companies of this study, the transition to the second generation occurred during the founder's lifetime. At Friesen Printers and Loewen Windows, the transition to the third generation followed the same pattern. John Loewen said of his father, C.P. Loewen, second generation president of Loewen Windows: 'He acted, he didn't discuss it. He gave the business to his kids. I don't know how much clearer you can communicate succession planning than actually doing it.'[175]

One of the difficulties of succession is adjudicating the hierarchy that exists among siblings involved in corporate leadership. The Friesen family appears to have avoided this problem. D.K. Friesen was the oldest sibling and the one who began the printing division of the company, and so was a logical choice for company president. The other two divisions of the company, stationery sales and yearbooks, became the responsibility of Ted and Ray respectively.[176] While differences of

Table 2.2. Annual sales and number of employees at Friesen Printers, Loewen Windows, and Palliser Furniture, 1963–2004

Year	Friesen Printers	Loewen Windows	Palliser Furniture*
1963	$1,013,706; est. 32–130	N/A; N/A	$630,000; 50
1969	$2,456,841; 130	N/A; N/A	$3,070,000; 170
1971	$3,036,479; est. 150	$5 661 385; 90	$4,000,000; 175
1974	$6,023,102; est. 150	$7,280,152; 180	$6,645,000; 245
1980	$17,730,919; est. 250–360	$18,436,004; N/A	$36,000,000; 600
1987	$36,153,227; est. 360–400	$41,552,244; N/A	$100,000,000; 850
1988	$42,409,310; est. 360–400	$42,410,159; N/A	$120,000,000; 1,600
1993	$52,433,810; est. 400–450	$47,172,686; est. 530–660	$192,900,000; 1,480
1994	$55,663,957; est. 400–450	$50,501,061; est. 530–660	$225,000,000; 1,800
1997	$73,500,000; est. 450–550	$55,820,679; est. 530–660	$330,000,000; 2,450
2003	N/A; N/A	$110,892,313; 1138	N/A; 3,800
2004	N/A; N/A	N/A; N/A	$500,000,000; 3,200

Sources: From documents held by Friesen Printers, Loewen Windows, and Palliser Furniture; *Steinbach Carillon News*; *Winnipeg Free Press*; *Winnipeg Tribune*; *The Binford Guide*; *World Link*; *Charlotte Observer* [North Carolina]; *Furniture/Today*; *Trade and Commerce*; *Mennonite Life*; *The Marketplace*; Toews and Klippenstein, *Manitoba Mennonite Memories*, 221; Mills, 'Gender, Ethnicity, and Religion,' 165, 195; McGuinness, *Friesens*, 121, 150, 154–5.
*Employee numbers are for facilities in Winnipeg only.

opinion among the brothers would occur and the 'older brother sometimes exercised his elder authority,' decisions usually were made by consensus.[177] Transition to the third generation of the Friesen family was simplified by the fact that David Glenn Friesen was the oldest and had the most experience.

Succession was more of a challenge at Palliser Furniture and Loewen Windows than at Friesen Printers. In the mid-1990s, as described above, there was some awkwardness as Frank and Art DeFehr bought out portions of each others' holdings in the company.[178] The third generation of the C.P. Loewen family consisted of four brothers and a sister, and hierarchies of age and gender played an important role in determining positions within the company. The youngest brother, John Loewen, explained: 'the oldest brother, twenty years older than [me], is there sooner ... Pragmatically, you know there's only one CEO position and three qualified brothers, at least three qualified brothers, to take that position.'[179]

The difficulty of establishing a hierarchy among the Loewen siblings was ongoing. The corporate accountant reminded the family in 1988 of 'their father's wishes that his children get along with one another, and he urged resolution of sensitive and controversial issues.'[180] A year later, the directors emphasized the need to clarify the distinction between Paul's role as chief executive officer and Charles's role as president of Loewen, as did Paul Loewen himself in 1994.[181] By 1999, only brothers Charles and Clyde Loewen were involved in management.[182]

The role of women in the management of these companies was quite limited. D.K. Friesen's wife, Mary T. Friesen, was a director of Friesen Printers in 1951, 1958 and 1959. Ted Friesen explained, however, that she 'only appears [on the list of directors] because [they] needed an extra body. She was never active.'[183] Sara Klippenstein Streimer Friesen, widow of D.W. Friesen, was a similarly inactive director from 1954 to 1959. Elizabeth Bergen, the first female employee at Friesen Printers, was a director in 1961–2. In the first decade after incorporation, board membership had included the three Friesen brothers and one or two shareholding employees. The Friesen family believed that share ownership necessitated a voice in the management of the business.[184] The decision was made in the early 1960s to limit board members to the three Friesen brothers and those in charge of the corporate divisions, a decision that resulted in there being no females on the board after 1963.[185]

As at Friesen Printers, there have been female directors at both Palliser Furniture and Loewen Windows. Until the 1990s, board membership at both these companies was limited to family members, and the female directors were members of the companies' founding families. A.A. DeFehr's wife, Mia Reimer DeFehr, was a director at Palliser

Furniture from 1966 to 1978. Daughter Irene DeFehr Loewen, president of the DeFehr Foundation, the family's charitable organization, has been a Palliser Furniture director since 1980. Art DeFehr's daughter, Shanti DeFehr, in management at the Logic Division, was a director from 1996 to 2000. His wife, Leona, has been a director since 1998.[186] At Loewen Windows, C.P. Loewen's only daughter, Che Anne Loewen, was a director until she sold her shares in the business in 1989.[187]

A perceptive insight into the difficulties of family corporate partnership, particularly for female family members, was offered by one of the co-owners of one of these businesses. Speaking of a female relative's departure from a leadership role in the business, he stated: 'I suspect [she] didn't feel much like an equal or respected partner ... Business language can be very macho, I suspect, and powerful; it uses lots of power elements.' He believed another sibling left the business 'because he felt rejected by his brothers.' The issue, he believed, was that qualities one appreciates in a sibling are not necessarily qualities one appreciates in a business leader: 'If there's only one leader, you might not choose the most patient or human of the two; in fact, you might pick the asshole who gets the job done.'

While existing in three different communities in Manitoba, the origins of these three companies are similar to each other and are typical of family-owned businesses of the early to mid-twentieth century in Canada. The rural businesses, Friesen Printers and Loewen Windows, emerged in response to local needs. The urban business, Palliser Furniture, was established in response to limits on personal upward mobility of the immigrant founder. There is nothing in the origins of these companies that is particularly unique or that distinguishes them as *Mennonite* businesses from their non-Mennonite counterparts in the province. Similarly, the structures of these businesses in their early years were in no way unique in ownership, management style, labour relations, or gender equity. Other Manitoba businesses exhibited similar characteristics, whether in their promotion of their humble origins, their decision to expand to serve a broader North American market, or in the assertion of the role of religious faith in their management decision-making process.[188] It was only the creation of a distinctively Mennonite corporate mythology at these businesses that differentiated them from other Manitoba workplaces.

3

Mennonite Corporate Mythology: The 'Reflections' Campaign

To varying degrees throughout their history, the management and ownership of three of Canada's largest Mennonite-owned businesses have represented themselves as 'Mennonite workplaces.' Such portrayals have drawn upon a number of mythologies, including that of the refugee immigrant turned successful business founder and of the transplantation of olde worlde European craftsmanship. Cultural critic Roland Barthes notes that such mythologies are rooted in history but have been mystified by a particular culture. The function of mythology, he declares, is the naturalization of ideology, and of bourgeois ideology in particular.[1] At Palliser Furniture, Friesen Printers, and Loewen Windows, a specific form of bourgeois ideology took shape. This 'Mennonite corporate mythology' was characterized by a strong work ethic, an emphasis on quality craftwork, and a combination of religious humility and yieldedness.

The examination of corporate mythology in this chapter meets a need that too often has gone unaddressed in business history. Kenneth Lipartito, historian of business and technology, asserts that business historians need to 'light out for the unknown territory of semiotics.'[2] He invokes anthropologist Clifford Geertz and historian Michel Foucault to argue that businesses should be read as texts 'to expose the cultural constructs they signify,' as well as their 'power to ascribe meaning, and thereby constrain, control, or claim to represent what is real.'[3] Communications historian Richard R. John argues similarly that business history needs to expand its horizons beyond the Chandlerian universe. He asserts that Chandler has overshadowed the valuable contributions of other business historians, such as Thomas Cochran's emphasis on culture, geography, and the environment; Martin Sklar's and James Livingston's connection of the rise of a managerial class to workers' loss of autonomy; and Oliver Zunz's treatment of the managerial class as a diverse group whose actions were designed to 'guarantee themselves a secure livelihood and a challenging career.'[4] John calls for a business history situated in a broader 'political, cultural, and social context' that incorporates cultural studies and semiotics into 'the comparative institutional approach to historical change that lies at the core of the Chandlerian tradition.'[5]

A cultural studies approach to business history in a Mennonite context, then, requires examination of the ideological creation and use of religious values for capitalist ends; that is, of mythology. Among North American Mennonites, one of the most pervasive mythologies is that of the Mennonite work ethic. The elements and operation of this ethic have received little attention from scholars. One of the few to investigate the Mennonite work ethic is economist Estel Wayne Nafziger, who does so in light of Max Weber's *The Protestant Ethic and the Spirit of Capitalism*. He defines Mennonitism in terms of historian Harold Bender's 'Anabaptist Vision': discipleship, nonconformity, love, and brotherhood.[6] He asserts that the Mennonite work ethic conforms to Weberian analysis in that, like the Protestants of Max Weber's classic study, Mennonites connect prosperity with righteousness, emphasize stewardship of wealth, and believe in the value of hard work and the accumulation of capital when used for spiritual ends.[7] Nafziger's study is confined to rural U.S. Mennonites in the decades of the 1920s and 1930s, and thus is of limited use in understanding the operation of the Mennonite work ethic in both post-war North American industrial capitalism and later twentieth-century globalized economies. Further, his reliance on Bender's categories for his definition of Mennonitism gives his interpretation an ahistorical fixity.

In addition to variations on Weber's Protestant work ethic, paternalism has proved a popular means of understanding workplace relations from the employer's perspective. Paternalism, the interaction of company values with class and gender inequalities, has been ably examined by Canadian historian Joan Sangster.[8] Male employers often sought to establish a community feeling in the workplace, 'often by equating the factory with an actual or imagined family,' with themselves as the dominant father-figure. 'Paternalism was intended to avoid labour unrest, to preserve managerial authority, and to satisfy a patrician sense of philanthropy. While often cloaked in a rationale of obligation, duty, or honour, paternalism essentially justified, extended, or at most modified existing power relationships.'[9] Sangster equates paternalism with the Gramscian notion of hegemony.[10] Ideology, defined as 'the production and articulation of systems of social meanings, values and belief systems,' is reinforced by social practices.[11] The power relationships established within the workplace by managers and owners are duplicated in the community and so become reified or naturalized. Class consciousness – the awareness of class inequality – is discouraged by the promotion of the 'illusion of community.'[12] Paternalism thus encourages 'consent to economic hierarchy as [an] inevitable part of daily life.'[13]

The composition of the town in which a company is situated plays a crucial role in the success of paternalism. In the small town atmosphere of Peterborough, Ontario, Sangster observed that paternalism was made effective by the 'geographical proximity of worker and manager in some neighbourhoods and churches, close knowledge of family networks, and a stable social hierarchy [which] bolstered the ideological hegemony operating within the factory, creating the illusion of an "organic community" in which class and community interest were one and the same.'[14] The absence of labour unions at Peterborough 'meant that workers did not have at hand institutional or ideological alternatives to the paternalist bargain.'[15] Instead, workers manipulated the paternalist arrangement for their benefit. 'Though on the surface paternalism seemed to symbolize deference to one's employer, a more negotiated accommodation was involved. While the paternalist bargain meant acquiescence, at least to some extent, to economic inequality ... at work, a distinct notion of dignity owed to workers and the respectability of their aspirations and lives ... was promoted and defended by the workers themselves.'[16] When paternalism was no longer able to 'deliver the economic goods,' deference – the 'moral legitimation of class domination' – collapsed.[17]

While the Protestant work ethic and paternalism are useful, they are insufficient for understanding workplace relations within a Mennonite context. What is proposed here instead is an examination of the creation of a workplace culture which assesses the role played by the religious component without neglecting change over time or the implications of the reification of ideology. Max Weber's work ethic, Patrick Joyce's understanding of deference, Joan Sangster's work on paternalism, and Roland Barthe's deconstruction of myth are all helpful here, but each of these scholars pays insufficient attention to the role of religion.[18] Scholars such as Lynne Marks and David Hall have produced interesting works on 'lived religion,' but there has been little in this field that does not focus on overt religious practices or religion within the context of family life.[19] The examination of Mennonite corporate mythology here will instead view religion not merely (and crudely) as the manipulative tool of a more powerful class of owners and managers. Instead, religion will be examined as the embodiment of faith or belief within the workplace, contributing to the creation of a corporate mythology that was shaped by Mennonitism.

The creation of a Mennonite corporate mythology at Friesen Printers began shortly after incorporation in 1950 and the assumption of managerial control by the second generation of the Friesen family. The religious heritage of the founder was invoked in memos, advertising, and in-house speeches. Employees were entreated to emulate the founder's frugality, honesty, effort, social conformity, and acceptance of authority.[20] A draft version of a corporate history, written by one of the business owners, states that founder D.W. Friesen had come from 'a simple, rural background. Hard work, plain living, conforming to the religious and social community, were not only expectations but necessities.'[21] Much as Mennonites were encouraged by their churches to pattern their lives after Christ, the workers at Friesen Printers were to be, in essence, disciples of the founder: 'We as Management want to renew and magnify that heritage [of our founder]. It is important that every employee fit into the pattern of this aim and policy. You are identified with the organization you work for; therefore, your conduct directly or indirectly will be a reflection on D.W. Friesen & Sons Ltd. We are confident that you will be happy and find satisfaction in working for our firm if you are in harmony with its objectives.'[22]

The founder's spiritual values were promoted by the owners to management and workers alike. Company president D.K. Friesen, for example, read a statement of corporate objectives at a shareholders meeting in 1955 that 'stressed that it was the wish of the executive that the employees of the company live a life consistent with [the founder's Christian] principles and thus honor the memory of the founder after whom the firm has been named.'[23] In a 1957 memo to staff, D.K. mentioned having read a 'creed' that he wished to apply to himself and share with the staff. He quoted: 'I believe in the work this business is doing, and in the fellowship of those who work with me in it, and in what it produces. I am willing to serve faithfully, to get together in solving problems, and to work harmoniously in getting the work done.'[24] The quotation is couched in the language of a religous confession of faith, which serves to elevate the values espoused. D.K. Friesen reminded employees that 'Business, if successful, must serve a purpose. That purpose is to serve fellow men. In serving others we find the greatest happiness, a service that makes life worthwhile.'[25]

A performance evaluation form dating from the 1960s provides further insight into the attributes which were valued by upper management at Friesen Printers.[26] The form addressed two areas: 'personal qualities and characteristics' and 'ability to manage an operation.' Qualities evaluated included honesty, integrity, personal appearance, maturity, judgment, initiative, leadership, cooperation with others, tact, and diplomacy. An employee's loyalty was examined by such questions as 'Does his job and the Firm come first over outside interests? Will he defend and support the Firm whenever necessary?'[27] An employee's involvement in community affairs must demonstrate 'an earnest desire to participate, not half-hearted.' Nor should this involvement be disinterested: 'Has his effort been good for the Firm?' The employee's home life was investigated: 'Does he live within his means? Has he a progressive attitude?' A progressive attitude was defined as a desire to be 'a success at his work, in his home, and in the community.'

The second area of evaluation, the ability to manage an operation, was assessed in four categories on this form. Employees' knowledge of operations and ability to produce results, their supervisory abilities, their aptitude in financial administration, and their skill with public relations were examined. An important aspect of supervisory skill was the ability to earn authority. 'Has he earned authority through gaining the respect of his employees,' the form asked, 'based on his own abilities to work with and through people harmoniously, yet decisively and fairly, without favoritism.'

In exchange for the loyalty and conformity of their employees, management promised to 'make [them] feel at home,' to respect them, and to provide financial security and the opportunity to develop individual talents.[28] 'Last but not least,' the company promised 'the development of a healthy community through the providing of goods and services, through deepening of spiritual values, and the strengthening and stabilization of the economic base.'[29]

Press operator and proofreader D.G. Friesen, a cousin of D.K. Friesen, recognized this integration of Mennonite religious beliefs with corporate ideology. In an interview conducted long after he had retired, he asserted that the religious faith of the owners at Friesen Printers 'was the top priority, especially with D.K. His father, David W., had been a very solid influence in those boys' lives. And especially D.K. tried to follow that up through his business practices. And in these [official corporate history] books that have been printed, it's mentioned a number of times, the basic principle: "Do good to your fellow man," which they've tried to instil in the management.'[30] This employee had internalized the Mennonite corporate mythology at Friesen Printers to such an extent that he referred to its promotion in company publications as proof of its validity and independent existence. Further, the power of the corporate mythology was such that it still influenced him years after he had left the company.

At Palliser Furniture, the founder's immigrant origins and religious values were emphasized in company promotional material as early as the 1970s. The company website in the early twenty-first century continued to trade upon those origins and the values they implied.

AT PALLISER WE BUILD VALUE WITH VALUES
The year was 1944. Abram Albert DeFehr, a Russian born immigrant to Canada, began making simple wooden pieces in the basement of his Winnipeg home ... Today, Palliser is Canada's leading home furniture manufacturer, providing a livelihood for over 4000 people, funding a philanthropic foundation that shares profits with communities around the world, and continuing to build value with values.[31]

Those values were further articulated in a section of the company's mission statement, created in 1997:

OUR VALUES
Building on a heritage of faith, we aspire to:
Demonstrate integrity in all relationships.
Promote the dignity and value of each other.
Respect the environment.
Support our community.
Strive for excellence in all we do.[32]

The company president and son of the founder, Art DeFehr, linked the Christian values and immigrant heritage of the founder with the largely immigrant nature of the company's workforce and environmentally friendly practices of the business in the late twentieth and early twenty-first centuries. In a message posted on the corporate website, he stated: 'There are approximately 4000 employees at Palliser from 70 nations who speak in 40 tongues. But we speak in only one voice as to our purpose and we live by one set of values. We believe that adherence to these values creates the best conditions to deliver genuine value to our retail partners and to consumers … God has blessed us and we seek to honor our Creator by being responsible in our business practices and our social and environmental impact.'[33] Such use of religious terminology was indistinguishable from that of mainstream evangelical Christian rhetoric.

The operation of Mennonite religious values in the workplace was not the simple equivalent of evangelical Christian values, however. While the end result may have been the same (worker deference in a non-union environment), Mennonite religious discourse in the workplace drew on the values of yieldedness in ways that evangelicalism did not. For example, the power of Mennonite corporate mythology at Palliser Furniture was strengthened by the decision of the DeFehr family to maintain their ties to Winnipeg's Mennonite community by living in a suburb that was a Mennonite ethnic enclave and by adjusting their consumption habits to meet Mennonite community expectations. Company president Art DeFehr asserted that his family made a 'deliberate choice' to remain within the Mennonite community and 'subject themselves to its judgment.'[34] Even at the height of the company's success in the 1990s, the DeFehrs continued to live and shop within North Kildonan (a Winnipeg suburb with a large concentration of Mennonites), he said, rather than 'fleeing to Tuxedo' (a wealthier Winnipeg suburb) as other successful businesspeople had done. By conforming to expectations regarding consumption and residence, for example, the family's perceived stewardship encouraged employee loyalty and conformity. Irene Loewen, daughter of company founder A.A. DeFehr, recalled: 'My father, when they had the means, loved to give luxuries to mother. But she didn't want them, she didn't feel comfortable with them. In the States when she was living there, she had learned to use make-up, she went to movies, even tried dancing. When she moved to North Kildonan she dropped all of it except her intellectual interests in order to fit in with the rest of the women. When dad wanted to buy her a fur stole she refused, feeling she would stand apart from the other women of the church. When she finally did get a fur coat it wasn't the luxury type that dad wanted to buy her.'[35] Such visible conformity served to reinforce the moral authority of the employer, an authority which extended beyond the workplace. Dave DeFehr, one of the founder's sons, declared: 'one of the pluses or one of the reasons why I think we have a fairly good culture at Palliser is that a lot of us, a lot of the executive and senior people [are] rubbing shoulders with regular employees in a church setting. We sit on the same bench at church or sit on the same [church] committees.'[36] Sharing a pew or committee responsibilities, of course, does not necessarily translate into equal social relations. In fact, it may serve merely to obscure those relations.

At Loewen Windows, the operation of Mennonite values took a highly visible form. A weekly fifteen- to twenty-minute chapel service for employees was provided, beginning in 1964, when employees requested an opportunity to gather for prayer after an employee died on the job.[37] Similarly, board meetings at the company always have begun with a devotional message and prayer. Company president Charles Loewen explained that such practices stemmed from a 'sense of a sacred obligation,' noting that he had 'been taught that the earth is the Lord's and everything in it.' He asserted that his family's access to 'power and money, assets' was a gift, as were their 'Midas touch ...,' wealth creation, leadership, the ability to attract followers in a worthy cause.' These gifts were from God, and the Loewen family was 'responsible to develop them' in order to 'perpetuate a wealth creation machine which [could] be beneficial to many, many people.'[38] Such declarations of Christian stewardship are more than simply an evangelical Christian religious gloss on age-old paternalist business philosophies: they draw on particularly Mennonite religious emphases, such as neighbourly love and the Benderian stress on discipleship.

At all three companies, the Mennonite corporate mythology was reinforced by the provision of social activities by the businesses and the involvement of business owners in the social and economic life of the broader community. Historians Joan Sangster, Joy Parr, Andrea Tone, Nikki Mandel, and Gerald Zahavi describe similar processes at work at factories in both Canada and the United States in the first half of the twentieth century.[39] Corporate social activities functioned as company rituals: picnics, Christmas parties, retirement dinners, multiethnic cultural festivals, boat cruises, golf tournaments, organized sports teams, and street parties were some of the many such activities.[40] These pursuits cultivated identification with and loyalty to the businesses that provided them. The indoctrination of Mennonite corporate mythology was fostered further by in-house publications, such as employee newsletters: the *Friesen Informer* at Friesen Printers, *Loewen Behold* at Loewen Windows, and an unnamed publication at Palliser Furniture. These newsletters not only provided information but helped shape workplace culture and encourage worker deference. The authority of employers at these companies was reinforced by the status and power that they had in the larger community. Friesen Printers president D.K. Friesen, for example, was mayor of Altona, a manager of both the local cooperative store and a vegetable oil processing plant, a member of the local water commission, a director of a number of local educational and health organizations, and a member of various local and national committees of his church. Similar lists of local, national, and even international involvement may be generated for the leadership, past and present, of each of the three companies in this study.[41]

There was a strong religious component in employers' efforts to shape workplace culture at these three businesses. Classic understandings and interpretations of paternalism do not address the manner in which these social relations were aided and abetted by religious belief. The semiological approach to mythology suggested by Roland Barthes provides a fruitful means of investigating the linkages between religion and capitalism. As a case study, a Barthian investigation of an early twenty-first century advertising campaign at Loewen Windows uncovers the ideological underpinnings of the Mennonite corporate mythology that existed not only at Loewen Windows but at all three firms.

In December 2002, Loewen Windows began a new advertising campaign known as 'Reflections.' The campaign consisted of four photo spreads, each consisting of a Loewen-made window in which a particular image is reflected. The first image is of a young girl wearing a dark coloured shirt under a high-necked, sleeveless black jumper. Her long hair is parted in the middle of her forehead and protected by a conservative white head covering. The text accompanying the image declares, 'There's a remarkable story reflected in every Loewen window.' The second image is of a small, white church, almost unidentifiable as such but for its modest steeple. Viewed through a window of gothic design, the church sits atop a sparsely treed prairie hill. The tagline reads, 'Once, we made church pews. We've been seeking perfection in our work ever since.' In the third image, a river meanders through a bucolic landscape as seen through a circular window. The text questions, 'Why can't a window be as much of a work of art as the landscape it frames?' In the final image of the series, rain streaks an arched window as it reflects a flash of lightning. The commentary reads, 'Windows designed to survive searing heat, arctic blasts, and something even less forgiving: the fickle winds of fashion.'[42]

While these images were used individually as advertisements in print publications such as lifestyle magazines, the series was also part of a promotional tool available from Loewen Windows and advertised on its website as the 'Soul' brochure.[43] The four images are described on the final page of the brochure as 'reflections of some striking photographs that reveal an essence of the Loewen brand. A young lady's intent gaze is returned by the glass in a Loewen Casement window; a lonely church atop a prairie ridge is captured in a Radius Top window with a Gothic grille; the Snake River is mirrored in a Loewen Round Top [window]; a Gulf Coast storm rages against the exterior of a stoic Picture Window.'

Following the first image in the series is an opening page of text which briefly places the company's origins in historical context: 'Every Loewen window mirrors a fascinating journey. It begins at the turn of the twentieth century on the lonely prairies of southern Manitoba. Here in the village of Steinbach, a group of Mennonite families, including the Loewens, had migrated from Russia to begin their lives anew.' The advertising copy then proffers an explanation for the success of the business: 'The key to our success is simple: while we've remained faithful to our roots – particularly in our deeply held traditional craft values and our work ethic – we've also grown to embrace new technologies and ideas from places as diverse as Europe, Japan, America and, of course, Canada. And so, we've become a company where seeming opposites exist in harmony: the old and the new, delicate beauty and a steely toughness, and pride in craft tempered by an abiding humility. The result is windows and doors that possess a rich heritage, a striking beauty, even a kind of soul you won't find anywhere else in the world.' Accompanying the remaining three images are a few pages of text extolling the virtues of the products, particularly their quality of manufacture, stylistic beauty, and technical strengths.

The first photo spread (see figure 3.1) plays with signs of Mennonitism in a deliberate manner. Though the brochure copy identifies her simply as a 'young lady,' this image contains multiple signs that connote Mennonitism: the conservative fashion of dress and hairstyling, the distinctive head covering. Even the choice of the window in which her visage is reflected is a sign: a casement window of simple lines rather than the comparatively ostentatious curves and flourishes, for example, of the company's round-top window. The decision to portray a 'young lady' rather than a 'young gentleman' is in part a nod to the general public's greater familiarity with the outward signs of female Mennonitism. The hat, plain coat, and knee boots of the conservative Mennonite *Praediger*, for example, may be recognized within a segment of the Mennonite community itself; among outsiders, such items of male dress are not well known. The choice of a youth rather than an adult is also interesting, as youth (particularly female youth) is a signifier of purity and innocence. Taken together, these signs denote simplicity, innocence, and humility.

Other elements of this image are more open to interpretation. What does it mean that the girl's portrait is in black and white? That the backdrop is of black emptiness? That the tagline for the advertisement is centred on the girl's jumper? These elements cannot be meaningless. The ad's text could just as easily have been placed over her shoulder in the inky blackness behind her, for example. Instead, the text is placed on her clothing, precisely where a T-shirt, say, would have a slogan or a logo. This conservative young woman would be unlikely to wear a branded T-shirt, yet here she advertises Loewen Windows. It is not her clothing, but she herself who is being 'branded,' marked, commodified.

There's a remarkable story reflected in every Loewen window.

3.1. Loewen Windows' 'Reflections' campaign: Mennonite girl
Source: 'Soul' brochure, December 2002, available from Loewen Windows, 'Pressroom: Advertising,' http://www.loewen.com/site.nsf/about/pressroom_ advertising (retrieved 29 January 2004; page removed).

Her Mennonitism, the 'remarkable story reflected in every Loewen window,' is what is being sold.

What of the colour and background? The black-and-white colour scheme conveys a sense of the past. This girl, this image, this advertisement – and hence this product – is part of a long-standing and persistent tradition, the 'remarkable story,' the 'fascinating journey' from Russia to Canada. The image's absence of a background makes it impossible to place the image in any specific time or place. Thus the product is made timeless: it is beyond trends; it will endure the ages.

The second photo spread (see figure 3.2) does not contain such obviously Mennonite signs. The 'lonely church atop a prairie ridge' would not be identified by an insider as a Mennonite church, at least not a Manitoban Mennonite one. Traditionally, Mennonite churches do not have a steeple; modern Mennonite church buildings in Manitoba, while generally still steepleless, are visually indistinguishable from Protestant churches. Here we see the necessity of the steeple and the choice of a gothic window: these are signs easily read by both Mennonites and non-Mennonites as distinctly religious. Yet this image does point to the Mennonitism of the previous image of the girl in the window: it is an isolated church, a prairie church, a small church, whose physical austerity signals an honest simplicity of faith. Viewed together, this overtly religious image reinforces the religious humility signified in the advertisement of the 'Mennonite girl.' Remarkably, a church that is clearly not a Mennonite church nonetheless references many aspects of Mennonite mythology.

The positioning of the church with respect to the window is worth noting. From the standpoint of the viewer, the church is slightly elevated. The advertising copy describes it as a church on a prairie ridge – in other words, a church on a hill. As such, for religious viewers, it immediately conjures up references to the 'city on a hill' in Christ's Sermon on the Mount: 'You are the salt of the earth; but if salt has lost its taste, how can its saltiness be restored? It is no longer good for anything, but is thrown out and trampled under foot. You are the light of the world. A city built on a hill cannot be hid. No one after lighting a lamp puts it under the bushel basket, but on the lampstand, and it gives light to all in the house. In the same way, let your light shine before others, so that they may see your good works and give glory to your Father in heaven.'[44]

Christ's 'city built on a hill' has become, in the parlance of the twentieth-century Christian community, the 'church on a hill.' The image links the values of the Sermon on the Mount with the Loewen Windows product. Beyond such obvious connotations of faith, the image also evokes subtle but specifically Mennonite references. The 'salt of the earth' has become a secular cliché for honest, hard-working, trustworthy, rural people. Not coincidentally, these are the very characteristics referenced as values in Mennonite corporate mythology – not only at Loewen Windows, but at Palliser Furniture and Friesen Printers as

Once, we made church pews. We've been seeking perfection in our work ever since.

3.2. Loewen Windows' 'Reflections' campaign: Church
Source: 'Soul' brochure, December 2002, available from Loewen Windows, 'Pressroom: Advertising,' http://www.loewen.com/site.nsf/about/pressroom_ advertising (retrieved 29 January 2004; page removed).

well. One of the owners of Loewen Windows, Clyde Loewen, himself noted the Mennoniteness of this particular image. Offering to provide me with a copy of the ad campaign's brochure during the course of our interview, I asked, 'Is this the one with the Mennonite young woman reflected in the window?' His honest reply moved us both to laughter: 'This is the young woman who is *portrayed* as a Mennonite.' He went on to explain that the ad campaign's images, particularly those of the church and the girl, related to 'strong cultural touchstones' that were 'probably recognizable in values' even to those unfamiliar with Mennonites. Those values, he noted, are sincerity and honesty.[45]

Only these first two of the four images in the campaign were highlighted on the Loewen Windows website in 2004. The Mennonite girl appeared on its homepage; the church image was used on the 'About Us' webpage. Clearly these two images were central to the advertising campaign, and not the other two – the river and the rainstorm. Indeed, Clyde Loewen's remarks mentioned above indicate as much. With their emphasis on quality and durability, the latter two images did little to differentiate Loewen's products from those of any other brand. Instead, what set Loewen Windows products apart was their 'soul.'

What, then, is the 'soul' of a commodity? The soul – the essence, that which is unique to an individual – is a religious notion. The products at Loewen Windows are invested with an invisible yet crucial quality that is not obviously discernible in either their physical appearance or their technical durability (the message of the last two images in the 'Reflections' campaign). That invisible quality is introduced by virtue of the nature of the individuals who manufacture the windows: these are products of a Mennonite family, the Loewens, and their primarily Mennonite employees, who remain 'faithful to [their] roots,' to their 'deeply held traditional craft values,' and to their 'work ethic.' They exhibit both 'pride in craft' and 'abiding humility.' They are constantly 'seeking perfection'; their work is in essence a spiritual quest.[46] The 'soul' of a Loewen window, then, is the commodification of the Mennonite corporate mythology.

Though less central to the campaign, the last two images in the series do serve to reinforce the signs in the first two photo spreads. The third image (see figure 3.3) is of a tranquil rural landscape. The lazy meandering of the river, the smoothness of the water's surface, signifies peace. The waterway is identified as the Snake River, the main branch of the Columbia River, which stretches across Idaho and Oregon. Why this particular river? Idaho is rural farm country, a state without a major urban centre; Oregon is noted for its forestry and wood production industries. Simultaneously, they reference both rural qualities (honesty, dependability, simplicity) and the natural substances (wood) from which Loewen Windows products are made. At the same time, these products are separated from the conditions of production. The landscape seen through/reflected in the window shows no signs of human habitation, much less industrial production.

3.3. Loewen Windows' 'Reflections' campaign: River
Source: 'Soul' brochure, December 2002, available from Loewen Windows, 'Pressroom: Advertising,' http://www.loewen.com/site.nsf/about/pressroom_advertising (retrieved 29 January 2004; page removed).

The text accompanying this image returns to the religious motif of the first two images: 'Why can't a window be as much of a work of art as the landscape it frames?' The work of art here is nature itself; God is the artist. The window, a human-made product, is equated with the Creation.[47] At the lower right of the image is the invitation: 'Discover the world's most inspiring windows at www.loewen.com.' The page of text that accompanies this image in the brochure elaborates on the 'inspirational' nature of the product: 'To our way of thinking, a window should be more than just a source of natural light and air. It should be a source of inspiration ... Perhaps the most important distinguishing feature of our windows, however, is the artistry and obsessive perfectionism of the people who craft them. In their skilled hands (aided by the most advanced production technology available), wood, metal and glass somehow magically meld, flow and even soar ... Which means you may have trouble deciding which is more inspiring: the view outside your windows or the windows themselves.'[48] Loewen Windows' products are not only *inspiring* but also *inspired*; in a word, they have 'soul.'

The final image of the series (see figure 3.4) depicts the elements of nature attacking a Loewen picture window. The product meets the challenge of the environment. But not only the rainstorm is held at bay, so too are the 'fickle winds of fashion.' Recalling the first image in the series, nothing could be further from fickle fashion than the conservative Mennonite presentation of the young woman. In contrast to the changing whims of society – inconstant, questionable, and unreliable – what is offered are the enduring values that emanate from the timeless, static, church-ordered society of the Mennonites. The product itself takes on these qualities: it is not merely a picture window, but a 'stoic' one, we are informed by the promotional text. Stolid, composed, calm, at peace – like the five-hundred-year tradition of the Mennonites themselves, these windows will 'stand the test of time.'[49]

The 'Reflections' campaign was designed by Loeffler, Ketchum, Mountjoy of North Carolina. Mitch Toews, advertising and corporate communications manager at Loewen Windows, explained the process that was the generation of the campaign: 'We said to [the ad agency], "We have an almost hundred year old company that has grown a thick layer of moss over what the true, the core of the company is. You know, our view is jaded. We don't know exactly what we are. You know, we're too close to it. So give us your impression."'[50] The agency conducted research not only at Loewen Windows but 'in the marketplace, through our dealers, through competitors, through architects, through builders' to devise a means of 'branding' Loewen Windows. 'And they came up with the heritage, the Mennonite heritage, which to them was striking ... We really had this good product, that enabled us to go into the luxury market in the U.S. and elsewhere and say, "We have a product for you, even though we're this humble company. We're not sophisticated like the marketplace, and yet we are because we have this wonderful

Windows designed to survive searing heat, arctic blasts and something even less forgiving: the fickle winds of fashion.

3.4. Loewen Windows' 'Reflections' campaign: Rainstorm
Source: 'Soul' brochure, December 2002, available from Loewen Windows, 'Pressroom: Advertising,' http://www.loewen.com/site.nsf/about/pressroom_advertising (retrieved 29 January 2004; page removed).

product. We really have the product." And that's what they saw.'[51] Of course, hiring an ad agency which develops a campaign that markets religious heritage is hardly a sign of a lack of sophistication.

'Reflections' was only the second advertising campaign conducted by Loewen Windows.[52] An earlier, more short-lived campaign was connected with the company's seventy-fifth anniversary celebrations in 1980 and consisted of a cartoonish spokesmodel named L. Porteous Fenster.[53] Fenster is depicted as an older male, mustachioed, wearing wire-rimmed glasses, flat cap, and overalls, with a ruler and pencil in his bib pocket.[54] The text accompanying the image reads, 'Traditionally crafted since 1905.' Mitch Toews considered the differences between the two campaigns, noting that the 'Reflections' campaign was a 'more stylized' and subtle way of presenting the same immigrant values as had the Fenster ads. The 'Reflections' campaign, however, 'was a little bit bolder' in that it referenced the religious dimension of Mennonitism. With the decision in the early 1990s to specialize in higher price-point wood windows, a change in advertising strategy was needed to target the new luxury market. Traditional carpenter Fenster was replaced with the stylized 'Reflections' campaign.

At first glance, it is difficult to discern how an advertising campaign that draws on images of a rural religious tradition can speak to a wealthy urban (and largely secular) audience. Clyde Loewen explained that the Mennonite heritage of the company's founder persisted in the work ethic of Loewen Windows employees, which he described as 'more than strong.' This ethic he described as incorporating friendliness, helpfulness, service, sincerity, honesty, and humility. It is this latter characteristic in particular that set up a conflict in the minds of the wealthy target market viewers of the company's 'Reflections' campaign. Clyde Loewen asserted that, as both Mennonites and Canadians, the company was 'a bit more humble' than its U.S. competitors. The decision to target the luxury market required the abandonment of humility, he noted. 'That market in the United States doesn't necessarily understand humility and all that,' he observed with laughter. Rather, the target market wanted to know the product was superior and wanted convincing reasons for its superiority. 'But that doesn't stop us from playing up a little bit of our heritage while we do it, because they still connect with traditional values a little bit,' he observed.[55]

The dissonance between the target market of the advertising campaign and the images conveyed in that campaign was deliberate. The images, 'eloquent in their simplicity,' would 'stop people in their tracks and let their natural curiosity lead them to learn more' about the story of Loewen Windows. 'We believe these messages respect the intelligence and inquisitiveness of the upscale market,' Mitch Toews declared. 'They are not an audience that you tell something to, but one that you allow to discover.'[56] It is the seeming contradiction between Mennonite humility and luxury goods production that would prompt viewers to examine the products more seriously. Contradictions such as this were the key to the campaign in the eyes of the marketing firm that developed it. Speaking of the marketing firm, Mitch Toews declared, 'They said what caught them off guard a little bit was our acceptance of risk, technology, very up-to-date management techniques ... It was that juxtaposition of old meets new that they thought was interesting about us.' The decision thus was made to make 'the mix of old and new' into 'the heartbeat of the brand.'[57]

The decision to use religious heritage as a marketing tool was not easily made, Loewen Windows management asserted. Commenting on the campaign, Clyde Loewen observed, 'It was with *some* degree of unease that we did that, because it felt a little, you know, at times, a little exploitative or something like that. Not overwhelmingly so, or we wouldn't have done it.'[58] Mitch Toews argued that it was the 'truth' of the campaign itself that was the deciding factor in choosing to go with the advertisements: the agency's pitch was accepted 'because it was true and because it was the unfiltered view' of the company.[59] While Toews did acknowledge that the advertisements were not so much about 'unfiltered truth' as about selling products, he argued strongly that the representations in the ads were accurate reflections of corporate reality. While noting that the job of the ad agency was to market the company, nonetheless he asserted that 'it was all true. You know, the things that they found about us are things that, if you're objective about it, if you can be, that yes, those are the things that are true about us.'[60] One wonders what Barthes would have made of Toews's assertions. 'Men do not have with myth a relationship based on truth but on use,' he writes; 'they depoliticize according to their needs.'[61]

Myths exist not to serve as descriptions of reality, but as obfuscations of it. Myths are ideological: they are public articulations of our understandings of ourselves. The reified beliefs that underlie those understandings, the 'forms of social consciousness' to use Marx's terminology, are shaped by the economic relations in which we find ourselves. The creation of Mennonite corporate mythology – both conscious and unconcious – serves capitalist economic needs by promoting worker assiduity, loyalty, and deference, and reinforces class relations. Invocations of religious humility, a component of Mennonite yieldedness, reifies these class relations by giving them a transcendent significance. As historian Roland Marchand has found, advertising served more than one audience, promoting a deliberate corporate identity to employees as much as to potential customers.[62] Philosopher John McMurtry notes that when a worker internalizes corporate mythology, 'the remarkable possibility of one who is objectively exploited by the social order comprehending the persistence of it as in *his* interests, achieves actuality.'[63] The use of specifically religious imagery to co-opt Mennonite workers makes this process particularly powerful.

The centrality of use rather than truth to mythology is evident in the discussion of the Mennonite corporate mythology and its attributes by the ownership of Loewen Windows. The 'Reflections' campaign is in fact a reflection of Mennonite corporate mythology with its portrayal of a static definition of Mennonitism emphasizing the values of peace, obedience, and humility. When interviewed by a fellow Mennonite, the Loewens were open about the limitations of these values for maintaining a profitable business. Charles Loewen recounted a story of a meeting with a customer in the northeastern United States. The customer told him, 'I don't know if it's a Canadian thing, whether it's a Loewen [Windows] thing, or it's a Mennonite thing, but you people are so nice.' As Charles Loewen was basking in the glow of the compliment, the customer continued, 'You're so nice, it undermines your performance.' He went on to explain that 'when our people tell your people a hard truth over the phone, by the time it hits the shopfloor, it's been "nice-fied" down to inaction.' This incident prompted Charles Loewen to reflect that 'there's another side, potentially, to ... the Mennonite ethos ... It's a little harder for Mennonites to be very, very frank and forthright and to expect remediation of nonperformance immediately.'[64] Peaceful tranquility and religious humility, made virtues in the advertising campaign, are here presented as liabilities.

Clyde Loewen highlighted yieldedness or the deferential obedience of Mennonites as another limitation on the ability to run an effective business. 'Sometimes, the other side of it is there's maybe a litle less ownership, accountability, ambition on the personal end ... There's a willingness to please the customer, but there's not always a great knowledge of what that really means or how to do it in a professional, competent manner.'[65] Sincerity and honesty, the content of the 'Reflections' campaign, are no match for professional efficiency and initiative.

Loewen family members themselves have had to re-examine how to be humble rural Mennonites in an urban capitalist world. John Loewen

observed that humility and yieldedness to community norms may have
been limits on the expansion of the business. He recalled his brother
Charles's interview of Neil MacKenzie, the first non-famiy and non-
Mennonite board member of the company. After Charles Loewen
described the company's recent successes, MacKenzie replied, 'Hey,
Charles, that's good, that's great. Let me ask you a question. What are
you doing to become a five hundred million dollar company?' In John
Loewen's words, 'That shut Chuck up. The universe shifted for him
and for all of us then.' John Loewen attributed the limits of the corporate vision to their Mennonite heritage: 'If we would have had more
outside influences or rubbed shoulders at the Manitoba Club with five
hundred million dollar silk tie boys ..., the question may have been
asked sooner.'[66]

The global nature of twentieth and twenty-first century capitalism
has necessitated a renegotiation of what it means to practice Mennonite
humility in a competitive marketplace. At a board meeting in 2001 to
discuss increasing sales, John Loewen asked, 'Will we like who we become?' The reply was, 'Yeah, of course, why wouldn't we?' In an interview recalling that incident, he reflected that such 'modesty, humility'
was a 'valid value to have,' but asked rhetorically, 'What's inherently
noble about staying at a hundred million? Add another zero, that won't
determine who you are ... The actual number is largely immaterial
when it comes to those values.' He noted that such questions were never
again raised, nor did they need to be. 'It's more important that you act
and behave modestly and responsibly with yourselves, the community,
and your employees.'[67] Company CEO Charles Loewen noted that his
brother John's question 'hangs to this day' and is a reflection of 'family
culture.'[68] He echoed his brother's observation that humility can be a
disadvantage when competing in a global marketplace: 'We don't blow
our own horn quite enough ... I remember once I taught Sunday School
... and I posed this theoretical question: "If you're a Mennonite, and
you make the best windows in the world, is it okay to say that? Or is it
wrong not to say it?" ... What's more important to a Mennonite: telling
the truth or their false humility?'[69]

Such questioning resulted in some changes in practice. The family's charitable foundation, begun in 1973, did not publicize its grants
in any way until 2000. The foundation's executive director noted that
this practice was a function of the New Testament adage that 'the left

hand shouldn't know what the right hand is doing.'[70] Publicity was considered not only an unseemly concession to pride but also could be poor stewardship. Stories circulate regarding C.P. Loewen's resistance to self-promotion. '[If he] would give a grant to a Bible college or some kind of an institution, they would say, "Can we put up a plaque with your name?" And he would typically ask, "Well, how much does a plaque cost?" And they'd say, "Thirty or forty dollars." And he'd say, "No, use that money where you need it. I don't need my name on a wall somewhere."'[71] The no-publicity policy came to an end in 2000. 'The employees were saying, "Well, we're working for a cheap company. They don't participate in the community. They're not a charitable kind of company." Which was not true at all.'[72] As the company expanded, communication between owners and shop-floor workers of necessity became more distant. The dissipation of paternalist bonds resulted in greater expectations on the part of employees for corporate accountability regarding profits.

Mennonite corporate mythology, then, operates in some contradictory ways. The necessity of competing in a global marketplace has required that the myth of the Mennonite corporate mythology be rendered in new forms to workers. At all three companies, with the expansion of the businesses and increased workforce diversity in the 1970s, the traditional paternalist bargain became untenable. Old-style appeals to the workforce to emulate the Mennonite values of the founders, to incarnate the Mennonite corporate mythology, became more difficult. The forms that the myth takes thus have undergone transformation. When necessary, as in the need for consumers to be able to differentiate their products from those of their competitors, management is willing to make use of the traditional forms of the Mennonite corporate mythology, as in the 'Reflections' campaign of 2002. Internally, the operation of the mythology makes some concessions to its status as myth without in any way undermining its effectiveness. Interviews with company president Charles Loewen and co-owner John Loewen show this clearly.

Asked to outline the ways in which the Mennonite heritage of the founder persisted in the day-to-day operation of the company, Charles Loewen offered several examples. He cited the provision of optional Tuesday worship services, company picnics, and Christmas banquets for employees; donations through the family foundation; the lack of cursing and raised voices on the shop floor; the absence of sexist or pornographic posters in private workspaces; and the decision not to serve alcohol at staff banquets. All of these existed at Palliser Furniture as well; all but the worship services were in operation at Friesen Printers. Loewen observed that his company was a place where 'it's not uncommon for people to bow their heads in grace before having a lunch in the cafeteria, where that kind of thing is deeply respected.' He noted the company's reluctance to take people to court when wronged, its reliance on people's word rather than contracts, its willingnes to service products beyond the limitations expressed by warranties. 'This is the Germanic or Dutch or whatever – Germanic Mennonite tradition, maybe even a craft or peasant kind of mentality, where you give full value.'[73] Similar statements could be made regarding the persistence of Mennonite heritage at Friesen Printers and Palliser Furniture.

John Loewen hastened to assert that such activities were not unique to Mennonites. 'It's a great testament, I feel, to the Mennonite faith. But I don't know that the Marvins and the Pellas and the Andersens [competing window manufacturers] of the world don't do that. I don't know if ... the fact that we're a Mennonite business necessarily makes us more generous or more ethical. I don't know about that.'[74] Is such a declaration a puncturing of Mennonite corporate mythology? Or has the myth merely been hidden in another layer of meaning, its signs converted into a new form? Is the humility of the Mennonite corporate mythology such that it refrains from claiming its own uniqueness?

Charles Loewen declared that he is not interested in the static preservation of a corporate culture rooted in Mennonitism.

I mean, I went to university, studied philosophy, so I'm an existentialist, I'm a postmodernist and, you know, we're all Marxists and so we're all – what do you call it. Unions and so on and so forth. I mean, once you become aware of those issues, you can't help but be influenced by them. And yet, we're finding what it means to be people of faith in our tradition, Anabaptist-Mennonite tradition. *Our* Anabaptist-Mennonite tradition, informed by those other learnings as well. And we're quite different than our father was, who had a much simpler and narrower exposure. Doesn't make mine superior. My children's will be different again. And the words that we have faith God gave to us will be interpreted differently at a different time in history. Inevitably. And we don't try to freeze that. That's part of what it means to me, part of my father's phrase, 'you don't rule from the grave.'[75]

A frozen representation of Mennonitism may be useful for advertising product, but within the company itself, the myth must find new forms. Charles Loewen insisted that 'in an age of diversity, we're not a Mennonite town anymore … we *never* call ourselves a Christian company.' While the Mennonite origins of the founding family were communicated to board members, there was no need to maintain some ethno-religious status quo. 'You know, if we were to have a plant in Indonesia dominated by Muslim workers, that we could allow and celebrate Muslim faith. Inspiration in that workplace could be part of a brand new interpretation and extension of the family culture in this community of faith.' Such an outcome was possible, Charles Loewen noted, 'in a postmodern age, in an age of diversity and international global understanding.'[76]

Such statements are not a demythologizing of Mennonite corporate mythology, but its reincarnation. As Barthes observes, 'It does not matter if one is later allowed to see through the myth, its action is assumed to be stronger than the rational explanations which may later belie it.'[77] The corporate mythology developed within these three businesses was shaped by the Mennonite heritage of their founders, workforces, and surrounding communities. As those communities and workplaces continue to evolve, the corporate mythology itself will be reinterpreted – though its purpose will remain the same. The myth exists to encourage conformity to the demands of capitalist production; such conformity is the ideology concealed by the myth. The religious vocabulary of the myth serves to place its content beyond doubt or question; what is depicted is not ideological need but sacred truth. Mennonite corporate mythology therefore could be transformed into a Muslim corporate mythology, if the needs of production demanded it.

Labour historians have been criticized in the past for giving scant attention to the role of employers in shaping the workplace. Business historian Michael Miller observes, 'Labor hisory has told us much about working-class movements, working-class lives, the nature of working-class work. But it has told us little about how the history of the workers has been molded by the values and concerns of the men who employed them.'[78] The examination here of the creation and operation of a Mennonite corporate mythology at Palliser Furniture, Friesen Printers, and Loewen Windows has avoided this problem. The signification of the myth has been explored through a close reading of a case study (the

'Reflections' campaign), which was used to expose the ideological values mystified by Mennonite corporate mythology.

Palliser Furniture, Friesen Printers, and Loewen Windows all have made use of their Mennonite heritage to ensure worker conformity, most obviously in the early years of their operation. The values of Mennonite corporate mythology have been represented as inherent to the Mennonite community, a process enabled by the use of religious idioms. Sociological and anthropological insights call into question such ahistorical portrayals as discussed in this chapter. Acknowledging that identity, culture, and ethnicity are historically contingent, cultural studies approaches provide access to the ideology underlying the Mennonite corporate mythology. The decoding of Mennonite signs in the 'Reflections' campaign reveals that humility and deferential obedience (forms of yieldedness), as well as honesty and sincerity, are among the values underlying Mennonite corporate mythology, a mythology whose power is difficult to overcome. Nonetheless, Charles Tilly's definition of identity as relational, cultural, historical, and contingent reminds us that such efforts to fashion an identity for the Mennonite worker through mythology are susceptible to challenge and reinterpretation.[79] Workers at Friesen Printers, Loewen Windows, and Palliser Furniture attempted to recreate a Mennonite identity in the late twentieth century that strove to challenge this Mennonite corporate mythology.

4

'You Had to Know Everything; Otherwise, You Weren't Fit': Worker Experience and Identity

Mennonite workers experienced and interpreted their workplaces in diverse ways. Those employed in the two rural businesses experienced a more homogeneous workforce of fellow Mennonites in a largely non-union environment. Those in the business located in the 'big city' had greater exposure to workers of diverse backgrounds and beliefs, and found themselves in an urban context that presented unions as a viable option for workers. Technological changes and the pressures of just-in-time production transformed their industries and further interfered with the development of a uniform worker identity. Religious beliefs and immigrant experiences reinforced the values of humility, deferential obedience, and pride in honest, quality work promoted by both the theology espoused by the Mennonite intellectual elite and by Mennonite corporate mythology. The unifying assumptions of this mythology were challenged, however, by generational differences among workers, by greater workplace diversity, and by the increasing pressures of the changing labour process itself.

The profile of workers at these three companies reflects the demography of the areas in which they are situated. Friesen Printers boasts that it 'relies heavily on the south central region of Manitoba for staff.'[1] The Mennonites in the area around Altona are primarily members of Mennonite Church Manitoba (earlier known as the General Conference Mennonites), although some also belong to the Mennonite Brethren Church, the Evangelical Mennonite Mission Church (EMMC), Reinland Mennonite Church, Church of God in Christ (Mennonite), and Sommerfeld Mennonite Church.[2] In addition to *Kanadier*, *Russlaender*, and Mexican Mennonites, the region has a small but significant French population and some non-Mennonite German immigrants who arrived at the turn of the millennium.[3] The overwhelming majority of workers at Friesen Printers has been and remains Mennonite.

Loewen Windows, southeastern Manitoba's largest employer, only began hiring non-Mennonite staff after 1979.[4] The Mennonite majority of their staff are drawn from denominations including Mennonite Church Manitoba, Mennonite Brethren, EMMC, Evangelical Mennonites (EMC), Evangelical Mennonite Brethren (EMB), Chortitzer Mennonites, Sommerfeld Mennonites, and Church of God in Christ (Mennonite).[5] In the last thirty years, the company also has employed many from the surrounding French communities, as well as immigrants from Germany who came to Canada under the provincial nominee program.[6]

Palliser Furniture, located in the urban centre of Winnipeg, not surprisingly had the most diverse workforce. The population of Winnipeg in the 1990s had a tremendous variety of ethnic origins, including Scots, Germans, Ukrainians, French, Irish, Poles, Aboriginal peoples, Dutch, Filipino, Icelanders, and Italians.[7] Palliser Furniture employees originally were the Russian Mennonite immigrants that settled the neighbourhoods in northeast Winnipeg known as the Kildonans. Area churches that served workers in this immediate post-war period included the Mennonite Brethren and Mennonite Church Manitoba.[8] By the late twentieth century, Palliser Furniture's workforce was 70 per cent new Canadians, representing seventy different national origins.[9] This diversity was the direct result of the decision in 1963 to enter the upholstery market, accompanied by the hiring of displaced Filipina garment workers.

For Mennonite workers who were immigrants to Canada or were refugees of the Second World War, their challenging life experiences and their religious commitments shaped their deferential attitudes in the workplace. Jakob Pries, employed at Woodland Supply, a Mennonite-owned cabinet construction firm in Winnipeg, mused that, as a refugee, he 'took all the chances that God was giving [him] to get ahead': 'I think those were enough for me; not exactly what I would wish, perhaps. But that's probably the best you will ever develop, so I did that.'[10] The religious belief that God was directing their lives, and the favourable comparison of their work life in Canada to their refugee experiences, explains these workers' deference. Hans Wiens, of Loewen Windows, spent a total of two years and seven months on two separate occasions in prisoner-of-war camps; nothing in his Canadian work experience was comparable. Peter Reimer, of Palliser Furniture, did not have career aspirations. Instead, he observed quietly: 'I just was very occupied with thinking, I always thought, said it very often to myself, asked the question, "Why did Stalin take away my dad?"'[11] Peter Reimer and Henry Wallman, both at Palliser Furniture, fled post-war Germany for Paraguay, only to discover the country was experiencing a revolution in 1947–8. 'It was very strange to come to Paraguay, and all of a sudden, we had to lie flat in the school where we were living at that time as refugees. Lie flat on the floor and the bullets were flying.'[12] Any difficulties on the job paled in comparison. Jakob Pries, of Woodland Supply, described the hazards of his post-war flight from Russia to Germany to Paraguay. He concluded, 'I wouldn't miss it even though we've talked about how difficult times have been. I would not miss them because they've shaped my personal life, my faith life, and all that. For me, that's part of my experience.'[13]

These workers were able to endure and come to terms with negative experiences because of their religious beliefs. As he summarized his life, Palliser Furniture worker Peter Reimer balanced both the positive and negative features of it, placing them in a religious context. He noted his childhood was happy, 'until [he] realized what the Communist regime was all about.' 'My father was taken away, and many others. So then it became very tough.' His efforts to avoid membership in Communist youth organizations and the trek he made from Ukraine to Poland were also difficult. 'Settling in Poland was not easy for mother and all the mothers, because most of the families were without fathers or husbands.' In addition, he was drafted into the military. The family chose to immigrate to Paraguay, though their preference was Canada. Settlement in the Chaco presented its own challenges: farming, establishing village life, forming a church, raising a family. He interrupted the chronology: 'But it was, for us, it was great. We were always thankful that God had protected us, that God was with us every day.' He continued with a description of his family's migration to Winnipeg, including the difficulties of finding work and repaying the travel debt. Again he interjected: 'And God has been very gracious to us.' He highlighted his enjoyment of church life and singing with the Mennonite Brethren Communications choir before concluding: 'Canada is the best place to be and to live. I have had the opportunity to see a number of countries and to travel quite a bit. I would not change. I hope and pray that God will grant us this beautiful country to live in for many more years, right?'[14]

Reimer's narrative choices reveal the role played by his religious convictions. Alessandro Portelli has proven the value of studying not only the content but the *forms* of oral history.[15] The cadence of the events Reimer relates is reminiscent of a religious conversion testimony, punctuated as it is by expressions of gratitude towards and trust in God. The narrative form he uses here was typical of many of the immigrant Mennonite workers interviewed. The form of a religious testimony presents all the aspects of one's life, both good and bad, as guided by divine authority. To regret an event, to complain, is to doubt God's wisdom. Negative events are thus valued equally with positive ones.

This narrative form is markedly different from that used by non-Mennonite workers. Michael Frisch, for example, observes that, for the workers interviewed by Studs Terkel in *Hard Times*, negative experiences were personalized while positive experiences were given universal meaning. Treating failure in this manner 'shelter[ed] them from deeper, more profoundly threatening historical truths.' Survival and success, meanwhile, became a 'self-validating message and a culturally validating legacy for the next generations.'[16] Similarly, Alessandro Portelli observes that communist workers in Terni, Italy, 'insist on the usefulness and success of their lives, by stressing the positive aspects of reality.'[17] The negative experiences of Mennonite immigrant workers like Peter Reimer, however, are crucial parts of the legacy to be transmitted, their meaning validated by their religious perspective.

Religious commitment was conveyed by actions on the job as well as by the content and form of oral interviews. For many Mennonite workers, work was an outlet for the expression of personal satisfaction, particularly since *hochmut* (religious pride) was unacceptable. Further, pride in work was a means of living out one's religious beliefs, of demonstrating discipleship and *Gelassenheit*, that sense of pacifist yieldedness. Various Bible passages were used by Mennonite theological leaders to promote this understanding:

And whatever you do, in word or deed, do everything in the name of the Lord Jesus, giving thanks to God the Father through Him. (Colossians 3:17)

Whatever your task, put yourselves into it, as done for the Lord and not for your masters. (Colossians 3:23)

Render service with enthusiasm, as to the Lord and not to men and women. (Ephesians 6:7)

The production of quality work without complaint was therefore a religious obligation. In this aspect, Mennonite religious identity reinforced Mennonite corporate mythology, in that pride in a job well done had the added advantage from management's perspective of fostering loyalty to the company on the part of employees. As Patrick Joyce observes, 'though not unambiguous in its effect, pride in work further fed the sense of commitment to it.'[18] D.G. Friesen, former press operator at Friesen Printers, corroborates this statement: 'I enjoyed and marvelled at the colour that came from the presses. Of course, you had to be very exact to get the colour to match. We did thousands and thousands and thousands of colour postcards one time. And there it was my job to match all four colours with the original colours; there were twenty-four on a sheet. So that was a challenge. And we could admit being proud of our production.'[19]

John Geddert exemplifies this pride of the craftsperson. Geddert worked as an assembler at Palliser Furniture for twenty-three years before retiring from the shop floor. He explained the gratification and dignity of his work as a chair assembler: 'Piecework, it's not for everybody. You have to be strong, and you have to know what you are doing, and you have to be very organized to make it productive ... You have to find out for yourself which way is the best way and the most productive way.'[20] Historian Ian McKay observes that often the pride in work of so-called unskilled labour goes unnoticed by everyone but the labourer him- or herself: 'For the vast indifferent bourgeois public, the coal miners' skills don't matter. They don't ever pause before a particularly appealing piece of coal and exclaim, "Ah, the craftsmanship of Glace Bay!" But the coal miner himself ... might well feel proud to be the miner who can produce the most on his shift.'[21] Such pride in work prompted Geddert to keep a record of how many chairs he assembled (see table 4.1). In his final fifteen years at Palliser Furniture, he as-

Table 4.1. Chairs assembled by John
Geddert at Palliser Furniture

Year	Chairs produced
1975	10,379
1976	10,455
1977	10,767
1978	16,920
1979	16,643
1980	18,273
1981	22,078
1982	22,680
1983	15,850
1984	16,278
1985	16,187
1986	14,935
1987	14,674
1988	13,732
1989	14,041
1990	5,716
Total	239,608

Source: Courtesy of John Geddert.

sembled almost one-quarter million chairs, ranging from a minimum of 5716 in one (partial) year to a maximum of 22,680 another year.

Ernie Dyck, a Canadian-born Mennonite factory worker at Friesen Printers, described his pride in his work in terms similar to those used by Geddert: 'I enjoy the satisfaction of a job well done. I also enjoy the unique challenges that each job presents to us, to me. And the variety that one encounters when working with print materials.'[22] Some of that variety, he noted, was the function of the materials themselves. An outsider may perceive the pushing of paper through a printing press as a repetitive and relatively unskilled task; Dyck argued otherwise. 'Working with paper is not like working with machines that cut wood, or trucks. There are always variables that come up. You can run the same paper for two days in a row, and you'll have different problems, like static, for example. It seems the machines sometimes have a personality.' Like McKay's Glace Bay miners, Dyck saw his work as more complex than the unskilled labour of an assembly line worker. He described the job process as a repeated negotiation among customers and various sectors of the printing plant: from price quotation by the office staff, to submission of the material by the customer, to pre-press production, and back to the customer for approval, then on to the press room, before finally ending in the bindery. He saw this process as markedly different from an assembly line, not only by virtue of the labour process but by virtue of the emotional investment of the workers themselves. 'In an assembly line, I picture a whole bunch of people standing or sitting in line and doing a little thing and handing it on. We become quite involved with our job. If I'm assigned a certain book, a certain job, I often – provided it isn't really large – I fold the whole job, every section, the whole quantity, from start to finish.'[23]

Dyck's unwillingness to identify as an assembly worker stemmed in part from his perception of himself as a co-owner of his place of employment. Friesen Printers, where he worked as a folder operator, is an employee-owned company.[24] Dyck owned shares in the business but had mixed feelings about employee ownership. He saw it as a 'good opportunity' and appreciated receiving dividend cheques, but wished his investments were more diversified. 'And sometimes I feel like – and this is just my personality, my background coming out – I should be treated with a little more respect sometimes.' He offered as an example the seemingly arbitrary changes to shift schedules that occasionally occurred. 'They don't take the trouble to explain adequately what the advantage to them or to us will be, and I sometimes feel we aren't being listened to, when it's very clear to us that the things they are saying about the change are going to affect us negatively, and them most likely as well.'[25] Though Dyck's percentage of ownership of the company was undoubtedly a tiny fraction of the total, he felt that, as a part owner, he was entitled to some say in the manner in which the company was run. 'I have no idea what the company is worth now and how much of it I own. I just know at this point that it's the single largest asset that I have.'[26] Though both Geddert and Dyck were workers, Dyck identified not as a worker but as a part owner.

Deferential acceptance of the conditions of work was not always a given. For some immigrant workers, the transition from small-business owner to wage labourer signified a huge loss of autonomy. Henry Froese had been self-employed in Paraguay; in Canada, he operated a machine in the cutting department of Friesen Printers. 'I hadn't worked for somebody for years. When I started here, that was hard.'[27] For years, he had told his own employees in Paraguay what to do. Now he was the one being told. 'That is just not the way you're used to ... But at work, then you have to do whatever they tell you.' Dyck dealt with the transition by working as independently as possible. 'That's much better now because I'm used to more stuff and I know my stuff to do and I don't wait for somebody that tells me what to do.' Thus he was able to refashion a work identity that gave him a sense of control.

For other workers, deference was learned slowly. Henry Wallman, of Palliser Furniture, was especially eloquent: 'To keep a job, I always found that if you tried to do your best, be honest, and don't act like a smart alec – at least, not from the beginning. Later on, maybe, you can do a little bit more, but not from the beginning.'[28] Wallman recommended that workers should listen, refrain from offering advice, and avoid asking questions. Such deferential acceptance of authority was a necessity for success on the job: 'That's what I have found the best way.' Any work satisfaction needed to emanate from within; workers could not rely on owners and managers for validation. Wallman recalled once asking a foreman's opinion of a job he thought he had carried out perfectly. The reply he received was, 'There's always room for improvement.' His co-workers, who had overheard the exchange, said, 'Why are you asking something like that? They will come and tell you when it's no good.' When he explained that he would like to receive an occasional compliment on a job well done, they told him, 'That doesn't happen much.' Both the necessity of deference to authority and the demonstration of a strong work ethic were reinforced for Wallman by his fellow workers.

The deference and work ethic that largely characterized the labour process in the first few decades of operation began to give way to other forces by the 1970s. In the early years, the organization of work at Palliser Furniture, Loewen Windows, and Friesen Printers was informal and non-hierarchical. A paternalist management style that assumed the deferential acceptance of social relations characterized these businesses from their founding until the early 1970s. This management style – and workers' response to it – was tested with the transformation of the labour process as these businesses expanded dramatically and more complex technology was introduced.

Of the three companies, Friesen Printers perhaps experienced the most technological change. From 1933 until the early 1940s, workers set type by hand to run on a hand-fed Gordon press. Circa 1944, typesetting became mechanized with the purchase of a Linotype machine. The conversion from letterpress to offset presses was made in 1954, and computerization of the press room occurred in 1979. Pre-press activities were computerized in the early 1980s. Henry Thiessen, hired as a camera operator in 1968, noted that at that time the company's only camera was a 320 Robertson. By the 1990s, cameras had been replaced by computerized scanners, and masking and stripping of artwork was no longer done by hand.[29] While press operation tended to remain a male occupation, the bindery had a preponderance of female workers.

At Palliser Furniture, workers built each product from start to finish when the business began in 1944. With the expansion of the product range and accompanying increase in sales, assembly-line production was initiated in the early 1950s. Separate divisions were created to manufacture particle-board, wood, or upholstered furniture, a process that began in the 1970s. The woodworking aspect of the business originally employed primarily men. The introduction of upholstery in 1963 resulted in the hiring of female employees to work the sewing machines – many of them former garment workers, many of them Filipina.

Loewen Windows began window manufacture in 1917, milling lumber to supply to house carpenters who then built windows at job sites. Ready-to-install windows were produced in a factory setting in 1955: men did the millwork, women did the glazing and office work. The workforce became more gender balanced by the early 1980s as a result of the automation of production in the 1970s. The development of a human resources department in the late 1970s, and the subsequent removal of hiring decisions from the purview of the immigrant Mennonite plant manager, resulted in a more ethnically and religiously diverse workforce.[30] For the first time, the company hired non-Mennonites from the nearby French-speaking communities of La Broquerie, Ste Anne, and St Pierre. Prior to 1979, hiring had been at the discretion of the plant manager, who (with the support of management) had chosen to hire only Mennonites.[31]

Until the 1970s, workers at all three companies received little on-the-job training. Henry Wallman's story is typical. When hired at Palliser Furniture in 1960, he was told he would work as a painter, much to his surprise. He received a week of training from the previous painter, but what most encouraged quick learning was the fact that he had to correct his own errors. 'In those days, you had to do the furniture with spray painting, and if you did a few mistakes, then you had to wash off those chests ... and then you found out pretty soon how to do a good job.'[32] Other Mennonite-owned companies in Manitoba operated in a similar fashion. Jakob Pries was also largely self-taught when he was hired in the early 1960s at Woodland Supply, a Mennonite-owned cabinet construction firm in Winnipeg. 'Job training? No, you had to know everything, otherwise you weren't fit,' he said, laughing. 'I mean, not the first day, mind you, but ... I just started with work that was simple and straightforward and then somehow you developed common sense and practical knowledge. You just adapt quite quickly to that.'[33]

By the 1970s, with the formation of corporate divisions and the expansion of the workforce, such informal training methods were no longer adequate. Palliser Furniture, Loewen Windows, and Friesen Printers developed employee orientation and training programs. These initiatives were spurred in part by the passage of the Manitoba Workplace Safety and Health Act in 1976, which required written safe-work procedures for each job. Employee handbooks were created at all three businesses in the 1970s and 1980s. Palliser Furniture produced training videos in the 1990s which highlighted the history of the company, the opportunities available to employees, and the quality-management program in use at the company. In cooperation with Red River College, Friesen Printers offered graphic arts courses at their factory to train their workers beginning in 1990–1. Similarly, Palliser Furniture hired professors from various colleges and universities in Manitoba to provide management training at their facility in the early 1990s.

Corporate growth was facilitated by the decision to specialize: full-colour books at Friesen Printers, customized wood windows at Loewen Windows, and upper price-point furniture at Palliser Furniture. Product specialization required reorganization of the shop floor. At Loewen Windows, just-in-time assembly line production was replaced by demand flow technology (also known as lean manufacturing) in the 1990s.[34] Workers were cross-trained so that all those under the same supervisor were able to do any job within a department.[35] Friesen Printers and Palliser Furniture both were certified in the 1990s with the International Organization for Standardization (ISO), a popular total quality management system.[36] ISO certification improved their ability to market to the European community.[37] Like lean manufacturing, ISO certification required management to take control of quality assurance through documentation of all policies and procedures.

As a consequence, at all three factories, job processes were timed and the work pace was determined by outside forces rather than by the workers themselves. Ben Funk, hired as a shop-floor worker at Loewen Windows in the late 1960s before becoming production manager in 1999, described the labour process there in the 1990s. Each job was 'timed and analysed' by engineers, who ensured that production was coordinated with delivery dates and trucking routes. 'All the lines have to be analysed and balanced [by the production engineers] so that all the product is finished at the same time.'[38] While such Taylorist timing was not in operation at Friesen Printers, film assembler Henry Thiessen noted that supervisors rather than workers established the work pace. 'Well, there's really no one standard how fast we need to work. It's hard to standardize some of the things. There are exceptions to every job. But yes, the supervisor is in charge of seeing to it that people don't waste time or loiter or spend too much time visiting and so on.'[39]

At Palliser Furniture, the compensation system further encouraged a rapid (and, at times, unsafe) work pace. Piecework, a system used until the 1990s at Palliser Furniture, took advantage of a worker's natural desire to earn a decent wage. When Henry Wallman began working as a painter at Palliser Furniture in 1960, he was paid by the hour. Once he was familiar with his job, he was transferred to a piecework system. 'Every piece of furniture had a certain price. And it was so priced that you made a little bit more than [if you were paid] hourly … But they also were very careful that they didn't give you too much.'[40] One of the advantages of the piecework system was that the motivation for increasing production speed came from the workers themselves. '[Management] didn't have to push you; you worked by yourself already as fast as you could … I had to work with [my co-workers] as fast as they did. And if I worked as fast as they did, then I could have that money, too.'[41] Such a system ensured that workers placed pressure on themselves to increase productivity.

Not all workers at Palliser Furniture prior to 1990 were paid according to piecework. Jake Ginter began work as an assembler at Palliser Furniture in 1967 and later became a supervisor. He noted that male and female workers were compensated differently in the early years of his employment due to the gendered division of labour. Assemblers, who were primarily male, were on piecework. Other workers, including most females, were paid by the hour. The difference in payment method translated into differences in worker productivity and resulted, at times, in conflict between the two groups of workers. 'The assemblers were on piecework. They pushed out a lot of units, and these people that supplied the assemblers, they were under a lot of pressure to supply these pieceworkers, because [the assemblers on piecework] wanted to earn their money, of course.'[42]

The piecework system at Palliser Furniture was replaced in 1989 or 1990 by a gainsharing plan, which linked compensation and productivity. The advantage of gainsharing over piecework, from a management perspective, was its emphasis on continuously increasing production. Under piecework, workers could conceivably be content with a certain level of pay and not exert themselves to exceed a given amount of production. Under gainsharing, groups of workers (called 'teams') would monitor line speed to ensure steady production: a modern twist on scientific management.[43]

This gainsharing system, designed by founder A.A. DeFehr's son Dave, was patterned after a similar system used at Lincoln Electric Arc Welders.[44] Workers were rewarded for exceeding quotas for production and productivity. Quality facilitator Bruce MacDonald explained that the gainsharing plan was based on both the amount of product produced and the efficient use of materials. 'So they know if they throw stuff away, it affects their paycheque. If they take too long to make [the product carefully] so they don't [have to] throw it away, that once again affects their paycheque. And as a result of that, people have less supervision because we're giving them the same tools to work with as the supervisor would with measurement and graphing and charting and so on.' The result, MacDonald asserted, was 'a yield much higher than the industry average' – he was told it was 'much more than ten per cent [more] than industry average.'[45]

A part of the gainsharing system was the calculation by management of an 'allowed time' for every product made at the factory. Peter Reimer, former packer and plant manager, noted that to get a product from the paint line to packing required between three and a half and four hours.[46] Reimer observed, 'As the workers group together, then they share the concern and also the quality. They make sure that no one in their group would waste too much time because they all pull in the same dollar.' Thus, although workers had some autonomy with respect to regulating line speed, the compensation system encouraged an ever-increasing level of production. Once a gainshare occurred, however, the lower time became the new allowed time. Workers were thus encouraged to participate in their own exploitation.

At Loewen Windows, compensation and production were not as clearly linked. For decades, individual managers largely used their own discretion to establish wages for the workers they supervised. Informal comparisons to other Mennonite-owned manufacturing firms in the province were made by management from time to time, however, though the results of such comparisons are not known. Compensation was formalized at Loewen Windows in 2002 when consultants were hired to introduce the Hay System.[47] The Hay System allocates points to jobs according to criteria such as physical difficulty and amount of decision-making authority. Jobs would be assigned to one of nine 'pay bands' based on the point rating, with manufacturing jobs allocated to the first four pay bands, administration to the first five, specialists to pay bands six and seven, and corporate leadership to pay bands seven through nine.[48] Each pay band had a starting and an end wage rate generated by comparison to other privately held companies within the geographic area. As a human resources office worker explained, 'Obviously for a town like Steinbach, paying market price if you were working in, living in Toronto isn't the same, right? You know, we're not paying $210,000 for a condo, so we don't need to be making [as much as a Toronto worker] – Like, there's that cost of living adjustment in there.'[49] Under the Hay System, workers at Loewen Windows had their wages reviewed at three- or six-month intervals to determine if their performance justified progression up the scale of their particular series of pay bands.

Economists Hugh Grant and Michael Rosenstock observe that census data indicate that Mennonites in Canada earn less on average than other Canadians (9 per cent less in 1991).[50] Their closer study of the data reveals, however, that 'within the Mennonite population the income gap between urban and rural residents, and between men and women, was larger than that found among the total Canadian population.'[51] Such studies suggest that the gendered distribution of labour at the rural plants (Loewen Windows and Friesen Printers) may mean that the wages of employees – and particularly of the female workers – were or are lower than those of non-Mennonite workers in similar industries. In the absence of detailed wage and salary data from the three companies of this study, more definitive conclusions are not possible. As privately held companies, such information was not available to this researcher. While some of the workers interviewed voiced the opinion that their wages were low, and managers asserted that wages were competitive for the area in which the plants were located, such evidence is anecdotal at best.[52]

Speedy production, promoted by supervisors and reinforced at some businesses by the compensation system, had an effect on worker safety at Palliser Furniture and Loewen Windows. While Friesen Printers had long made use of large paper cutters, which presented a small element of danger, the various wood saws operated at Palliser Furniture and Loewen Windows made work at these companies more hazardous. Manitoba's Workplace Safety and Health Act, passed in 1976, mandated detailed record-keeping by the provincial government of on-the-job hazards at workplaces in the province. No incident or inspection reports on Friesen Printers were filed by Workplace Safety and Health officers from 1976 to 2004.[53] There were six incident investigation reports on Loewen Windows and ten on Palliser Furniture filed during this same period.[54] The absence of publicly available accident reports before 1976 preclude study of safety issues at these companies before that date.

Reports were filed on six accidents at Loewen Windows that occurred between June 1999 and October 2002. The workers involved were four women and two men, whose experience at the company ranged from one month to eight years. Four of the incidents involved cuts and amputations of fingers. In three of the incidents, improvement orders were issued, including a stop-work order in one case. The reports note that company management took action in two cases despite the absence of improvement orders.[55] In a number of other incidents, improvement orders were issued by safety officers. In these instances, contributing factors were the high turnover in the position of safety manager at Loewen Windows, the inability of a non-English-speaking employee to read safety procedures in English, and in the words of an investigator, 'a workplace concept' that clearing jammed material from equipment while in operation was 'an acceptable practice' and reduced machine downtime.[56] A culture that encouraged speed over safety thus existed at Loewen Windows, at least since the late 1990s.

With a workforce five times that of Loewen Windows, it is perhaps not surprising that Palliser Furniture should have more incident reports on file; what is more unusual is the criticism of management practices at the company in some of these reports.[57] An investigating officer in 1992 expressed concern about management actions. He observed that the company did not have 'a written policy and procedure in place on the safe operation of machinery, reporting of maintenance requirements or the use of equipment without safeguards.'[58] In one instance, although a piece of replacement safety equipment was in storage, it was not installed on the machinery until after an accident occurred. The workers interviewed by the investigator claimed that the machinery's existing safety equipment had been inoperative for three or four months prior to the accident. Management told the investigator that the replacement safety equipment had been ordered from Germany two months prior to the accident. The German manufacturers disputed this account, however, asserting that the order was placed a week after the accident.[59]

After a worker severed a finger while adjusting a mitre saw in 1999, the incident investigator observed that management at Palliser Furniture were not following the company's safety policy. The injured worker, the investigator noted, 'felt he was under pressure to be productive and was at risk of losing his job. He felt that he needed to get going and therefore did not take time to inform his Lead Hand of the malfunction of his machine ... The Lead Hand had stated his productivity was poor and he could be replaced.'[60] As at Loewen Windows, the work culture at Palliser Furniture encouraged minimizing machine downtime, even at the expense of worker safety. In another incident the same year, the trainer of a worker who severed two fingers while adjusting a powered machine explained to the investigator that 'this method was acceptable as long as one was careful ... By not shutting the machine off productivity was maximized.'[61] Clearly safety at times took a back seat to the demands of rapid production, a philosophy which was reinforced to some extent by the company's gainsharing system.[62]

Workers' autonomy, their sense of personal control over not only their work but their personal lives, was challenged by these changes

in the labour process. Increased investment in technology and the demands of global competition necessitated the introduction of shift work
at Friesen Printers in 1969, and later at Palliser Furniture and Loewen
Windows. The role of work in these workers' lives was transformed as
a consequence. For many, shift work was the aspect of their job that
most affected their lives, and which they consequently liked the least.

Ernie Dyck, folder operator at Friesen Printers, explained how shift
work affected him physically and socially. 'You're always adjusting
your sleeping patterns ... It also has affected my life personally, in the
sense that I can't commit to something in the middle of the week, as
far as church commitments are concerned or going out with friends, on
a regular basis. It just can't happen until the weekend.'[63] Jake Rempel,
press operator at Friesen Printers, disliked shift work but was able to
justify its necessity. 'I haven't had to do much shift. I'm one of the
luckier ones. And I see that it is necessary for the company to run more
than one shift, because if you have equipment that is that expensive,
you need to run them more than eight hours a day.' Dan Klassen, hardcover machine operator, described the effect of shift work on his personal schedule. 'We work from six to two – six in the morning until two
in the afternoon – and two to midnight. So for me, I have to be at work
at five thirty, get the line going by six. So that means getting up at five.
That means being in bed by ten. So it's kind of tough to be out until ten
or eleven like most people around.'[64] The pressures of these changes
to the labour process extended beyond the shop floor to affect not only
the workers' social lives, but their home and family lives as well. John
Geddert, chair assembler at Palliser Furniture from 1967 to 1990, noted
the personal toll taken by his employment: 'I had sleepless nights, I had
dreams, and it always was because of the pressure from the workplace
... I should have dealt with this sooner, because it's even not good for
your health ... and for your family life. Even the family feels it ... that
there is something that should be different. You start getting nervous,
and you are so tired.'[65]

The distancing of management from workers as the companies expanded in the 1970s was another change to the labour process to which
workers had to adjust. As the size of the workforce increased, a for-
malization or bureaucratization of the lines of communication resulted.
Employees had worked side by side with the business owners when
the companies were small. Henry Wallman recalled that when he be-

gan work at Palliser Furniture in 1960, owner A.A. DeFehr would stop by regularly and ask how he was doing. 'And then he heard our complaints.' This personal involvement continued when DeFehr's sons began work in the company. Workers, managers, and owners would often sit together in the lunch room and engage in casual conversation. 'But I don't think that's the case anymore, at least not at that place.'[66] With employers visible and accessible, workers had the opportunity not only to voice complaints but offer suggestions, thus exerting some control over the labour process itself. Wallman commented that management and workers used to be 'closer, working closer together': 'I found that very good, that we as workers count more and were not just a number. As a worker, if there was something that we thought, "Maybe we should do it this way," we didn't hesitate to say, "Well, could we try this way? Could we try that way?" And our boss actually liked that. I mean, we would still do what he wants and that was, of course, his shop, but we always could give suggestions.'[67] When owners and management were compelled by the increasing complexity of the business to limit their role to administration in the 1970s, shop-floor workers saw them less frequently. Opportunities to share concerns freely and informally with their employers were lost. Wallman noted that his wife asked him why he continued to work there, given how frequently he and his co-workers would complain about the job after hours. He observed that he was not actually unhappy, because 'those days, we actually could say all kinds of things still ... But now ... well, you hardly talk at all to the boss.'[68]

When the businesses were small in size, and the owners had a regular presence on the shop floor, workers addressed their concerns directly to the company owners. With expansion, more formal grievance procedures were introduced in the 1990s. Workers were expected to address their complaints first to their immediate supervisor, then to management, and if still unsatisfied, to the company president. Employee handbooks from the 1990s at these three companies mention that workers were free to present their concerns directly to the CEO, if they preferred. Few of the workers interviewed for this project stated that they had ever done so. Instead, the informal and individualistic conflict resolution methods of an earlier time continued to be used.

Conflicts on the shop floor were usually resolved on a one-to-one basis. Mennonite workers at these companies almost never took a col-

lective approach. Conrad Stoesz, a former assembler at Floform Industries (a Mennonite-owned countertop factory in Winnipeg), recognized
that supervisors were not always aware of conflicts. 'If it got too out of
hand, then the supervisor would call you into his office. But he didn't
always get wind of things that happened either. Kind of like a principal,
you know. You don't go and tattle to the principal about what's happen-
ing and stuff at school.'[69] Stoesz explained that at Floform, shop-floor
workers rarely addressed their concerns to management and would
resolve their own differences instead. Jakob Pries discovered that his
position as manager at Woodland Supply made him a sort of father
figure to employees. 'At the beginning we were small, and everybody
came to me with their problems. Whether it was personal problems or
problems at home or whatever, they would come to me and tell me their
hurts or whatever it would be.' As the company grew larger, grievances
were dealt with in a more formal manner: 'They had to go through the
proper channels. I didn't accept any complaints from the floor, because
they had to go through their supervisors and foremen, and they had to
solve it.'

A combination of paternalistic management and deferential workers was particularly effective at staving off conflict. Henry Kroeker,
foreman at Loewen Windows, remarked that he had a simple solution
for conflicts. 'When a worker didn't want to do the job [that] I gave
him, then I just tell him, "Go to the manager and tell him that you
don't want to do that." And then they fire him. In fifteen years, just
one man [did this].'[70] Jakob Pries said that his non-Mennonite German
supervisors at Woodland Supply recognized and valued the obedience
of Mennonite immigrant employees: 'Those people are happy workers.
They work hard, they don't complain, they do what you tell them ...
You can trust them that they won't do behind your back what you don't
like, or just loaf around when you're not there as a formal supervisor.'
Peter Reimer, manager at Palliser Furniture, believed that socializing
with employees made a difference in their acceptance of work discipline. 'When I went to seminars in Montreal or in Toronto ..., managers would ask, "How are you doing it in Winnipeg?" And I'd say ...,
"If at all possible, I visit with them on Sundays, I play dominoes with
them, I golf with them, I go to weddings." And they would say, "What?
How can you do that? Because, you know, that's not the way we do it.
There's a big gap between management. You know, we're up here and

the employees are over there." And I'd say, "No that's not my ... way of working with people."' Of course, such social interaction was made easier by a shared ethno-religious heritage. As the ethnic composition of the workforce diversified, informal social interactions like these became more difficult.

Henry Thiessen, while assistant supervisor at Friesen Printers, noted that workers would sometimes ignore the established hierarchies and procedures for conflict resolution in favour of their own, more direct methods. He described one 'almost impossible situation' he had been forced to deal with as a result. As the supervisor 'lacked communication skills,' workers would address their concerns to Thiessen and ask him to represent their views to the supervisor. The supervisor was greatly offended by this system, so Thiessen told the company president he 'no longer wanted to be bridging the problems all the time' due to the stress. The solution for Thiessen was to change his position within the company: he became a film assembler and ceased to work as an assistant supervisor.[71] On occasion, then, workers were able to circumvent the established chain of command when it was in their interest to do so.

Worker acceptance and manipulation of methods of conflict resolution at their workplaces in part explains their reluctance to unionize. Loewen Windows, Palliser Furniture, and Friesen Printers were not unionized during the twentieth century. In accordance with provincial safety legislation of the 1970s, each of these businesses had a workplace safety and health committee, composed of an equal number of management and worker representatives.[72] Employee committees also existed since the 1980s at these companies to direct the actions of production teams. A few workers, when questioned about unionization, explained that union representation was unnecessary given the existence of such committees. Others took a more equivocal stance on the benefits of the absence of a union. While believing employee committees to be 'just as good' as unions, Henry Wallman also stated that he did not think such committees made any significant difference at Palliser Furniture. 'We had – what do you call it? A shop union? It was similar, a little bit like a union.' Each department elected a worker representative to meet with management to discuss wages and other issues. 'So yes, we had a little say, but I don't know, I always thought it didn't make a big difference ... Wages, when it came to wages, they were higher than it would have been if we had been a unionized shop.' Asked how he knew this to be the case, he explained, 'They gave us those [union wage] books. No, no, we saw that [for ourselves].' Wallman himself served on the employee committee for a number of years. 'For a worker, that was just as good as if it was from outside [i.e., from a union]. And then we had to deal with just our office personnel, not with outside people [such as union representatives].' A shop-floor worker who later became a manager, Wallman completely accepted the argument of the ownership of Palliser Furniture that union representation was an intrusion of external forces rather than the manifestation of the agency of Palliser Furniture workers themselves.

If the hierarchization of the 1970s took a toll on workers, it was also difficult for those in management who had begun their careers on the shop floor. Once the workforce had expanded beyond a handful of employees, owners were no longer able to oversee all aspects of the business themselves. Another layer of management – lead hands, supervisors, and plant managers – became necessary. Until the 1990s, most of these positions were filled by immigrant Mennonites who had risen from the ranks of the shop floor to supervisory positions. For some, this transition was difficult. Henry Wallman spent twelve years at Palliser Furniture as a painter and two years there as a manager. He joked, 'If it wouldn't have been for the money, I wouldn't have worked there.' The transition to management was 'very hard.' His desire remained to 'be [his] own boss ... to do what [he] wanted.' As a painter, he found that he could work somewhat independently. In management, he 'had to tell people to do this, do that. And that [he] found very hard.' 'You have to know how to handle people. You had to please your boss, and you couldn't be too harsh to the workers also. That was quite stressful.'[73] Jakob Pries negotiated a similar transition when he moved from cabinetmaker to foreman to manager at the Mennonite-owned Winnipeg cabinet factory, Woodland Supply. He left the company before he reached the age of retirement. The stress caused by the conflict between his need to 'maintain profitability' for the owners of the business and his desire to be 'fair to the workers' was, he said, ultimately too great.[74]

Dan Paetkau noticed that his move from the shop floor to the office altered his relationships with his former co-workers. He had risen from the ranks of glazier to supervisor at Loewen Windows. 'Once you're in a leadership role, it's fair to say there's a certain amount of change,' he observed.[75] He added that this change was more pronounced in the early years of the business than it was in the 1990s since it used to be that the company was 'probably more like a family.' When asked how circumstances had changed, he replied, 'It's like the rest of the world. Is church the same as it used to be?' The change is 'not necessarily negative' but he 'wish[ed they] could have had it [the way it used to be] longer.' He noted that this was partly nostalgia for the 'good olden days.'[76]

Ben Funk observed that the interests of management and the interests of workers were not the same. He had been hired as an assembler at Loewen Windows and was promoted to production manager. 'As soon as you get into management, that separates you from the regular workers. And not that you don't have a relationship with them, but the environment, with your responsibility [for] the people on the floor … automatically changes your interest.'[77] John Geddert was offered the job of lead hand at Palliser Furniture, but he declined it. He turned it down because, in his words, he wanted to keep his friends and feel free to say what he wanted to the boss. As lead hand, 'you have to say what the boss wants you to say.'[78]

As plant manager at Palliser Furniture, Peter Reimer found his position of authority sometimes conflicted with his sense of personal responsibility. Reimer had begun work as a packer and shipper before becoming a supervisor and then plant manager. He described the most difficult aspect of his job as laying off workers during slow periods. 'That was the toughest job, because they have to make payments, they have to feed their family. When a man would come into my office, and say, "Well, now what shall I do? It's wintertime," that was tough.'[79] Whether they gave up independent business ownership for shop-floor employment on arrival in Canada, or were promoted from the shop floor to management within the company, such changes were difficult and challenged these workers' identity.

Henry Froese, paper cutter at Friesen Printers, was aware that there were differences of self-perception and identity between workers like himself and management. 'Well, when you work with people, some people, they think my job is higher and, they maybe think, more important. And from a certain point it's probably true. But you have to have workers for everything, and they're all important. That's what I think. That's not just sweeper on the floor or that or that. That is a sweeper on the floor, they have to do – that has to be done. When nobody does it, it's pretty dirty. So I think every work is important. But some people, it goes to their head when they are higher up. That's the way I find it.'[80] Abe Toews, of Loewen Windows, also commented on differences in status between workers and management. He believed too many supervisors were interested in maintaining their distance (and thus their separate identity) from workers. By contrast, the interests of workers, he asserted, were simply to earn a good wage and be treated with respect. He told the story of a co-worker with ten years' experience who received a trivial wage increase and quit in protest. A high worker turnover rate meant that Loewen Windows contacted him after a year and offered to hire him back. 'And he said, "Only if you give me that much money, then I'm coming back. Otherwise, not. And treat me like a human being."'[81]

Toews observed that lead hands, workers who received supervisory (though non-management) positions, sometimes misidentified their status. Without using the specific terminology, he nonetheless incorporated class consciousness into his explanation of the difference between 'good' and 'bad' lead hands. The good ones were those who continued to identify as workers rather than as managers. They 'went to the front [to the shop floor], they don't want to be sitting in the back [in the office] there anymore.' A bad lead hand is one who has 'no smile on his face' and 'won't help.' When he first began working at Loewen Windows, he said the lead hands were helpful, which made the work easier. Later, 'the others were mostly snobs. Like, "I am now the lead hand and you are the worker. You have to listen to me, not nobody else."'

Toews left his job at Loewen Windows more than once in an effort to find better paying and more satisfying employment.[82] Each time, his search was unsuccessful and he returned to the company. A conflict with a supervisor resulted in his final departure from the business. 'I quit after that [because the supervisor] gave me actually shit for what I didn't even do. That was night-shift work, the night shift's fault.' Toews believed a production problem was unfairly blamed on him because of his unfamiliarity with English. The supervisor approached Toews and asked him to read some instructions. 'I wasn't very good with reading at that time, and he gave me a big word ... I couldn't read that, and he went back to his office.' Toews then realized that his supervisor had asked him to read in an attempt to determine who was responsible for the production problem. He approached the supervisor and declared, 'Now you want to think I can't read this one word, and it's all my fault now?' Angered, Toews asked to have the night-shift worker included in the discussion, and the three men returned to the factory floor. Toews then was taken to task by the supervisor for not having the correct number of pieces of wood at his work station. Toews protested that he learned the process from 'the best cutter, the moulder operator, the best one there' and that the night-shift worker's station was set up in the same manner. The supervisor did not accept this argument, so Toews told him, 'We are both workers here. We both work on these machines. He only is working nights and I am working days. You're giving me shit but not [him].'

Abe Toews believed the stress of such workplace conflict was, perhaps, unavoidable. 'That shit on my head, I can do it somewhere else than over there [at Loewen Windows].' What he perceived to be the inadequacy of the wages at the company failed to compensate for this stress. 'You have to give [workers] more – a lot more money than what they made at that time. That [low pay] doesn't work anymore.' Interestingly, Toews did not hold upper management accountable for conditions on the shop floor. 'They just come in there and look. "Okay, it runs nice." And then they go out and do something else again. And if they would know a little more [about shop-floor conditions], I think maybe it would be a little more changed.'

In an effort to lessen the increasing distance between management and workers, new means of communication were introduced at all three companies. Staff newsletters were initiated at Loewen Windows in 1975, and at Palliser Furniture in 1981; they had been in use at Friesen Printers since 1964. Beginning in 1982, the latter had kept employees informed by providing them with an annual 'Goals and Objectives' booklet that included a financial summary and outlined management's plans for the coming year. Christmas parties, summer barbecues, camping trips, and sporting events were other, less formal channels of communication used at all three companies in the late twentieth century. Palliser Furniture, which began hiring Asian immigrants in the 1970s, attempted to build community within its increasingly multicultural staff through 'Pallorama.' This celebration of ethnic foods and customs, begun in 1992 in response to a morale problem caused by lay-offs, was a corporate version of Winnipeg's multicultural festival, 'Folklorama.'[83]

A communication method unique to Loewen Windows was their provision to employees since 1988 of a chance to meet with the company president at birthday lunches and dinners for employees.[84] The meal was followed by a question-and-answer session with the company president, Charles Loewen. 'So you get to ask the boss anything you want. And people do ask anything. "How much do you make?" You know. "How come my parking spot is so far from the door?" "So-and-so is grouchy on Mondays and Fridays." Whatever. From soup to nuts.'[85] The company president took full advantage of this opportunity.

> Charles [Loewen] does a really good job. One of his greatest qualities is that communication setting. He just – he's a star in that setting. He gets a lot of information out there, and then, of course, there's a ripple effect. You know, you drop a pebble, when the boss says something in that meeting. And he knows that and leverages it. He does it very effectively. I get the sense that the employees have a strong feeling of connection in that forum because it's very personal. Especially after the first half hour or so and someone's asked one of those dumb questions: 'How come we don't have a smoking lounge?' or something like that. And Charles will give them a straight-from-the-shoulder reply. And then everybody sort of loosens up and you can get a really good dialogue going sometimes.[86]

Such meetings were an opportunity not only to share information but, even more importantly, to reinforce corporate mythology.

Generational differences further divided the workforce at these companies. As the businesses expanded, more (and younger) workers were hired. This younger generation of Mennonite workers had not experienced the vagaries of life as immigrants or war refugees, and so the challenges of work life were viewed more seriously by them than by the earlier generation. In addition, the changes to workplace hierarchies and technology that accompanied the expansion of these businesses meant that these younger workers could no longer count on the lifelong employment and opportunities for advancement that their fathers and grandfathers experienced when they immigrated to Canada. Dan Paetkau, of Loewen Windows, described how his thirty-two-year-old son told him 'with tears in his eyes' that he 'would never have his [father's] work experience despite his education. Today you can't choose a job and make a thirty year career of it.'[87] Paetkau agreed with his son, and asked rhetorically, 'How many of them at Loewen Windows today in their mid-twenties will do that work thirty years from now?' He said he had recently spoken to three or four young Loewen Windows workers. One worker had told him there should be a thirty-year-service award, and another replied that it was not needed because no one would make it. 'And there aren't many' that do, agreed Paetkau.

David Strempler, a young Canadian-born Mennonite employed as an assembler at Palliser Furniture, expressed a similar longing for the job mobility and promotional practices of the pre-1970s period: 'It used to be that if you were Mennonite, then you were guaranteed a management job.' By the late twentieth century, managers at Palliser Furniture, Loewen Windows, and Friesen Printers were more likely to be hired from outside the company than promoted from the shop floor, and many were non-Mennonite.[88] Such changes to promotional practices further fractured the unity of the Mennonite working class.

The labour process at all three factories was nonhierarchical until the 1970s, when corporate expansion and technological innovation made change necessary. Employee training was accordingly transformed, and the labour process was timed. A shift from piecework to gainsharing in the 1990s at Palliser Furniture encouraged continuous improvement in productivity. This change in the compensation system contributed to safety issues at Palliser Furniture, a problem also present, albeit to a lesser extent, at Loewen Windows. Despite the introduction of more formal procedures in the 1990s, workers at all three companies continued to rely on informal methods of conflict resolution.

The deference many Mennonite workers exhibited on the job was shaped by their past experiences and future hopes. Deference was reinforced by the ethno-religious community, both as social organization and source of religious values. British historian Patrick Joyce notes that deference is the 'moral legitimation of class domination,' whose roots are found in the community and the home.[89] Deference is rooted in dependence, the economic necessity of work, and population stability.[90] It legitimates the existing social hierarchy by converting 'power relations into moral ones.'[91] The present arrangement of power is hegemonized: 'is becomes ought.'[92] There are, however, limits to hegemony because there is always 'the danger of deference being "seen through."' If paternalism fails to 'deliver the economic goods,' deference will collapse.[93] Employers must be careful not to extend their power too far, lest the moral basis of deference be eroded.[94]

Mennonite workers viewed themselves and their work in ways that both complied with and challenged the theological identity promoted by the Mennonite intellectual elite and the identity created by Mennonite corporate mythology. They did not always act with deferential obedience to their employers, in conformity with Mennonite religious emphases on obedience and community cohesion. Despite signs on the part of some employees of the crafting of a unique identity for themselves *as workers* apart from the identities manufactured for them by Mennonite academics, theologians, and business owners, Mennonite workers remained largely uninterested in unionization.

Although class has been virtually ignored by scholars of Mennonite history, economist Roy Vogt concludes that a study of class division is necessary for an understanding of Mennonite-owned business, as 'the working relationship between employer and employee shows all the signs of a fundamental class division.'[95] This examination of the labour process and worker identity at Friesen Printers, Loewen Windows, and Palliser Furniture reveals that the social relations of production Marx described were, indeed, present at these companies. Though the workers interviewed may not have expressed their views in class-conscious *language*, the *content* and *narrative form* of their remarks, particularly with respect to the labour process and their autonomy, points to the existence of the class division Vogt remarks upon. The nature of their employment as factory workers affected not only their job mobility and security, the speed of their work, their sleeping patterns, and their social lives, but also their identity.

With the transformation of Friesen Printers, Loewen Windows, and Palliser Furniture from small family businesses to large corporations, the relationship between Mennonite workers and their employers was reinterpreted. Employers made use of Mennonite religious motifs to craft a common ethos, but increased ethnic diversity in the workforce, together with the transformation of the labour process, resulted in some splits in the unity of the Mennonite workplace. The creation of a unique Mennonite worker identity to contest Mennonite theological identity and Mennonite corporate mythology was hampered by differences between generations and differences in migration histories. The challenges of just-in-time production and the differing class interests of workers and owners paled in comparison to the horrors of life as a war refugee, to economic hardship in Mexico, or to the difficulty of taming the so-called green hell that was the Paraguayan Chaco, for example.[96] It was the broader social and economic challenges faced by the province of Manitoba in the 1970s that ultimately catalysed a redefinition of Mennonite worker identity.

5

Unequally Yoked: Manitoba Mennonites and the Schreyer Government

The decades of the 1960s and 1970s were years of dramatic social and economic transformation. A recession in the 1970s introduced 'stagflation' to North Americans' vocabulary – the devastating combination of inflation and high unemployment. Wage and price controls were implemented in the United States by President Nixon in 1973 and in Canada by Prime Minister Trudeau in 1975. Public confidence in authorities and institutions was eroded by the events of 1968: the Democratic National Convention riots in Chicago, the Soviet invasion of Czechoslovakia and the violent crushing of the Prague Spring, the defeat of the May 1968 movement in France, as well as the assassinations of Martin Luther King, Jr, and Robert Kennedy. The ongoing war in Vietnam, the Kent State shootings in Ohio in 1970, the FLQ crisis in Quebec of that same year, and the 1972 Watergate scandal further threatened people's sense of peace and security and their faith in the established social order.

In Manitoba, the decade of the 1970s was notable for its labour activism. The New Democratic Party, under the leadership of Edward Schreyer, was elected to office for the first time in the province in 1969. The Manitoba Labour Relations Act was revised in 1972, granting more favourable terms to workers regarding compulsory union dues check-off, unfair labour practices, and union certification. High inflation, together with wage and price controls, resulted in a record number of strikes in the mid-1970s, both provincially and nationally (see table 5.1).[1] These events, together with the election of Trudeau to a minority

Table 5.1. Strikes and lockouts in Canada and Manitoba, 1974–6

Year	Locale	Total no. of strikes	Strikes begun that year	No. of workers involved	Days lost
1974	Canada	N/A	1173	580,192	N/A
	Manitoba	23	18	8,571	143,940
1975	Canada	N/A	1103	506,443	N/A
	Manitoba	33	32	4,693	161,070
1976	Canada	N/A	921	1,570,941	N/A
	Manitoba	30	25	8,935	98,190

Source: Labour Canada, *Strikes and Lockouts in Canada*, 1974–5, 1976.

government in 1972 with the balance of federal power held by the NDP, meant that among Manitoba Mennonites – ironically by employers and employees alike – the strengthened labour movement of the 1970s was a concern.

Manitoba as a whole was divided on the question of organized labour, a split that dated back to the 1919 Winnipeg General Strike. Lloyd Stinson, formerly a Winnipeg city councillor, member of Manitoba's Legislative Assembly, and provincial leader of the Cooperative Commonwealth Federation (or CCF, the forerunner of the NDP), asserted that the 1919 strike 'divided the city into two hostile camps' of 'the Establishment and Labor, owners and workers.' He noted that the line between these two groups, though 'somewhat blurred,' nonetheless persisted in the mid-1970s.[2] The division was also evident in the geography of the city and the province. The north largely was populated by blue-collar workers and those employed in resource extraction industries; the south had a significant population of business owners and farmers. Farmers shared the anti-union sentiments of many business owners, as they had 'no comprehension of the problems of urban workers.'[3] These divisions were reflected in the 1969 provincial election: northern Manitoba and north Winnipeg voted for the NDP; southern Manitoba and south Winnipeg voted for the Progressive Conservatives.

Mennonites in Manitoba were not united in their assessment of the candidates for political office in the 1969 election. James Urry notes that while Mennonites in Manitoba became more involved in politics (both voting and running for office) in the 1960s and 1970s, they did not vote as an 'ethnic bloc.'[4] Manitobans in general, however, tended to vote as 'geographic blocs.' In the 1969 provincial election, rural southern Manitoba voted overwhelmingly for the Progressive Conservative party. North of Winnipeg, rural voters elected New Democratic Party candidates to the legislature, with very few exceptions. This north-south divide was replicated in Winnipeg itself, with the northeastern electoral districts returning NDP MLAs, and the southwestern districts electing Progressive Conservatives.[5] Mennonites in Manitoba voted similarly to the non-Mennonite population: Mennonites in the rural south elected Progressive Conservatives, and those in north Winnipeg elected New Democrats (see tables 5.2 and 5.3).[6] Joe Friesen's study of polling stations in Mennonite enclaves in Winnipeg suggests that the election of Premier Schreyer may have been 'a turning point in terms of Mennonite attitudes to the political left.'[7] He attributes this shift to the increased urbanization of Manitoban Mennonites, though he notes that Mennonites' suspicion of the left, occasioned by their negative experiences of Russia after the Russian Revolution, remained a significant force in the community.[8] Doubtless, Manitobans' collective memory of the violent crushing of the 1919 strike, which resulted in a dialectic of worker activism and worker resistance to activism, played a role as well.

As North American Mennonites became more urbanized, their opposition to union membership declined, particularly among more educated urban Mennonites of higher socio-economic status. Surveys conducted in the late 1980s found 54 per cent of Canadian and American Mennonites did not oppose union membership.[9] Nonetheless, the percentage of North American Mennonites who actually were members of labour unions remained very low. Five per cent were unionized in 1972, six per cent in 1989; by comparison, twenty to thirty per cent of the general population was unionized in these decades.[10]

Mennonites in North America had long objected to union membership, a position which stemmed from similar religious objections to communism and socialism. North American Mennonite churches and institutions were unified in their stance against socialism and labour unions in the 1930s, but this attitude softened by the 1970s.[11] The earliest resolution against communism was passed by a national meeting of General Conference Mennonites (the largest of several Mennonite denominations in that year) at their annual conference in 1937.[12] The

Table 5.2. 1969 Manitoba provincial election results in electoral divisions with a significant Mennonite population

Electoral division	PC	LIB	NDP	Other	Member elected
Elmwood (urban)	1526	1053	**3803**	0	Russell J. Doern
Kildonan (urban)	1876	851	**4589**	0	Peter Fox
Rossmere (urban)	1746	631	**4089**	238 Independent	Edward Schreyer
Emerson (rural)	**2467**	2014	695	237 Social Credit	Gabriel Girard
Gladstone (rural)	**3000**	2583	1064	0	James Robert Ferguson
Lakeside (rural)	**2532**	2190	573	0	Harry J. Enns
La Verendrye (rural)	1051	**1933**	721	0	Leonard A. Barkman
Morris (rural)	**2472**	1183	712	0	Warner H. Jorgenson
Pembina (rural)	**2823**	1815	336	521 Social Credit	George Henderson
Rhineland (rural)	1853	782	181	**1981 Social Credit**	Jacob M. Froese

Source: Province of Manitoba, General Election, 25 June 1969, Summary of Results.

Note: The political party receiving the most votes in a particular electoral division has its tally in bold. For tables 5.2 and 5.3, the following abbreviations are used: PC (Progressive Conservative Party), LIB (Liberal Party), NDP (New Democratic Party). Rural electoral divisions presented in these tables are those that include significant portions of the former Mennonite West and East Reserves. Urban electoral divisions are all in Winnipeg, and are those that most closely correspond to the distribution of Mennonites in Winnipeg (Werner, *Imagined Homes*, 96, figure 5; 103, figure 6).

Table 5.3. 1969 Manitoba provincial election popular vote in electoral divisions with a significant Mennonite population

Electoral division	PC (%)	LIB (%)	NDP (%)	Total votes
Elmwood (urban)	23.8	16.4	**59.3**	6,417
Kildonan (urban)	25.6	11.6	**62.5**	7,338
Rossmere (urban)	26.0	9.4	**60.8**	6,723
Emerson (rural)	**45.3**	37.0	12.8	5,440
Gladstone (rural)	**45.0**	38.7	15.9	6,672
Lakeside (rural)	**47.7**	41.2	10.8	5,311
La Verendrye (rural)	28.2	**51.8**	19.3	3,732
Morris (rural)	**53.6**	25.6	15.4	4,613
Pembina (rural)	**51.2**	32.9	6.1	5,513
Rhineland (rural)	**38.5**	16.2	3.8	4,815
Urban average	25.1	12.4	**60.9**	20,478
Rural average	**44.9**	34.6	11.9	36,096

Source: Province of Manitoba, General Election, 25 June 1969, Summary of Results.
Note: The political party receiving the highest percentage of the popular vote in a particular electoral division has its tally in bold.

Mennonite interpretation of the Christian faith and the philosophy and goals of communism were seen as diametrically opposed, despite the attraction of leftist views for some Mennonites. 'In this socialistically and economically turbulent age there may be some Mennonites who are carried away with Marxistic [*sic*] socialism under the guise of so-called Christian socialism. But such deluded persons do not represent the doctrines, teachings nor practises of Christian faith and life as held by Mennonites in general nor as taught by the church.'[13] North American Mennonites had heard first-hand of the atrocities of life under Stalinist rule. Many personal letters from Mennonites in Russia to relatives in Canada and the United States were printed in Mennonite-owned German-language publications such as *Der Bote*. Most of the leadership of the Mennonite churches in Russia, and many Mennonite farmers in Ukraine, had been exiled to Siberia. Such circumstances undoubtedly shaped the critique of Russian communism expressed in the resolution: '[The Marxist] ridicules Jesus Christ; burns God in effigy'; and destroys churches. Marxists 'exterminate' farmers and 'assassinate or execute' those who even 'seem to disagree' with the communist government. 'There is in this heartless, brutally selfish despotism no vestige of love, pity or sympathy ... There is no peace, happiness or contentment left to the exploited, oppressed and enslaved millions of Russian hapless people.' The statement concluded forcefully that 'no spiritual, social or economic relation or cooperation [is] possible, nor does any exist between Russian Communism (Marxian Socialism) and truly faithful Mennonite Christians.' Christianity and historical materialism were incompatible, for 'it is impossible to serve God and Mammon simultaneously.'

By the 1950s, rather than simply condemning communism, there was recognition that socialist philosophies expressed valid critiques of injustice. Mennonite Central Committee (MCC), a relief, service, and peace organization supported by various North American Mennonite church conferences (and by the Brethren in Christ church conference), issued a 'Report on Communism' in 1952. MCC recognized the positive aims of communism as 'a worldwide campaign for social and economic justice to be realized in an all-embracing community of men.'[14] Communism was described as 'a judgment' on western civilization that 'requires of Christians a self-criticism which will enable them, in a cold-war situation, to see clearly their relationship to those aspects of national, cultural, and economic life which would tend to continue the conditions which have contributed to the cause of Communism.' Christians were called to respond, not by embracing 'atheistic' communism, but by practicing 'a close relationship of non-resistance and the way of the cross to self-denial in ... economic life.'

Accordingly, a more nuanced response to communism was made by the (Old) Mennonite Church and the General Conference Mennonite Church, the two largest Mennonite denominations at the time, which passed identical resolutions on communism in 1961 and 1962 respectively. Again, communism was critiqued for its atheism.[15] Nonetheless, the Mennonite authors of the anti-communist resolutions saw their responsibility, as a minority religious alternative to mainstream Christianity, to offer material aid, prayer, and the gospel to everyone, including 'reputed enemies' and 'those who suffer for Christ behind the Iron Curtain.' This responsibility was to be met even if it meant being accused of harbouring communist sympathies. Further, the Mennonites called upon 'Christians' to 'urge upon governments such a positive course of action as may help to remove the conditions that contribute to the rise of Communism and tend to make people vulnerable to Communist influence.' The document rejected the equation of Christianity 'with Americanism or with any particular economic, political, or materialistic system,' or with anti-communism. 'Although we teach and warn against atheistic Communism, we cannot be involved in any anti-Communist crusade that takes the form of a "holy war" and employs distortion of facts, unfounded charges against persons and organizations, particularly against fellow Christians, promotes blind fear, and creates an atmosphere that can lead to a very dangerous type of totalitarian philosophy.' As in the 1952 statement by MCC, communism was described as a judgment on unfaithful Christians.

By 1964, there were signs that the equation of Christianity with anti-communism was seen as problematic by North American Mennonites. The (Old) Mennonite Church that year, in a statement titled 'Anti-Communism on the Radio and in the Press,' criticized the methods of anti-communists, whose attacks were often unchristian in style and untrue in substance. 'To lend such movements our support would constitute involvement in the use of evil means for the opposing of evil.'[16] Citing McCarthyism as an example, the committee observed that 'time has proved that extremist views of the past have frequently been wrong.' The rumours of communist influence in the Warren Commission, the equation of American capitalism with Christianity, and the derision of the American civil rights movement as communist-inspired were all condemned, 'the more so when they purport[ed] to be made in the name of Christianity.' Christians were to 'witness against' such actions, even at the risk of being labelled 'subversives.'

Changing Mennonite attitudes towards socialism and communism were paralleled in their position on trade unions. Union membership was rejected in part because the threat of strike action was considered an exercise of force on the part of labour. Management's use of force, through the control of labour conditions, terms of employment, and the ability to terminate employees, was rarely critiqued in the same manner.[17] The (Old) Mennonite Church passed a resolution against union membership as early as 1937.[18] Several Bible passages were cited in support. Some verses declared that the highest authority for Christians was God – not the union oath of membership. Others suggested that Christians should not press demands for justice or seek to establish the kingdom of God on earth. Scriptural references to non-resistance were used to argue that the coercive nature of strikes and the adversarialism of collective bargaining were incompatible with Christian values.[19]

The resolution made reference as well to the most frequently cited scripture passage used by Mennonites to defend their position against organized labour. Christians should not join unions because of the apostle Paul's admonition: 'Be ye not unequally yoked together with unbelievers: for what fellowship hath righteousness with unrighteousness? and what communion hath light with darkness? And what concord hath Christ with Belial? or what part hath he that believeth with an infidel? And what agreement hath the temple of God with idols? for ye are the temple of the living God; as God hath said, I will dwell in them, and walk in them; and I will be their God, and they shall be my people.'[20] The resolution concluded that church members could not join a union. In an effort to be balanced, church members who were also employers were informed that they 'should by fairness and liberality seek to forestall labor dissatisfaction among their employees.' Somewhat unrealistically, it was noted that the church itself should, 'in anything that savors of class strife,' maintain impartiality, 'not favoring the unscriptural practices of either capital or labor.'

The Brethren in Christ Church and the (Old) Mennonite Church approved a similar statement against union membership in 1941. Class conflict was condemned as a power struggle emanating from 'an absence of the Christian principle of love.'[21] The statement echoed Guy Hershberger's advocation of passive meekness, declaring that 'Biblical nonresistance enjoins submission even to injustice rather than to engage in conflict.' As a consequence, Christian employees could not be involved in unions because of the threat of force implied in 'the monopolistic closed shop, the boycott, the picket line and the strike.' At the same time, Christian employers were not to join manufacturers' associations if the associations existed to counteract the labour movement through use of 'the lockout, the blacklist, detective agencies, espionage, strike-breakers and munitions.' Mennonite employees were to be assisted in negotiating their exemption from union membership through the (Old) Mennonite Church's creation of a Committee on Industrial Relations.[22]

Ten years later, a study conference of the (Old) Mennonite Church acknowledged that members were not adhering consistently to the 1941 statement.[23] What was needed, conference members argued, was the production of educational literature that would instruct Mennonites on the types of employment contracts that were compatible with their religious beliefs. The conference report reiterated that Christians could not be union members. The inconsistency with which the 1941 statement was being followed was 'weakening the position of the church on the entire question of nonresistance and the recognition [the church sought] to obtain for that position.'

Three years later, the (Old) Mennonite Church accepted the realities of post-war industrial society and softened its position. The Committee on Economic and Social Relations (formerly the Committee on Industrial Relations) acknowledged in 1954 that unions 'serve a useful purpose for the maintenance of justice and a balance of power in a sub-Christian society.' Mennonites were free to 'cooperate with the union (as ... with the state) in so far as doing so [did] not conflict with ... Christian testimony.'[24]

Other Mennonite groups followed suit. The Church of God in Christ, Mennonite (also known as the Holdeman Mennonites) had opposed union membership in 1953.[25] By 1967, the denomination left union membership to the individual as 'a matter of conscience.' Employment in union shops was permitted if the equivalent of dues could be paid to charity and if Mennonite employees refrained from voting on certain union issues (presumably strike votes).[26] Similarly, the Mennonite Brethren Church (the third largest Mennonite denomination in North America at the time) decided in 1969 not to forbid union membership. Mennonites were warned, however, that they should not engage in union-related violence or intimidation.[27] The prejudice against unions had not completely disappeared: the original motion had included the phrase 'nor should we judge or condemn those who are members of unions' – wording that was omitted when the motion was finally voted on and accepted.

Thus, by the 1970s there were few, if any, Mennonite denominations that explicitly prohibited union membership.[28] The 1963 Confession of Faith of the Mennonite Church made no mention of union membership in the article that tradtionally would have included it (Article 18: Love and Non-resistance), merely noting that love and non-resistance must be applied 'to personal injustice, to situations in which people commonly resort to litigation, to industrial strife, and to international tensions and wars.'[29] The same article in the 1975 Confession of Faith of the Mennonite Brethren Church also omitted reference to unions, declaring that Christians seek 'to practice Christ's law of love in all relationships, and in all situations, including those involving personal injustice, social upheaval and international tensions.'[30]

Despite the various Mennonite church conferences' change in attitude with respect to organized labour, some Mennonites in Manitoba remained sceptical of the possibility of combining Christian commitment and union membership. At several Manitoba workplaces in the 1970s, some Mennonite workers – often with the encouragement of Mennonite business owners and some members of the Mennonite intellectual elite – strongly resisted unions, seeking exemption from membership on the basis of their religious convictions. Whether their rejection of unions was in fact grounded in religious convictions or whether their political views were the real reason is debatable. John Redekop's study of voting patterns from 1940 to 1960 within the Mennonite Brethren Church and James Urry's discussion of the politics in the riding of Rossmere in the 1970s suggest that there were no clear correlations between Mennonites' denominational membership, socioeconomic position, and political allegiance.[31] Whatever the case, united in opposition to unions, these Mennonites requested the intervention of the Manitoba chapter of MCC.

The organization took action in 1974. MCC Manitoba board chair Peter Peters and MCC Peace and Social Concerns Committee members Diedrich Gerbrandt and Harold Jantz met with Russell Paulley, minister of labour, on 17 December. They asked the minister to guarantee workers' rights to reject union membership on the grounds of conscience. Section 68(3) of the Labour Relations Act allowed employees working under collective agreements to remit their dues to a charity rather than the union, provided that they had religiously based conscientious objections to joining and paying dues to a union.[32] MCC asserted that the Manitoba Labour Board had been 'turning down all applications for exemption' under this section. 'Among the eight or so cases heard by the board during the past months have been three Mennonites.'[33] Paulley responded with a letter in January 1975, observing that the delegation's concern was with the Labour Board's interpretation of Section 68(3) and not with the legislation itself. He advised them to address their concerns directly to the Labour Board.[34]

One of the Mennonite workers who sought exemption under Section 68(3) was Henry Funk, a baker, whose cause was taken up with vigour by the editor of the *Mennonite Brethren Herald*. Funk was fired from his job at McGavin Toastmaster in Winnipeg for his refusal to join the union as was required by the collective agreement. He applied to the Manitoba Labour Board in 1975 for an exemption. As a Mennonite Brethren, Funk declared he had religious objections to 'the violent tactics of unions' and to taking an oath of membership. His application was dismissed as the relevant section was not applicable to his circumstances: Funk had been hired in violation of the collective agreement, which had a clause requiring new employees be hired only after signing an application to join the union.

Even in the absence of this clause, the chair of the Manitoba Labour Board, Murdoch MacKay, observed that Funk's application would not have been successful. The Mennonite Brethren Church had no official stance against unions at that time, and so Funk's opposition to joining one was founded upon personal rather than religious beliefs, MacKay contended. Both Funk and his church minister testified to the fact that North American Mennonite churches were changing their position on organized labour. While the official Mennonite Brethren Church position no longer condemned union involvement, the old attitudes remained. Funk's church did not forbid union membership, though Funk himself 'felt that the tone of the sermons were against unions.' Funk's minister testified that 'most ministers of his Church would suggest that unionism was contrary to their beliefs but would not specifically preach against unions.'[35] MacKay concluded that union membership did not break any church rules 'and is only detrimental if the conscience of the adherent feels that way.' As such, MacKay was confident that Funk's objection was merely personal and not, in fact, religious.

Though objecting to the coercion of unions, Funk was not opposed to the coercion of the courts; he took his case to the Manitoba Court of Appeal, which ruled in his favour in 1976.[36] The question the court had to decide was whether the Labour Board had adjudicated on the basis of Funk's personal beliefs or those of the Mennonite Brethren Church to which he belonged; if the latter, then the board had overstepped its bounds. The court found that the position of the Mennonite Brethren Church on union membership was irrelevant; since Funk believed that union membership violated his personal religious beliefs, he was exempt under Section 68(3) of the Manitoba Labour Relations Act.

Even before Henry Funk received his favourable judgment from the courts, his case became a cause célèbre in the Manitoba Mennonite community. He was invited to describe his experience at a meeting of the Canadian Mennonite Health Assembly (CMHA) in April 1975. The group met in Winnipeg to discuss the role of labour unions in Mennonite-operated hospitals and personal care homes.[37] The assembly raised seven hundred dollars to fund Funk's appeal, believing his court case 'could well set a precedent in [its] position to organized labor.'

Funk's case was not the only one discussed at the CMHA meetings. Two Mennonite nurses described their experience with the Manitoba Nurses Association and a representative of a Mennonite nursing home outlined 'his board's position in the event that a union organized his staff.'[38] While the proceedings do not detail either the nurses' experience or the board's position, the use of 'outsider' language to describe the decision to unionize makes it clear that the perspective was not pro-union. In addition, John Redekop, professor of political science at the University of Waterloo and a member of the Mennonite Brethren Church, delivered a lecture on labour-management relations from a biblical perspective.[39] The event culminated in a recommendation by those assembled that MCC and the CMHA 'should work together to make' their Mennonite constituency 'more aware of the labor laws of the areas' in which they lived and how they 'could best respond to them.'[40]

The question of union membership accordingly was raised at the annual meeting of MCC Manitoba in Winnipeg on 22 November 1975. The meeting was attended by 327 official delegates of Mennonite churches in the province and 250 guests.[41] Peace and Social Concerns committee member Harold Jantz requested that Mennonite churches examine the question of whether church members should join unions and suggested that churches offer assistance to 'conscientious objectors' to unions.[42] The choice of language here was deliberate, in that it equated refusal to join a union with refusal to fight in the military – a position for which many Mennonites had made significant sacrifices historically. Jantz was also editor of the *Mennonite Brethren Herald*, the official magazine of the Mennonite Brethren Church (produced in Winnipeg), a publication in which Jantz had been promoting Henry Funk's cause. Jantz advocated the use of the courts and writing to the government as methods whereby Mennonites could seek exemption from union membership.

Other Mennonites testified to their own negative experiences with unions. Jake Neufeld, Altona postmaster and president of his union local, stated that he had 'refused to call the 17 members to a strike' when indoor postal workers struck nationally in the summer of 1975.[43] June Buhr, a Mennonite employed at the Winkler hospital, explained why Mennonite nurses objected to unions.[44] Strikes left patients without care. A Mennonite's allegiance was to God and Christ, not the union. Further, the Bible taught people 'to be content with their wages, and not to "render evil for evil or to exercise vengeance."'

Not everyone at the meeting, however, agreed with the wholesale criticism of unions offered by presentations like these. The proceedings note that Jantz's presentation 'sparked a discussion which indicated that Mennonites have differences of opinion on the degree to which they should become involved in secular structures, such as unions, courts, and political parties.' In addition, some Mennonites present at the meeting 'cautioned employers not to take advantage of employees and a suggestion was made that churches should speak to the matter of underpaying employees also.' The resolution passed by the assembly was worded carefully to reflect the absence of consensus, neither condemning nor endorsing union membership. It stated that MCC Manitoba's Peace and Social Concerns Committee was to be given a mandate to 'be a resource and to represent individuals and groups who request assistance' on the issue of labour relations.

MCC, an organization that had been founded in the 1920s to assist Mennonite famine victims in Russia, thus became involved in mediating Manitoba Mennonites' moral debates regarding labour unions. MCC Manitoba's constituency, composed of representatives of the province's Mennonite churches and other supporters of the organization, had demanded action. MCC responded by organizing a seminar on labour-management relations. This seminar was held in Steinbach on 27 January 1976, and repeated in Winkler on the twenty-eighth and Winnipeg on the twenty-ninth. A total of more than two hundred Mennonites attended, including representatives from Loewen Windows, Triple E (a Mennonite-owned manufacturer of recreational vehicles in Winkler, MB), and the Mennonite owner of Kitchen Gallery (a cabinet manufacturer in Winnipeg, MB).[45]

While the resolution that had been passed at MCC Manitoba's annual meeting had been phrased neutrally to request education and assistance, the leadership of that organization chose to present a clearly anti-union position at the seminars. The seminars were advertised in Mennonite church bulletins throughout the province: 'With the present unhappy spirit in relations of labor and management toward one another, many Christians are increasingly asking themselves what their response ought to be. These seminars will attempt to give some answers, from a biblical understanding, of the kind of relationships which acknowledge the Lordship of Christ and bring about reconciliation.'[46] The pastor of Steinbach's Grace Mennonite Church explained to the local newspaper that the motivation for the seminars in part was 'the unhappiness of the postal strike' of 1975. The question of Mennonite participation in organized labour had been prompted by Mennonites' post-war movement to the cities, he maintained. 'While we didn't want to become part of the labor unions because there's something about the power strategy that we didn't like, urbanization has simply demanded involvement.'[47] MCC's Harold Jantz declared, 'There is no reason why we have to buy the adversary concept' promoted by unions.[48] MCC had planned to invite, as speakers, people who were working in 'a business or industry where they do not have a union but rather some alternative means of relating to management.'[49] Presumably they were unable to find anyone who met these criteria: the speakers ultimately chosen were political science professor John Redekop (a Mennonite) and Gerald Vandezande of the Christian Labour Association of Canada, neither one of whom were admirers of labour unions.[50]

At the seminars, Redekop presented the case against unions. He described Canadian labour-management relations in the 1970s as being 'in a very sorry state.'[51] The responsibility for this situation lay with workers consumed with materialist desires, for whom 'quitting time [was] the only highlight of the working day.' Professionals, whom Redekop placed in a separate (and superior) category, also suffered from this 'lack of purpose.' Workers of all sorts were preoccupied with the false notion that 'society owes [them] a constantly improving living standard.'[52] The labour movement was criticized for its militancy and disrespect of signed contracts and the law. While 'the average taxpayer who strays from the straight and narrow path of the law' was quickly brought into line by law enforcement, strikers were 'blatantly' ignoring back-to-work orders. 'This seed of dereliction can bear only bitter fruit,' Redekop warned.[53] After proffering this negative assessment of labour, he continued with a critique of both Christian employers and employees. Among Christians, 'class antagonism, selfish individualism, unchristian capitalism, sloth, insensitivity, economic blackmail, exploitation, and the propensity to see employees as commodities rather than people are much too common.'[54] He declared that Mennonites did wrong to ignore the biblical command not to be unequally yoked with unbelievers – a veiled condemnation of Mennonite members of labour unions, as this passage was often invoked in Mennonite church statements against unionism. And yet some of his other comments suggested contradictorily that Mennonites should attempt to transform unions from within: 'As employees have we tried to influence union policy? Do we attend meetings? Do we speak up and spell out our principles? Do we stand for elective office? Or do we merely draw back and complain?' At the same time, workers were encouraged to see things from 'management's point of view.' Employers were also asked: do you 'honestly try to see issues from the other side of the table? As employers do we indulge in hatred and innuendo provided these are directed against unions? Do we ever seriously look for positive dimensions of unionism?'[55] Though Mennonite employers were told that they had moral obligations to their workers, the Mennonite workers' responsibility to their employers far outweighed their right to demand the fulfilment of such obligations on the part of employers.

Redekop concluded with his interpretation of the Bible's view of labour. Work was part of the order of creation, part of a meaningful life and service to God. Again his comments were somewhat contradictory. He repeated his reference to 2 Corinthians 6:14–16, observing that a Christian 'weighs very carefully the entire matter of being yoked together with materialistic pagans.'[56] The implication was that Christians could not be union members. And yet he declared that since love rather than non-resistance was a biblical imperative, then both management and labour, 'as a last resort, have the right to use power, short of physical violence or psychological destruction, to press their claim for justice as they see it.' In Redekop's view, business owners were free to lock out workers ('slothful employees') and even to close their businesses permanently in response to labour issues. Workers could strike but could not prevent scabbing. 'In this manner both sides can exercise freedom of choice for themselves but they have no right to force their decisions on others.'[57] Thus Redekop implicitly rejected the compulsory dues check-off of the newly revised Manitoba Labour Relations Act. On balance, for all his qualifications and evasions, Redekop's presentation was decidedly anti-union.

Speaker Gerald Vandezande was even more direct in his condemnation of unions. He distributed a list of objections to unions by the Christian Labour Association of Canada (CLAC). These objections included their 'acceptance of coercion and force,' the practice of closed shops, membership oaths, and adversarial relations with management.[58] A further objection was to the Manitoba Labour Board's rulings regarding Section 68(3) that an official church statement against unions was needed before a church member could claim conscientious objection to union membership. The ruling 'fail[ed] to recognize the nature of the church as a voluntary association ... [and] fail[ed] to recognize as well that the exercise of conscience is precisely the practice of taking a general teaching of the church and applying it to a particular situation.' The document concluded that Christians should not have to become 'economic martyrs' by quitting jobs that required them to join a union, though they should be willing to do so. While Vandezande was not a Mennonite, his views were supported by the Mennonite speaker, John Redekop. Redekop expressed sentiments similar to those of Vandezande, asserting that 'some might have to change vocations or deny faith and ethics.'[59] Both Redekop and Vandezande promoted the CLAC, arguing that too many unions 'demand allegiance above God' and that the CLAC advocated 'reconciliation' rather than adversarialism.

The audience at the seminars were provided with copies of documents that the presenters believed supported their case against unions. In addition to the CLAC handout, audience members received copies of Section 68(3) of the Manitoba Labour Relations Act and the similar Section 39(1) of the Ontario Labour Relations Act, as well as the 1969 Mennonite Brethren Church statement on 'The Christian and Labor Unions,' and the 'Reasons for Decision' in the case of Henry Funk's application under Section 68(3) to the Manitoba Labour Board. The membership oaths for the International Brotherhood of Electrical Workers, Canadian Union of Public Employees, Canadian Union of Postal Workers, and the Bakery and Confectionery Workers' International Union of America were distributed. A copy of a letter from Egon Frech, special assistant to Manitoba Premier Edward Schreyer, in reply to Gerald Vandezande's questions on Section 68(3) was also presented. Frech noted that the government's support of the Rand Formula had been modified by a discussion of the views of the Plymouth Brethren in a legislative committee reviewing the proposed revision of the Manitoba Labour Relations Act. The Plymouth Brethren 'would in fact sooner quit their jobs than to pay dues to a union,' and so the act was amended to allow exemption for reasons of religious belief. Frech emphasized that the amendment 'was designed to make allowances for specific religious – i.e., ecclesiastical – beliefs, and not to exempt everyone who is morally opposed to unions.'[60]

Three years after the MCC Manitoba seminars, North American Mennonite business owners offered their own interpretation of the relationship between religious belief and union involvement. Mennonite Industry and Business Associates (MIBA), forerunner to Mennonite Economic Development Associates (MEDA), argued that adversarial relations could be avoided and workplace harmony achieved through a scriptural approach. MIBA issued a report on labour-management relations on 20 October 1979, which outlined biblical principles for labour relations. These principles were justice, love, honesty, and integrity, the peaceful resolution of differences, reverence for work, and reverence for personhood. Justice required the 'fair and considerate treatment' of subordinates '*because* of their dependent position.' 'Justice is to be given because it is commanded, not because persons deserve it or have earned it, i.e., it is not a contingency based on performance or power.'[61] The ethic of love necessitated service in lieu of 'exploitation ..., domination ..., class consciousness and stratification.'[62] Employers and employees alike were called to avoid 'deception, misinformation, misleading intentions, misrepresentation, or stealing which can include unfair wages, withholding advancement, etc.'[63] A biblical approach to conflict resolution was advocated. Violence, including social and psychological violence, as a means of dispute resolution was inappropriate. Personal respect meant that class conflict was rejected as 'foreign to the Bible.' Even terms like 'management' and 'labour' were to be avoided as they 'den[ied] the Biblical worth and reality of the person.'[64] Interestingly, the provision of employee stock options and profit sharing were suggested as means of demonstrating reverence for personhood.

Some practical suggestions for Christian labour relations were proffered. Employers were cautioned to avoid 'a wide disparity in their life style when compared to their employees.'[65] The warning was not against a wide disparity in incomes, merely against its public display. This organization of Mennonite business owners also recommended, among other techniques, the adoption of 'management/employees committees' as alternatives to unions, the provision of 'breakfast, lunch or coffee with "the Boss,"' the expenditure of 'a day a month on a menial task concept' (when the owner would do the work of a particular employee), and the employment of an 'industrial chaplain.' Also promoted were profit sharing, employee share ownership, and employee representation on the board of directors.[66] A number of these options were taken up by Friesen Printers, Palliser Furniture, and Loewen Windows – many of them in response to unionization attempts in the 1970s and later.

The efforts of the CMHA, MCC Manitoba, and MIBA reveal that there was no unity among Mennonite church leadership, business owners, and workers in the province in the 1970s regarding the morality of organized labour. While church conferences had ceased to prohibit union membership, North American Mennonites largely continued to refrain from joining unions. Urban and rural Mennonites voted for different parties in the 1969 provincial election that brought the NDP to power for the first time. The NDP's changes to the Labour Relations Act were seen as an opportunity by some Mennonites to declare their conscientious objection to unions. Resistance by the Manitoba Labour Board, the provincial government, and the courts led to their defeat. Efforts by the Mennonite intellectual elite – including MCC Manitoba leadership, Professor John Redekop, and MIBA – to unify the Mennonite response to organized labour met opposition from Mennonites who did not share the elite's political and religious views.

The 1970s saw a revitalized labour movement and a growing distrust of institutions and authority in Canada as elsewhere. Mennonites, now thoroughly embedded in urban society, had to re-examine the connection between their religious beliefs and the exigencies of late twentieth-century industrial capitalism. Manitoba Mennonites reinterpreted their religious commitment to pacifism in their new context as an industrialized workforce under a left-leaning government. The conclusion of the Mennonite intellectual and corporate elites in Manitoba was that union involvement on the part of Mennonite workers would result inevitably in the dilution of their religious commitments. Mennonite workers themselves were less certain.

6

'No One Is Always Happy with His Environment': Union Drives and Corporate Responses

Mennonites in North America exhibited contradictory attitudes towards the labour movement in the last half of the twentieth century. Official church pronouncements, passed with the approval of representatives of the laity, reflected a new acceptance of unions. Mennonite business, professional, and charitable organizations, however, made efforts to limit Mennonite involvement in the labour movement. There was little unity among Mennonites in Manitoba on the question of unions. Nonetheless, the debate did result in some changes within the three workplaces of this study: unsuccessful attempts to unionize were followed by redefinitions of ownership rights and their meaning for workers with respect to profit sharing and employee share ownership.

It was within this climate that an attempt to organize the workers at Friesen Printers was made. The expansion of the business and attendant introduction of a more formalized chain of command strained communication between the owners and the shop-floor workers. In the 1930s and 1940s, D.K., Ted, and Ray Friesen had worked side by side with their few employees. By the 1970s, the size of the business was such that it was impossible to maintain these personal contacts.

Tensions were apparent already by the end of the 1960s. The introduction of a staff newsletter in 1968 and company Christmas party speeches by the president proved inadequate substitutes for face-to-face interaction on the shop floor.[1] An internal company newsletter in 1968 explained that while such 'employee bulletins' had been issued sporadically in the past, a new and more concerted effort to communi-

cate was needed. 'The need for such a publication is vital, as we feel
that communication between front-office and staff is often sadly lack-
ing, so we will try again.'[2] Despite the existence of the staff newsletter, company president D.K. Friesen observed in 1973 that 'relations
become more impersonal no matter how hard' the company tried.[3] In
such a large company, the open-door policy for resolving grievances
did little to minimize the distance between management and staff. In
a speech in 1968, D.K. told employees that he understood that taking
advantage of the open-door policy was 'not easy for [employees] to
do, and management decisions [were] therefore not always understood
the way they were intended.' The result was 'misunderstandings and
sometimes resentment.'[4] Such misunderstandings and resentment were
the particular property of the younger workers, as D.K. noted in 1971:
'I *wonder* about the young. They may not know exactly what they want,
but they are certain they don't have it now. What will they be 30 or 40
years from today?'[5] D.K. Friesen held up his rural background as a
model for these youth. On the farm, he had learned that 'honest labour
was a satisfying experience, and that you get nothing free that is worthwhile,' whereas '*much* of the rebellion of youth in towns and cities now
is due to the fact that they have not enough to do.'[6]

Impersonal employer-employee relations and generational differences were not the only causes of employee dissatisfaction at Friesen
Printers in the late 1960s and early 1970s. Shift work was instituted in
1969. The paid workday was shortened by half an hour to compensate
for slower sales in 1970. Time clocks were introduced (though later removed) in 1971.[7] Plant additions and departmental expansions resulted
in transfers of employees between divisions.[8]

Dissatisfaction among some workers at Friesen Printers culminated
in an effort to unionize in 1972. It is unclear who instigated the organization drive. The records of Winnipeg Local 191 of the International
Typographers Union (ITU) show that they had been interested in organizing Friesen Printers workers as early as 1952.[9] Ray Rudersdorfer,
the ITU representative who led the 1972 drive, asserts it began at the
behest of a nephew of the owners of Friesen Printers, who was president of an ITU local in Alberta at the time. Former press operator D.G.
Friesen claims it was not Friesen employees but 'outside influence' that
was responsible for the drive.[10] Former Friesen Printers employee Isby
Bergen attributes the initiative to a worker in the printing department

who did not live in Altona. 'I don't know if he was asked to leave or whether he left on his own ... Anyway, he was the instigator.'[11]

Whatever the origins, management was aware of the union's efforts by April 1972. A memo to staff that month coupled a discussion of wage increases with an explanation of management's attitude towards unions.[12] The memo made comparisons of union wages to recent wage increases at the company, emphasizing that Friesen Printers' wages equalled those of the Winnipeg Lithographers' and Pressmen's International Union and were higher than those of the ITU. The memo also included a section titled 'Some reasons why we are non-union.' A union was unable to provide skilled workers in a town the size of Altona; equipment at Friesen Printers was more sophisticated than that at unionized plants in Winnipeg; few Manitoba printing plants were unionized; employer-employee relations would deteriorate since 'management would have to deal only with the shop steward, or the union organizer' instead of all employees. 'We have no objection to unions, if they could guarantee our employees a job here, higher annual wages or other benefits. *This is up to employees*. However, it is up to management to generate jobs, unions offer no help there.'[13] D.K. Friesen concluded, 'Indications from our employees are that they are not interested in a union, as long as we treat them as fairly as we have in the past.'[14]

Despite this anti-union rhetoric, Friesen Printers' management took Winnipeg union demands into consideration when examining wage increases in Altona. In August of 1972, the directors considered increasing salaries. Wages at the company had been based on the Lithographers' and Pressmen's International Union (LPIU) scale. The LPIU had gone on strike at some Winnipeg plants, but was now negotiating, and some plants had made wage increases. 'What do we do?' D.K. Friesen asked his directors. 'Do we wait until next April with increases, or do we adjust this fall *for a further year* on the basis of the new rates?'[15] A further consideration was the fact that the 'ITU have just gone into negotiations, and the Letterpress and bindery rates have not yet been established.' The decision was made not to make any wage increase.[16]

Meanwhile, Friesen Printers' employees were 'talking union.' Two meetings – possibly more – were held to discuss the situation. A dozen press operators from Friesen Printers met at the hotel in Gretna, near Altona. A member of management declared he did not recall 'much in the way of response' from management. He himself was at the Gretna hotel the night in question: 'When these fellows came down the stairs following their meeting they were somewhat embarrassed seeing me there.'[17] The owners of Friesen Printers had their own meeting with the ITU representative, however.

Ray Rudersdorfer met with D.K. Friesen, Ray Friesen, and Harold Buhr (manager of the manufacturing division) on 17 November 1972. Rudersdorfer had sent literature to some employees, held discussions with them, and advertised in the *Altona Echo*. Company management claimed to be aware of most of his activities. According to D.K. Friesen, Rudersdorfer 'also said that he could see no way of organizing [Friesen's] employees except with the assistance of management, and requested [management's] assistance.'[18]

Management summarized the meeting in a memo to staff on 28 November 1972. After listing the benefits available to Friesen Printers employees, they stated in the memo: 'Unless [Rudersdorfer] could satisfy us that the employees would be better off with a union than they are without one, we would oppose his organizing to the best of our ability.'[19] The memo noted that D.K. Friesen had suggested that both he and Rudersdorfer distribute handouts to staff outlining their positions on unionization. Friesen wrote, 'To date we have heard nothing further from [Rudersdorfer], and I thought our employees would be interested in what happened, as many of them knew of his visit.'[20]

Rudersdorfer's recollection of the meeting differed in some significant aspects from the perspective presented in the memo from D.K. Friesen. A joint oral presentation to staff by management and union representatives on the advantages and disadvantages of unionism was planned. This presentation was cancelled by Ray Friesen when Rudersdorfer declared his intention to equate unions with cooperatives and credit unions.[21] Rudersdorfer believed that Friesen felt such a presentation had too great a chance of success, given that the Friesen brothers were active supporters of local cooperatives.[22]

A month after the unsuccessful meeting between Friesen Printers' management and the ITU representative, D.K. Friesen delivered one of the longest of his Christmas party speeches. Referring to the assembled people as 'fellow employees,' he acknowledged the dissatisfaction that existed among some staff. 'No one is always happy with his environment, or day-to-day work. And they shouldn't be, or there would be no progress.'[23] The imperative to comply with company policies and rules remained. In the absence of compliance, management was 'apt to scold and admonish a bit, but like a parent, [they tried] to do this gently and instructively, bearing in mind that we all make mistakes, and doing it confidentially with each employee, to benefit both himself and the Company.' D.K. Friesen expressed concern regarding 'any friction between employees, or between management and staff,' encouraging workers to address grievances to the board of directors.

D.K. directly addressed the recent failed organization drive in his speech. 'There has been some discussion of late about Unions, and we feel this matter should be discussed ... *We sincerely believe* that outside unions are not in the best long-term interest of the employees.'[24] He proposed instead that workers elect representatives to form an 'employees' association.' The advantages of an association over a union, he suggested, were the avoidance of 'union dues, strike pay, loss of wages, and ... destroying the personal relations we now have with each other.'[25] Management would assist in the creation of the association, which he proposed would negotiate wages and work hours. 'I am certain we would deal much more sympathetically with your representatives than we would with an outside organizer,' he concluded.[26] Nonetheless, an employee association was never formed.

Unions remained a concern of Friesen Printers management. Historian Esther Epp-Tiessen notes that Altona business leaders worried that the development of other large businesses in the town could lead to labour problems. She cites D.K. Friesen's remarks at a 1978 Chamber of Commerce meeting that the large companies attracted to southern Manitoba's non-union workforce could themselves become 'the perfect breeding grounds for union activity.' He questioned 'whether this was desirable.'[27] Two years earlier, D.K. Friesen had commented to *Winnipeg Tribune* reporters that 'the fact that there are only so many jobs available in Altona has a steadying influence on the labor force.'[28] This opposition to the organization of workers was not atypical of Mennonite business people, nor even of Mennonite employees. Newspaper reporter Gerald Wright cites as an example the employees of a Steinbach area cooperative poultry plant who succeeded in their application to the Manitoba Labour Board to have their plant's union certification overturned in 1989.[29] It may or may not have been the Mennonite workers at Friesen Printers who sought unionization, though their Mennonite employers' position against unionism was clear. Management at

Friesen Printers, however, never made overt use of religious beliefs to argue against the organization of labour.

Two decades later, it was not such moral opposition to unions by Mennonite workers but rather non-Mennonite workers' opposition to imposed spirituality that prompted, in part, the attempt to organize a division of Palliser Furniture. The owners of Palliser Furniture took a more aggressive stance against the efforts of their workers to organize in 1996 than did Friesen Printers in 1972. A group of twenty-two workers at Palliser Furniture's Logic Division (which manufactures particle board and laminate casegoods) sought union representation in 1995. These employees – Canadians of Métis, Aboriginal, Asian, Laotian, and Cambodian backgrounds – did not share the Mennonite ethnic and religious identity of their employers. They spent four or five months exploring their options, contacting the Canadian Auto Workers' union, the United Steelworkers, and the United Brotherhood of Carpenters and Joiners of America (UBCJA). They ultimately decided that UBCJA Local 343 would best represent their interests. An organizing drive was launched during the first three months of 1996.[30]

The motivations for the 1996 drive, according to the union representative, were objections to management paternalism and mandatory chapel attendance. A report in the *Winnipeg Free Press* ascribed the drive to employee disagreement with 'the company's faith heritage' as exemplified by the chapels. Palliser Furniture's 1970 employee handbook stated explicitly that 'Everyone is expected to participate in this Chapel Service.' Quoting Matthew 4:4 ('Man does not live by bread alone, but by every word that proceedeth out of the mouth of God.'), the handbook noted that the chapel provided 'spiritual food' and encouraged employees to inform management if they knew of a pastor who could deliver a message in English or German at the service.[31] The 1993 employee handbook renamed the chapel an 'assembly' and emphasized that the time spent in assembly was paid time. The purpose of the assembly had expanded beyond solely religious concerns, though religion remained a theme. Assemblies were now held to discuss production reports and changes in benefits or policies, to introduce new personnel, to provide information on methods of stress reduction, to address chemical dependencies, as well as to provide spiritual or personal growth.[32]

Wages were another, though lesser, motivation for organizing. A union newsletter distributed at the plant declared, 'We believe Palliser Furniture falls below industry standards in terms of wages and working conditions.'[33] UBCJA Local 343 claimed to have spoken to all four hundred employees at the Logic Division and found that everyone made under ten dollars an hour, whereas the company claimed the average hourly wage was at least eleven dollars.[34] While gainsharing may have been part of the company's wage calculations, the union dismissed this benefit. Gainsharing at Palliser Furniture was tied to performance and was 'no substitute for a fair wage.' Employees could lose their share if they were late or committed some other infraction more than three times in a pay period. A flyer distributed to workers outlined the union objections to gainsharing in detail, arguing that profit-sharing and gainsharing 'schemes' were inadequate substitutes for wage increases linked to inflation. Without a voice in corporate management, workers should not have to 'share the risks brought on by bad decisions or corporate greed.' Until such time as workers were paid a good wage, profit sharing and gainsharing at Palliser Furniture were 'for suckers.'[35]

Another significant issue during the union drive was the company's description of government-mandated benefits. The union believed that statements about such programs as the Canada Pension Plan and Unemployment Insurance in the 1993 employee handbook could be interpreted, particularly by the many immigrant workers for whom English was a second language, as claiming these benefits to be exclusive to Palliser Furniture rather than universal. The handbook noted that the 'cost of these programs, paid by PALLISER, is significant.'[36] The Canada Pension Plan was described in the handbook as a 'mandatory government pension plan ... For every dollar you contribute to this plan, PALLISER contributes another dollar on your behalf.'[37] As for Unemployment Insurance, the handbook stated the 'Federal Government of Canada administers' the program, to which Palliser Furniture contributed $1.25 for every employee dollar contributed.[38] Worker's Compensation was also detailed in the handbook. 'As a Palliser employee, you are covered by a Worker's Compensation program ... The Company pays for the entire cost and provides this coverage at no cost to you beginning with your first day of work.'[39] The union's response was to assert in their newsletters that these benefits were not 'provided by an employer out of generosity' but 'required by law' and that 'benefits are not benefits if the Company charges you for them.'[40]

Corporate management was not silent in the face of this criticism by the Carpenters' Union. Henry Wallman, former painter and later manager at Palliser Furniture, had retired from the company before the 1996 attempt to unionize. His contacts with other employees kept him informed of the situation, though. 'The boss had told them ... "If you guys elect, let in a union, then the next morning, there will be a lock on the door."'[41] Union documents support Wallman's claim that the response of company management was to threaten to close the Winnipeg plant and create an extra shift at their branch plant in North Carolina.[42] The union leafleted the North Carolina plant to warn of these tactics. Two issues of the newsletter distributed to Palliser Furniture's Winnipeg workers addressed the concern that production would be transferred to the United States if the union drive was successful. At first, workers were reminded of their 'legal right to unionize.' The union noted that Palliser Furniture would not jeopardize the 'millions of dollars in federal and provincial loans' it had received for expansion in Manitoba.[43] A month later, the stakes were raised. The union noted that workers were being asked to sign a management-led petition against the union. Workers were encouraged by the union to sign the petition in addition to their union cards, as a means of protecting themselves from reprisals. 'The Labour Board will not recognize the petition. They will recognize your Union card. Be patient and be careful.' Management were also warned that they were 'in for a surprise' if they transferred production to Troutman, as the Carpenters' Union would organize there as well. 'It's a race to the bottom to see who will work for less ... International Unions are the only way for workers to protect themselves.'[44]

In the end, less than 65 per cent of employees signed union cards, and so a vote on union certification could not be held.[45] The union claimed a partial victory in that pay raises followed the failed organization attempt.[46] Patrick Martin, former business manager of UBCJA Local 343 and later member of parliament, asserted that Palliser Furniture management became more respectful as well. Prior to the union drive, he did not 'think Art and Frank [DeFehr] knew what assholes they had on the assembly line' as supervisors. Future union drives at Palliser Furniture may be more successful with the changing composition of the workforce. Henry Wallman noted, 'I think they [management] tried always to please so that [workers] were not too anxious to get a union. But those, at that time, were mostly, like I said before, immigrants to

Canada from Paraguay, Germany. But now they have younger people, so I don't know, that could change there.' Many of these younger people were Indo-Chinese Canadians who formerly were employed in the unionized garment factories in Winnipeg. Their history of unionism and non-Mennonite background may make them more receptive to future union drives.[47]

Union activity at Loewen Windows was much more limited than at Friesen Printers or Palliser Furniture, though just as unsuccessful. Company CEO Charles Loewen recalled that, at some point in the 1980s, a shop-floor worker approached him with a copy of a business card that was reputedly on 'every old-model automobile in the parking lot' of the factory. The card had the question, 'Want a union?' followed by contact information. The worker offered to remove all the cards, but Charles Loewen declined. 'I said, "If we're that vulnerable that all it takes is one business card, then we deserve this." That's the last organization attempt that I've been aware of here in Steinbach.'[48] Charles Loewen asserted that employees had never been interested in unionization, though occasionally 'disgruntled employees' who left the company would 'threaten' to contact union organizers.[49] Though management was 'not led by fear,' they preferred that the business remain non-union. '[It is] no secret we would prefer not to have a bargaining agent or an intermediary that brings bureaucracy to, and potentially an adversarial climate within, the company. We have a strong sense that we have lots of competitors and if we want to be adversarial, there's lots of adversarial relationships that we engage in every day with our competitors.'[50] As did the Mennonite intellectual and corporate elite discussed in the previous chapter, Loewen here depicted unions as an external force, rather than a representation decision made by workers themselves. Later in the interview, however, he presented the opposite viewpoint, connecting union membership with his religious heritage in a uniquely positive way. He noted that 'freedom of assembly' was 'one of the freedoms that motivated [his] ancestors' to immigrate to Canada, and that it was highly valued within the Mennonite church. If workers decided to organize, management would 'adapt.' While noting that 'not all bargaining agents are adversarial,' many were, and if necessary, management would 'become a little more adversarial, too.' 'But our preference is that we don't need that inefficiency, if we are in good communication, and are sensitive and fair.' Loewen here presented a contradictory approach to the integration of Mennonite faith claims with labour relations. He connected the principle of collective bargaining with Mennonite religious and historical commitments to freedom, yet asserted that confrontational union representatives would be met with confrontation in kind.

Mennonite business leadership, under the auspices of MIBA, had recommended a variety of methods for staving off attempts at unionization. Of the methods recommended in their 1979 report on labour relations from a Mennonite religious perspective, two of the more radical methods – profit sharing and employee ownership – were adopted to varying extents at Friesen Printers, Loewen Windows, and Palliser Furniture. Profit sharing began at Friesen Printers in 1960. The plan was modelled after that used by Hilroy, a Canadian school supplies company, which had in turn based their plan on that of Eastman Kodak of Rochester, New York.[51] Roy Hill, the president of Hilroy and a supplier to Friesen Printers, had described his company's plan to the Friesen brothers. Management at Friesen Printers explained their motivations regarding the plan at a shareholders' meeting, commenting that it had 'long been in [their] thinking as the *right* way of conducting [their] business affairs together with [their] employees.' Earlier implementation had been 'delayed for various reasons,' but despite other demands on their capital, management 'felt to postpone this [plan] further was unfair to … employees.'[52] Management was prompted in part by their commitment to producer cooperatives; profit sharing was seen as a natural outgrowth.[53] In addition, profit sharing was a means of combatting the potential for 'relationships to grow impersonal' as the business expanded.[54]

Employees at Friesen Printers were eligible for profit sharing after five years of employment, though this requirement was lowered to three and a half years by 1981. Profits after taxes were split fifty-fifty between shareholders and employees.[55] In 1981, profit was shared on a sliding scale among those employed five years or more, those employed four and a half years, and those employed three and a half years.[56] In the mid-1980s, the profit-sharing formula was changed to a point system. Workers received one point for every one thousand dollars they had earned in the previous five years. Points were totalled for all workers, then divided into the employees' share of profits (10 per cent of profits before taxes) to obtain the value per point.[57] Management warned employees that absenteeism and late arrival at work, as well as poor 'housekeeping, conduct and attitudes,' may be taken into account in calculating an individual's profit share.[58] Management apparently never acted on these warnings, and doing so was unnecessary given the corporate culture. As the president explained, 'The whole business world was much more paternalistic then and the company was much smaller ... Everyone arrived here at eight or it was believed the president would know it and it would influence profit sharing. To this day, [starting early and working late] are strong cultural tenets of the company.'[59] Mennonite corporate mythology held such sway among the employees that external monitoring was largely unnecessary.

Statistics on profit sharing at Friesen Printers are available from 1973 (see table 6.1). The total profit distributed to employees was three-quarter million dollars by the mid-1990s. The average amount per employee was approximately two thousand dollars since the mid-1980s. Of course, given that the profit share was calculated on the basis of one's salary, this average value provides little information. Lower paid employees presumably would have received much less than two thousand dollars per year; those in management might have received considerably more.

Palliser Furniture introduced a profit-sharing plan in 1981. Under this plan, 20 per cent of profits were set aside before taxes for distribution among employees. The amount an employee received was determined by 'his/her level of earnings, the success (or lack of success) of the division in which he/she [was] employed, years of service with the company, and level of responsibility.'[60] Full-time workers were eligible for participation after nine months' employment. Half the bonus was distributed as cash; half was deferred until retirement.[61] Management stressed that profit sharing would not serve as a 'substitute for adequate levels of pay' or future raises.[62] Management gave as reasons for initiation of the profit-sharing plan the desire to allow employees to share in the company's success and the belief that profit sharing would serve as a 'catalyst' for greater 'cooperation and understanding among employees.' Workers were warned that the profit share was 'an incentive bonus and not an automatic cheque.'[63]

Loewen Windows has had profit sharing since 1984.[64] Two explanations of the origins of this plan were provided by individuals in management at the company. The former vice-president of finance ex-

Table 6.1. Friesen Printers profit-sharing statistics

Year	Total profit distributed to employees	No. of employee participants in profit sharing	Average amount per employee
1973	$14,000.00	N/A	N/A
1974	$19,000.00	N/A	N/A
1975	$38,845.00	N/A	N/A
1976	$41,250.00	N/A	N/A
1977	$46,310.00	135	$343.04
1978	$32,158.00	N/A	N/A
1979	$110,208.00	N/A	N/A
1980	$212,821.00	N/A	N/A
1981	$227,194.00	N/A	N/A
1982	$230,851.00	N/A	N/A
1983	$286,638.00	N/A	N/A
1984	$434,896.00	189	$2,301.04
1985	$455,888.00	192	$2,374.42
1986	$402,222.00	187	$2,150.92
1987	$399,546.00	184	$2,171.45
1988	$571,540.00	259	$2,206.72
1989	$654,845.00	N/A	N/A
1990	$660,378.00	270	$2,445.84
1991	N/A	310	N/A
1992	N/A	340	N/A
1993	$731,000.00	355 (est.)	$2,059.15
1994	$780,000.00	355 (est.)	$2,197.18
1995	N/A	450	N/A
1996	N/A	N/A	N/A
1997	N/A	N/A	N/A
1998	$1,280,000.00	N/A	N/A
1999	$1,390,000.00	555	$2,504.50

Sources: Friesen Printers Board of Directors' and Shareholders' meeting minutes, 1973–1994; '1999 Annual meeting report,' *Paper Trails* (Friesens Corporation employee newsletter) 11, no. 2 (April–June 2000): 12.
Note: Average amount per employee calculated by dividing total profit distributed by number of employees.

plained that profit sharing was a way of assuaging the Loewen family's 'sense of responsibilty to share the good fortunes of the company with the employees' while avoiding worry about the ongoing sustainability of simply providing higher rates of pay.[65] The vice-president of human resources swathed the origins of the plan in legend, attributing the idea to C.P. (Cornie) Loewen's wife, Annie: 'In one year in particular, they had a lot of profits and they were sitting down at the kitchen table one evening, and Cornie's wife said, "Well, we can't keep all this. What are we going to do with all this money? We just can't keep it all. And we need to really recognize the employees who have helped get us here. We need to give some of this stuff back." So it was actually at the kitchen table, that [Annie Loewen] said, "Hey, let's develop some sort of way to give some of this back to employees." That was kind of it. That's folklore, anyway.'[66]

Full-time employees at Loewen Windows were eligible for profit sharing after one year's employment. Since 2002, part-time workers also were eligible.[67] At first, the profit-sharing plan had a minimum payout of one hundred dollars. This minimum was replaced in the mid-1990s by a percentage based on years of employment: the equivalent of 1.5 per cent of base pay (after one year) to 2.5 per cent (after ten years). This guaranteed portion was deposited biweekly in a deferred profit-sharing plan. The balance of the profit share was determined by first calculating an adjusted profit figure: net profit minus an approximately 10 per cent dividend for the owners of the company.[68] In good years, 15 per cent was distributed to employees, half as a cash bonus.[69] Over the years, this cash bonus has ranged from 0 to 20 per cent of a worker's income.[70] The other 50 per cent was distributed as matching contributions among those employees who voluntarily contributed to a group Registered Retirement Savings Plan (RRSP).[71] Any remaining profit was again shared among employees on the basis of salary and years of employment.

Profit sharing and the voluntary group RRSP were offered in lieu of a company pension plan at Loewen Windows. The company's vice-president of finance acknowledges that the absence of a pension plan 'is very unusual in a Canadian workplace environment for a company this size' and that the profit-sharing plan does not always compensate as well as a pension plan would. 'So we, to a certain extent, are not fully funding what would normally be a pension plan for employees'; though, in particularly profitable years workers would receive 'in excess of what a pension plan typically would pay.'[72] At Friesen Printers, a pension plan was provided in the 1990s; participation was voluntary for those hired before 1984, compulsory for those hired after that date.

Table 6.2. Loewen Windows profit-sharing statistics

Year	Profit share as percentage of salary	Average profit share	Total profit share
1987	N/A	N/A	$774,743.00
1988	N/A	N/A	$299,359.00
1989	N/A	N/A	$336,029.00
1990	N/A	N/A	$347,495.00
1992	N/A	N/A	$109,250.00
1996	N/A	N/A	$457,838.00
1997	N/A	N/A	$583,281.00
1998	N/A	N/A	$860,042.00
1999	20	N/A	$2,184,424.00
2000	20	N/A	$1,905,425.00
2001	16	$1,300.00	$1,385,595.00
2002	N/A	$1,900.00	$1,103,957.00

Sources: 'News in brief,' *Canadian Mennonite* 4, no. 6 (20 March 2000): 32; 'Loewen Employees Garner Big Bonuses,' *Steinbach Carillon* (26 February 2001): 1; 'Company Announces Profit-Sharing Payout,' *Steinbach Carillon* (18 February 2002): 14A. Total profit-share statistics courtesy of Loewen Windows.

Employees made contributions to the private company pension plan of 3.5 per cent of their earnings up to the maximum pensionable earnings per year as defined by the Canada Pension Plan, and 5 per cent of their earnings over that amount; these contributions were matched by the employer. Palliser Furniture did not have a pension plan in the 1990s; an optional group RRSP was available. In addition, those employed five years or more received a bonus of 2 per cent of their earnings, invested in a deferred profit-sharing account.[73]

During the late 1980s and early 1990s, there were four or five occasions when there was no profit share in excess of the guaranteed minimum at Loewen Windows. These were years when the company's market share was eroded by the introduction of polyvinyl chloride (PVC) windows by competitors. The company responded by moving into the United States market and specializing in wood windows.[74] In 1999 and 2000, profit sharing amounted to the equivalent of up to 20 per cent of an employee's annual salary (see table 6.2). 'Still, a recent workforce survey showed widespread disenchantment with salaries. So Loewen hiked its payroll by $1.5 million in October [2002], or about

$2000 annually per full-time employee.'[75] In 2003, the strong Canadian dollar resulted in a decrease in profits despite an increase in sales; no profit share (apart from the guaranteed minimum) was distributed. As profit sharing was a replacement for a company pension plan, such vagaries in payouts were problematic for employees.

According to a study conducted in 1992, there were three types of profit-sharing plans in use in Canada. Some paid the profit share immediately (in cash or shares or both), some were deferred plans, and others were a combination of the two. Nationally, only 18 per cent of private companies had profit-sharing plans in the late twentieth century. Of those companies, 75 per cent had cash-based plans. The majority of them were created in the 1980s and allocated profit share according to a fixed percentage ranging from 1 to 33 per cent with a median of 10 per cent. Only 30 per cent of private companies with profit-sharing plans allocated the payout according to employee salary. In the majority of these plans (73 per cent), all full-time employees were eligible participants (see table 6.3).[76] Friesen Printers' plan is considerably older than the average Canadian profit-sharing plan and has a longer service requirement for employee quailfication. The plans at Loewen Windows and Palliser Furniture are more typical in all aspects except that these companies distribute a higher percentage of profit than the national average.

Employee share ownership at Friesen Printers also set this company apart from the average Canadian corporation. In the early 1990s, only 4 per cent of privately held Canadian companies had employees as shareholders.[77] Of those companies, 83 per cent issued voting stock to employees – as did Friesen Printers. Palliser Furniture's employee share ownership program did not issue voting stock and thus was in the minority of such plans (see table 6.4). Friesen Printers was unique among Canadian companies both in the extent of employee ownership (100% versus a national median of 11%) and in the age of its plan (a decade older than the national average).

Even as profit sharing was advocated by MIBA as a means of ensuring harmonious workplace relations, employee share ownership at Friesen Printers was viewed as one reason for the defeat of the 1972 union drive at that company. Isby Bergen, former Friesen Printers employee, explained that by being a shareholder, 'you're not just an employee; you put yourself into it.' By identifying as an owner instead of just a worker

Table 6.3. Profit-sharing plans at Friesen Printers, Loewen Windows, and Palliser Furniture compared to Canadian average

	Canada (% of companies)	Friesen	Loewen	Palliser
Profit distribution	Cash (75)	Cash & Shares	Cash & Deferred	Cash & Deferred
Allocated by salary	No (70)	Yes	Yes	Yes
All full-timers eligible	Yes (73)	Yes	Yes	Yes
Service requirement	Yes (72)	Yes	Yes	Yes
Length of service required	1 year (majority)	3.5 years	1 year	9 months
Profit distributed (%)	10 (median)	10	15	20
Date of creation	1980s (60)	1960	1984	1981

Source: Canadian average data from Long, 'Incidence and Nature of Employee Profit Sharing and Share Ownership in Canada.'

Table 6.4. Employee share ownership at Friesen Printers and Palliser Furniture compared to Canadian average

	Canada (% of companies)	Friesen	Palliser
Voting shares	Yes (83)	Yes	No
All full-timers eligible	Yes (81)	Yes	Yes
Service requirement	Yes (66)	Yes	Yes
Length of service required	3–12 months	3.5 years	10 years
Sale of shares on retirement or termination	No (83)	Yes	Not on retirement
Percentage of company owned by employees	11 (median); 31 (mean)	100	Unknown minority
Date of creation	1980s (63)	1972	1982

Source: Canadian average data from Long, 'The Incidence and Nature of Employee Profit Sharing and Share Ownership in Canada.'

in this way, the company 'never had a strike, or a union.' Bergen thought 'having the opportunity to become shareholders ha[d] prevented this.'[78] Though the union drive failed, it may have been partly responsible for the change in share structure in May 1972. Workers had been eligible to purchase non-voting shares at Friesen Printers in 1965, provided they had been employed for at least a year.[79] In 1972, voting shares were made available to employees who had worked a minimum of five years at the company and were deemed a 'key person' by the board of directors.[80] In September 1973, voting shares were made available to all employees who had been at the company a minimum of five years.[81]

Further changes to the share structure at Friesen Printers occurred in the 1980s. Shares from relatives of the owners, local auto dealers who received them in exchange for vehicles, and farmers interested in investing were all purchased by the company in 1982, so only those employed at the company could hold shares.[82] In 1987, employees were allowed to purchase shares if employed three and a half years.[83] Until 1985, majority control was in the hands of the Friesen family; after that year, the board of directors held 52 per cent of shares. By 1990, company president David Glenn Friesen was the only individual to own more than 10 per cent of shares, as other members of the Friesen family retired and had to sell their stock (see table 6.5).[84]

By the early 1990s, 60 per cent of Friesen Printers employees had purchased shares in the company.[85] To encourage greater participation in share ownership, the profit-sharing plan was altered in 1992. Twenty per cent of the payout was allocated as company shares. This percentage was increased to 30 per cent in 1993 and 40 per cent in 1994.[86] While employees were free to sell these shares (though not to non-employees), the majority chose to keep them.[87] The escalating value of shares led to numerous share splits in the late 1990s (see table 6.6). Henry Froese, paper cutter, explained the personal value of the shares. He expected the Canada Pension Plan to decline in value over the years, and hoped to supplement his retirement income with profits from the sale of his shares. 'That would make it a little easier. And I think the people are more satisfied in the company when they have something to look forward to.'[88] Eugene Letkeman, graphic arts instructor, agreed with Froese's assessment. He asserted that shares were a better investment than low interest savings accounts and safer than purchasing stocks.[89]

Table 6.5. Owners of 10+% voting shares in Friesen Printers

Year	Shareholder	No. of shares (%)
1978	Ted Friesen	18
	Ray Friesen	12
	Northbend Investments*	11
1979–80	Ted Friesen	17
	Ray Friesen	12
	Northbend Investments	11
1981–2	Ted Friesen	16
	Ray Friesen	11
	Northbend Investments	11
1983	Ted Friesen	18
	Ray Friesen	13
	Northbend Investments	12
	David Glenn Friesen	11
1984	Ted Friesen	15
	Ray Friesen	10
	Northbend Investments	12
	David Glenn Friesen	13
1985–6	David Glenn Friesen	23
	John Victor Friesen	12
	Tim Friesen	12
1987–8	David Glenn Friesen	N/A (min. 10)
	Tim Friesen	N/A (min. 10)
1989	David Glenn Friesen	N/A (min. 10)
	Friesens Employee Trust	N/A (min. 10)
1990–6	David Glenn Friesen	N/A (min. 10)
1997	David Glenn Friesen	30
1998–2003	David Glenn Friesen	N/A (min. 10)

Sources: Manitoba Companies Office, Friesens Corporation, File #8253,
Annual Returns, 1979–2003; Gordon Sinclair Jr, 'Printer's Story Real Page-
Turner,' *Winnipeg Free Press* (30 March 1997): A1.
*Northbend Investments was an investment company held by D.K. Friesen.

There has never been employee ownership of shares, voting or non-voting, at Loewen Windows. Ownership of the company remained in the hands of C.P. (Cornie) Loewen and his children (see table 6.7) until its sale in 2010 to Denmark's VKR Holding.

Palliser Furniture began offering shares to senior employees in 1982; unlike at Friesen Printers, the stock offered has always been non-voting.

Table 6.6. Friesen Printers share statistics

Year	Shareholders' equity	Dividends paid	Equity per share	No. of employee shareholders
1975	$919,650.00	$0.34	N/A	N/A
1976	$1,137,752.00	$0.36	$8.15	N/A
1977	$1,381,614.00	$0.43	$9.90	N/A
1978	$1,588,403.00	$0.45	$11.36	N/A
1979	$2,128,525.00	$0.50	$15.15	N/A
1980	$3,159,722.00	$1.00	$22.39	N/A
1981	$4,320,011.00	$1.50	$30.67	N/A
1982	$5,706,829.00	$2.00	$40.52*	55
1983	$6,286,754.00	$1.10	$9.57	100
1984	$8,140,640.00	$1.50	$24.47	N/A
1985	$9,712,198.00	$2.00	$37.95*	97
1986	$10,797,760.00	$0.22	$4.83	136
1987	$11,942,075.00	$0.24	$5.95	N/A
1988	$13,777,037.00	$0.27	$7.68	N/A
1989	$16,156,816.00	$0.30	$9.82	150
1990	$18,468,698.00	$0.44	$12.80*	N/A
1991	N/A	N/A	$1.08	N/A
1992	N/A	N/A	$1.24	N/A
1993	N/A	N/A	$1.45	300
1994	N/A	N/A	$1.65	N/A
1995	N/A	N/A	$1.82	N/A

Source: Friesens Corporation Five-Year Financial Summaries, 1975–95.
Courtesy of T.E. Friesen.
*Shares were restructured or split in these years

Before making this decision, the DeFehr family and their lawyers debated what form employee share ownership should take. Should shares be offered to those with seniority, those with a particular position in the corporate hierarchy, or those who management deemed would see share ownership as 'an incentive ... to improve productivity and stay with the company as well as a reward for services rendered?'[90] The DeFehrs were warned by their legal counsel that employees who became shareholders often underwent an attitude change, becoming unwilling to 'accept directions, authority and instructions from senior management.'[91] Company expansions and acquisitions would become more difficult because workers would question or critique management deci-

Table 6.7. Ownership of Loewen Windows

Year	Shareholder	Shares (%)
1991	C. Paul Loewen Holdings Inc.	25
	Charles N. Loewen Holdings Inc.	25
	R.C. Loewen Holdings Inc.	25
	J.R. Loewen Holdings Inc.	25
1992–9	C. Paul Loewen Holdings Inc.	20
	Charles N. Loewen Holdings Inc.	20
	Stuart R. Loewen Holdings Inc.	20
	R.C. Loewen Holdings Inc.	20
	J.R. Loewen Holdings Inc.	20

Source: Manitoba Companies Office, C.P. Loewen Enterprises, File #2527405, Annual Returns, 1991–9.
Note: Further details on the ownership of Loewen Windows are not available from the Manitoba Companies Office. Prior to 1991, Loewen Windows was not incorporated but registered as a business under the Manitoba Business Names Registration Act and thus did not file annual returns (which contain shareholder information) with the Companies Office.

sions. Workers would ask 'to see financial statements' and might ask about executive perquisites 'real or imagined' such as 'travel abroad.'[92] Making shares available to employees would not necessarily increase their loyalty to the company, the company's owners were cautioned. However, 'presumably some good will would be created among those employees who would be permitted to purchase shares. Hopefully this good will could be translated into higher productivity by all of the employees.'[93]

The DeFehr family discussed the possibility of setting differences in the initial distribution of shares to compensate for the different degrees of seniority among employees (see table 6.8).[94] Offering stock to long-term shop-floor employees (Group IV) was viewed as the least likely possibility. Ultimately the decision was made to make non-voting shares available to those 'with extra responsibility' after ten years' employment and to all others after fifteen years' employment.[95] Those eligible received an initial gift of shares equal in value to ten weeks' pay. In 1989, the eligibility requirement for all employees, regardless of level of responsibility, was set at ten years of service.[96] Only a small

Table 6.8. Suggested employee share ownership plan, Palliser Furniture, 1979

Group		Number in in group	Minimum seniority	Participation (%)
I	Senior management	5	5 years	100
II	Middle management	16	5 years	30
III	Foremen & senior sales	31	10 years	10
IV	Long-term employees	N/A	10 years	5

Source: Palliser Furniture, Executive Committee meeting minutes, 19–20 January 1979.

Table 6.9. Palliser Furniture share statistics

Year	No. of shareholders	Total no. of employees	Shareholders as % of total staff
1987	87	850	10
1989	125	N/A	N/A
1990	157	N/A	N/A
1991	188	N/A	N/A

Sources: Palliser Furniture, employee newsletters 8, no. 2 (July 1989); 10, no. 7 (May–June 1991): 5; 6, no. 1 (July 1987).

fraction of Palliser Furniture employees were shareholders in the late 1980s (see table 6.9); it is unknown to what extent employee share ownership continued after that period.[97] Majority control of Palliser Furniture remained in the hands of the DeFehr family (see table 6.10); in 1996, Art DeFehr bought out his siblings, eventually selling back one division of the company (DeFehr Division) to his brother, Frank.[98]

At one of these three companies, employee share ownership and profit sharing were initiated by comments from a member of the founder's family. In a letter to his family, this individual argued that the family's religious beliefs necessitated the implementation of such programs. Reducing economic disparity between workers and owners would be 'looked upon favourably' by workers. Such practical gains were not the main reason for his suggestions, however. Christian teaching emphasized that wealth was 'ultimately owned by God' and 'to be used to God's glory.' Whether employee share ownership and profit-sharing

Table 6.10. Owners of 10+% voting shares in Palliser Furniture

Year	Shareholders	Shares (%)
1978	A.A. DeFehr & A.A. DeFehr Holdings Ltd.	49.52
	David DeFehr	12.38
	Arthur DeFehr	19.05
	Frank DeFehr	19.05
1979	Frank DeFehr Holdings Ltd.	33.00
	Arthur DeFehr Holdings Ltd.	33.00
	David DeFehr Holdings Ltd.	33.00
1980–7	A.A. DeFehr Holdings Ltd. (aka 95230 Canada Inc.)	10.00
	Frank DeFehr Holdings Ltd. (aka 95232 Canada Inc.)	30.00
	Arthur DeFehr Holdings Ltd. (aka 95223 Canada Inc.)	30.00
	David DeFehr Holdings Ltd. (aka 95225 Canada Inc.)	30.00
1988	A.A. DeFehr Holdings Ltd.	0.54
	Frank DeFehr Holdings Ltd.	1.63
	David DeFehr Holdings Ltd.	1.63
	Arthur DeFehr Holdings Ltd.	1.63
	95224 Canada Inc.*	26.06
	Palliser Furniture Investments**	68.50
1989	A.A. DeFehr Holdings Ltd.	0.74
	Frank DeFehr Holdings Ltd.	2.21
	David DeFehr Holdings Ltd.	2.21
	Arthur DeFehr Holdings Ltd.	2.21
	Palliser Furniture Investments	92.64
1990–1	A.A. DeFehr Holdings Ltd.	10.00
	Frank DeFehr Holdings Ltd.	30.00
	David DeFehr Holdings Ltd.	30.00
	Arthur DeFehr Holdings Ltd.	30.00
1994	Frank DeFehr Holdings Ltd.	30.00
	David DeFehr Holdings Ltd.	30.00
	Arthur DeFehr Holdings Ltd.	30.00
	95224 Canada Inc.	10.00
1996	Palliser Furniture Holdings Ltd.***	100.00
1997	N/A	N/A
1998–2001	Cape Jersey Holdings Ltd.	53.40
	David DeFehr Holdings Ltd.	33.70
	95224 Canada Inc.	7.80
	Joanne DeFehr Holdings Ltd.	1.70
	Andrew DeFehr Holdings Ltd.	1.70
	Richard DeFehr Holdings Ltd.	1.70
2002–4	Palliser Furniture Holdings Ltd.	100.00

Sources: Manitoba Companies Office, A.A. DeFehr Manufacturing, File #4786662, Annual Returns, 1978–9; Manitoba Companies Office, Palliser Furniture Ltd., File #0504262, Annual Returns, 1980–96; Manitoba Companies Office, Palliser Furniture Ltd., File #3814743, Annual Returns, 1998–2004.
*Likely owned by a member of the DeFehr family.
**Comprised all employee owners of shares (including the DeFehrs).
***Owned by Art DeFehr.

plans were necessary outgrowths of a Mennonite faith that emphasizes mutual aid, as this person suggested, or conditions for preserving a non-union workforce, as MIBA and others argued, is debatable.

Profit-sharing plans were believed by many business owners (and, indeed, some workers) to have helped prevent unionization. The reformation of profit sharing (and the introduction of share ownership) at Friesen Printers coincided with the attempt to organize in 1972. The promotion of profit sharing as a way to stave off union organizing attempts had been made in Manitoba as early as 1953, when representatives of the Council of Profit Sharing Industries spoke at a Winnipeg Rotary Club meeting. A Manitoba businessman was quoted in the *Winnipeg Tribune* in 1967: 'No unions. We don't need them. Walter Reuther, the Detroit labour leader, says if all companies operated on our basis [providing profit sharing], unions would be obsolete.' A *Tribune* article in 1976 observed that companies with profit-sharing plans tended to be non-unionized, while a 1975 editorial contended that profit sharing was 'Capitalism's answer to Marxism.'[99] For Manitoba Mennonite religious and corporate leaders, such promises to deter unions and challenge leftist political parties would have been compelling reasons to introduce such plans.

The 1970s saw a revitalized labour movement in Canada. Mennonites, now thoroughly embedded in urban society, had to re-examine the connection between their religious beliefs and the exigencies of late twentieth-century industrial capitalism. The Mennonite employers of this study remained firm in their opposition to the organization of their workers. The expansion of these businesses, though, meant that Mennonite corporate mythology could no longer be relied upon to mitigate the demands of workers. Workers attempted to organize in 1972 at Friesen Printers and in 1996 at Palliser Furniture. In both cases, they were unsuccessful. A renegotiation of sorts took place, however, as owners acknowledged their employees' concerns by implementing and transforming profit-sharing and employee share ownership plans. As the studies by Richard Long reveal, the provision of such plans set these companies apart, to a degree, from the majority of Canadian businesses.

Profit sharing and employee share ownership were beneficial to employees so long as the company was profitable. Of course, employees had to take on faith management declarations regarding the state of company finances in the absence of both employee representatives on the board of directors and full disclosure of financial statements. The real test of such plans, however, was tough economic times. When their profit share declined because of circumstances beyond their control (a rising Canadian dollar, for example), shop-floor workers were punished financially to a degree that management and owners rarely were.

The tension between late twentieth-century Mennonite emphasis on social responsibility, as exhibited by labour's demands for economic justice, and early twentieth-century Mennonite insistence on avoidance of confrontation was evident in the struggle of Manitoba Mennonites with their response to unions. Pacifism had often been dismissed as passivity in the past; now the adherence to the principle of non-violence could be seen as an excuse for accepting economic exploitation. The Mennonite emphasis on justice and neighbourly love could have translated into support for labour unions, but in late twentieth-century Manitoba, it did not. Perhaps Mennonite workers recognized that national unions had limited effectiveness in a global capitalist system – as evidenced by Palliser Furniture management's coercive threat to transfer production to the United States. Whatever the reason, though North American Mennonites' attitudes towards unions may have undergone change during this period, they continued to avoid becoming union members.

Conclusion

In 1976, when MCC Manitoba held its series of seminars to address their constituents' concerns about the NDP government's revision of provincial labour legislation, I was only five years old. I thus have no personal memory of the Schreyer years. Nor do I have a communicative memory of that time period: neither my parents nor my church congregation discussed those events during my subsequent youth or young adulthood. Yet, I do have a collective memory of Mennonitism and labour relations.[1]

This collective memory has been shaped by the particular circumstances of my family and my work life. My father, at various points in his life, worked as a farmer, a mechanic, a service station owner, a lay minister, a vocational instructor at a community college, and an author of automotive textbooks. The dinner table and the television set were two settings in our home where work, ideology, and religious belief – both in the news and in our own lives – were the subjects of vigorous debate. I was raised in an atmosphere that suggested that these subjects were intrinsically related.

My own work experience has been limited to Mennonite employers. From my penultimate year in high school until my entry into graduate school, I waited tables in a Mennonite-owned restaurant. An incident in my early twenties brought home to me the diversity of Mennonite experiences and understandings of labour relations: I bought a T-shirt commemorating the seventy-fifth anniversary of the Winnipeg General Strike – an event that had not been discussed in my high school or university history classes to that point. Somewhat naively, I wore the shirt to work one day, thinking to make a statement about my love for history, oblivious to how others may interpret it as a comment on labour issues. I was genuinely puzzled by my employer's negative reaction: I had assumed that, as fellow Mennonites, we shared a common viewpoint. That incident was one of many that shifted my perspective from an essentialist understanding of Mennonitism to one that recognized the contextual, historical, contingent, and constructed nature of identity – and, indeed, of the plurality of identities even within a seemingly unified ethno-religious community.

This study has argued that the religious values and competing identity claims of Mennonites complicated their relationship to each other – and to capitalism – in ways that many non-Mennonites did not experience. Their examination of how to be a Mennonite and a participant in economic life – how to be 'in the world, but not of it' – was transformed, but not resolved. Nor did Manitoba Mennonites in the late twentieth century pose a systemic challenge to the existing economic system. Ideological understandings of ethno-religious identity on the part of Mennonite intellectuals, business owners, and workers, while rooted in different social and ideological contexts, resulted in acquiescence and accommodation to the established order, as revealed in the limited responses of Manitoba Mennonites to the labour militancy of the 1970s.

The Christian religion certainly has offered resources of resistance that predate capitalism's transformation of the labour process. Though Thompson's 'chiliasm of despair' thesis on Methodism is an oft-cited portion of his classic *The Making of the English Working Class*, he also speaks favourably of the revolutionary potential of dissenting Christian traditions and of the organizational contribution made by Methodism to working-class political movements.[2] Religion can be repressive, he notes, but it can also be an 'imaginative resource' or (as the Bible was to William Blake) 'a Poem of probable impossibilities.'[3]

As this study has shown, Mennonitism did not constitute such a resource for factory workers in twentieth-century Manitoba. Nor had all Mennonites abandoned their concerns regarding organized labour by the century's end. John H. Redekop, whose anti-union presentations at sessions organized by the Mennonite Central Committee in Manitoba in 1976 were discussed earlier, still viewed union membership as a threat to Anabaptist Christian understandings of non-violence in 1989. The *Global Anabaptist Mennonite Encyclopedia* entry on labour unions, which he updated, concludes that Mennonites have had 'major difficulty successfully relating the peace position to their interaction with labor unions.' He speculates that 'ethical issues dealing with labor unions will be one of the most important practical testing grounds of Christians committed to the way of peace and reconciliation.'[4] It may be argued, however, that the challenges of industrial capitalism – rather than the question of union membership – are more worthy of critical attention by Mennonites and others.

Theological resources exist within Mennonitism that would allow for such a critique of capitalist society; whether twenty-first century Mennonites and others will make use of those resources is a matter for conjecture. The experience of many Mennonites in Russia under Stalinism makes some Mennonites suspicious of any such critique, equating it with a commitment to godless communism. In a globalized culture, Mennonite encounters with the broader world will only increase, and with time, the suspicions of the generation that survived Stalin will fade into the past. A five-century history of insistence on the 'priesthood of all believers'[5] means that Mennonites will continue to engage in debate about their role in the world, recreating their identity as necessary.

While not proffering a definitive answer to the problems of industrial capitalism, this study has examined the historical recreation of Mennonite identity in the context of twentieth century capitalism as practiced in three Mennonite-owned firms in Manitoba. In doing so, this manuscript addresses lacunae in both Mennonite history and the social history of the working class. Though nearly one in four North American Mennonites are members of the working class, little has been written about their experiences.[6] In addition, this work contributes to the nascent conversations among oral historians, scholars of lived religion, business historians, and practitioners of the social history of the working class. Perhaps its greatest contribution lies in its attempt to bring these diverse groups into conversation with one another.

Competing claims of ethno-religious identity were made by the Mennonite intellectual elite (including church leaders, theologians, and academics), by Mennonite business owners, and by Mennonite workers in the last half of the twentieth century. The dramatic changes in Manitoban society in the 1970s and the synchronous attempts by North

American theologians and business owners to address the upheavals and transformations of post-war capitalism explain why Mennonite workers in Manitoba did not develop a firm sense of class consciousness in this period.

Mennonite business owners, by contrast, had a keen understanding of the necessity of reducing the potential for class conflict, crafting what I have termed a Mennonite corporate mythology. While they made use of typical paternalist arrangements such as company social events and sports teams, they also integrated religious values with business practices in a manner that reinforced the hierarchy of labour. The deference of workers was encouraged not only by employer paternalism but also by Mennonite religious understandings of 'yieldedness.' The 'Reflections' advertising campaign at Loewen Windows, discussed in chapter 3, is but one example of this process.

Religion was not only a tool that could be used to ensure worker loyalty and conformity; the religious beliefs of workers also acted to some extent as a check on the behaviour of owners, limiting their conspicuous consumption, for instance, as was the case with the DeFehr family. Religion also could function in contradictory ways, as when owners implemented profit-sharing and employee share ownership programs. Such programs were both an example of the owners' religious commitment to justice and fairness and a means of securing the deference of workers.

Historian Joan Sangster notes that the absence of labour unions from Peterborough, Ontario, before the 1940s 'meant that workers did not have at hand institutional or ideological alternatives to the paternalist bargain.'[7] A similar situation existed for much of the twentieth century in the rural communities of Steinbach and Altona, the homes of Loewen Windows and Friesen Printers respectively. Sangster notes that Peterborough workers manipulated the paternalist arrangement for their benefit: deference to authority was coupled with 'a distinct notion of *dignity owed* to workers and the respectability of their aspirations and lives.'[8] It was only when the benefits of paternalism to workers were on the wane, as in Manitoba in the 1970s, that employees took a serious interest in unionization.

At times of acute stress, such as the high inflation rates and increased labour militancy of Manitoba in the 1970s, efforts to secure worker conformity were insufficient. Though many Mennonites in Manitoba, whether labour or management, were opposed to union membership, a minority saw unions as a means of redressing injustice. Attempts to organize at Friesen Printers and Palliser Furniture were unsuccessful, but owners heard the message that was delivered, and changes to wages and benefit programs were made.

The experiences and perspectives of Mennonite workers and Mennonite owners, even within the same factory, clearly differed. There was a lack of unity on the Canadian Mennonite position with respect to labour activism. This lack of consensus stemmed from the different class positions of Mennonite workers and their employers, as well as from the diversity of belief within the Mennonite faith itself. While nonconformity and autonomy were emphasized, so too were humility and deferential obedience or 'yieldedness.' Some Mennonite workers supported unionization; most did not. Mennonite employers answered the challenge of worker discontent by implementing profit-sharing and employee share ownership programs and by recreating Mennonite corporate mythology.

The result was that, far from presenting a challenge or critique, Mennonite religious understandings in twentieth-century Manitoba served to reify capitalist economic and social relations. Readers would be wrong to infer, however, that such reification was the inevitable consequence of religious belief. Robert Orsi reminds us that 'religious creations are not stable ... They subvert the intentions of those who would manipulate them for their own ends ... Religious idioms can be appropriated for ends quite the opposite of those sought by power.'[9] Whether the twenty-first century will see Mennonite workers appropriate their religious heritage for such purposes remains to be seen. What does seem certain is that religious identity will continue to be contested, and that those debates will be conducted not only in theological treatises and church pews but also in the workplace.

Notes

Abbreviations

CCA	Consumer and Corporate Affairs
CTL	C.T. Loewen & Sons, Vertical File, 1980
DWF	D.W. Friesen, Vertical File, 1981–2
GAMEO	*Global Anabaptist Mennonite Encyclopedia Online*
MCC	Mennonite Central Committee, Manitoba Collection
MCO	Manitoba Companies Office
MHC	Mennonite Heritage Centre
NRSV	New Revised Standard Version
UBCJA	United Brotherhood of Carpenters and Joiners of America.
UMA	University of Manitoba Archives

Introduction

1 See, for example, Iacovetta, *Such Hardworking People*; Campbell, 'Cult of Spontaneity'; Stone, *Jewish Radicalism in Winnipeg*.

2 Redekop et al., *Mennonite Entrepreneurs*; Redekop and Redekop, *Entrepreneurs in the Faith Community*; Epp, *Mennonites in Canada*; Regehr, 'From Agriculture to Big Business'; Regehr, *Mennonites in Canada*; Loewen, *Family, Church, and Market*.

3 Bainton, 'Left Wing of the Reformation.'

4 Six per cent of Mennonites in North America were union members in 1989. Kauffman and Driedger, *The Mennonite Mosaic*, 92, 207–8.

5 The Brethren in Christ denomination was formed by Anabaptist Mennonites in Pennsylvania in the 1780s in response to pietist revivalism. This
   revivalism emphasized crisis conversion (salvation achieved as the result
   of a personal 'decision for Christ' rather than salvation as the hoped-for
   end of a life of discipleship) and the visible work of the Holy Spirit in
   the believer's life. C. Nelson Hostetter and E. Morris Sider, 'Brethren in
   Christ Church,' *GAMEO*, 1990, http://www.gameo.org/encyclopedia/
   contents/B748ME.html (retrieved 11 October 2004).
6 The United States and the Democratic Republic of Congo had the largest
   groups of Mennonites. These numbers include only those who are baptized members in Mennonite and Brethren in Christ churches. According
   to Mennonite World Conference, in 2003 there were 127,348 Mennonites
   in India, 323,329 in the United States, and 194,119 in the Congo. Two
   American Mennonite groups formed the Congo Inland Mission (later
   known as Africa Inter-Mennonite Mission) in 1910. This organization
   provided schools for abandoned and orphaned children as well as children
   freed from slavery, and translated the Bible into local languages. Checole
   et al., *Global Mennonite History*, 69–81; Mennonite World Conference,
   'MWC-2003 Mennonite & Brethren in Christ World Membership,' http://
   www.mwc-cmm.org/Directory/mbictotal.html (retrieved 3 October 2003;
   page removed). In 2001, 191,465 Canadians recorded their religion as
   Mennonite. Statistics Canada, 'Selected Religions, for Canada, Provinces
   and Territories – 2001 Sample Data: Canada,' 1 April 2003, http://www12
   .statcan.ca/english/census01/products/highlight/Religion/Page.cfm?Lang
   =E&Geo=PR&View=1a&Code=01&Table=1&StartRec=1&Sort=2&B1
   =Canada&B2=1 (retrieved 3 October 2003).
7 Statistics Canada, 'Selected Religions, for Census Metropolitan Areas and
   Census Agglomerations – 2001 Sample Data: Winnipeg (CMA), Man.,' 1
   April 2003, http://www12.statcan.ca/english/census01/products/highlight/
   Religion/Page.cfm?Lang=E&Geo=CMA&View=2a&Code=602&Table
   =1&StartRec=1&Sort=2&B1=602&B2=1 (retrieved 3 October 2003);
   Statistics Canada, 'Selected Religions, for Canada, Provinces and Territories – 2001 Sample Data: Manitoba,' 1 April 2003, http://www12.statcan
   .ca/english/census01/products/highlight/Religion/Page.cfm?Lang=E&
   Geo=PR&View=1a&Code=46&Table=1&StartRec=1&Sort=2&B1=46&
   B2=All (retrieved 3 October 2003). There are some difficulties with rely-
   ing on church membership statistics. Since Mennonite churches practice
   adult baptism, such statistics omit children and young adults who may
   self-identify as Mennonites as well as those adults who attend Mennonite

churches without having joined them as members. Thus the 2001 Canada census records some 60,000 more Mennonites in Canada than does the Mennonite World Conference.

Another problem with these statistics, and with the study of Mennonite history generally, is the definition of the term Mennonite. Indeed, Mennonites themselves have difficulty defining a Mennonite. Royden Loewen argues that it is possible to categorize six different Mennonite written discourses of ethnic identity: embrace of Mennonite ethnicity and de-emphasis of religious tradition; simultaneous embrace of ethnicity and Canadian evangelicalism; urban rejection of ethnicity and embrace of social activism; conservative rural connection of faith and ethnicity; and simultaneous embrace of ethnicity separated from religion. Loewen, 'Poetics of Peoplehood.'

8 Rempel, 'Examination'; 'Mennonites and the Jobs'; 'Mennonites Better Represented.'

9 J. Winfield Fretz and Calvin W. Redekop, 'Business,' *GAMEO*, 1989, http://www.gameo.org/encyclopedia/contents/B86ME.html (retrieved 2 March 2010); Calvin W. Redekop, 'Work Ethic,' *GAMEO*, 1989, http://www.gameo.org/encyclopedia/contents/W675ME.htm (retrieved 2 March 2010).

Anabaptism was the collective name given to a series of religious movements that emerged in the sixteenth century in Switzerland and the Low Countries. The name is derived from their practice of adult baptism (re-baptism). Though there were some variations in beliefs, most Anabaptists were committed to a radical separation of church and state (referred to as a 'two kingdom' worldview), the rejection of violence, and living one's life in accordance with the teachings of Christ (termed 'discipleship').

10 Hershberger, 'Nonresistance and Industrial Conflict'; Thiessen, 'Mennonite Business in Town and City.'

11 'Lived religion' requires viewing 'all religion as lived experience' and not separating religion from other aspects of daily life, from other cultural institutions and public discourses. It acknowledges that sacred spaces include workplaces as much as churches and mosques, and examines power relations within communities. Orsi, 'Is the Study of Lived Religion Irrelevant,' 172.

12 Chandler, 'Luck,' 3. See Fogel and Engerman, *Reinterpretation of American Economic History*.

13 Cuff, 'Notes,' 123.

14 Amatori and Jones, 'Introduction,' in *Business History*, 4–5. Clark and

Rowlinson note that organizational studies in the early twenty-first century were shifting from economics and sociology to history, though there was resistance and suspicion. Clark and Rowlinson, 'Treatment of History,' 331–2, 346–7.

15 Hofstede, 'Cultural Relativity,' 88.

16 Laird, 'Introduction,' 686. Laird defines social capital as 'assets based on personal connections and connectability.' Ibid., 685.

17 Redding, 'Thick Description,' 149.

18 Walton, 'New Directions,' 3–6, 8–9. See, for example, Richard Whittington's introduction to a special issue of *Business History* in 2007, which 'argues for the central importance of the managerial revolution for business historians.' Whittington, 'Introduction.'

19 Walton, 6. Walton claims that innovative and multidisciplinary work in the field is discouraged by the structure of university disciplines and academic presses. Ibid., 7.

20 Hackett et al., 'Forum,' 1–2; K'Meyer, 'I Just Felt Called,' 728–9.

21 Pasture, 'Role of Religion,' 117.

22 K'Meyer, 725.

23 Hackett et al., 21.

24 Orsi, 'Everyday Miracles,' 18.

25 K'Meyer, 732.

26 Orsi, 'Is the Study of Lived Religion Irrelevant,' 174.

27 Harris, *History of Trucking*.

28 Mysyk, *Manitoba Commercial Market Gardening*.

29 H. Klassen, *Business History of Alberta*. A pictorial history of Manitoba businesses does exist: Coates and McGuinness, *The Keystone Province*.

30 DeFehr, *Memories of My Life*.

31 Redekop et al., *Mennonite Entrepreneurs*; Redekop and Redekop, *Entrepreneurs*; Driedger, 'Mennonite Business in Winnipeg.'

32 Vogt, 'Myth.' Vogt argues that Mennonite business owners were far from being exceptions to traditional Mennonite occupational patterns. From the sixteenth century to the present day, 'the pursuit of individual wealth was generally more encouraged than inhibited' among Mennonites. In Canada, he asserts, Mennonites have been 'singularly aggressive in their pursuit of economic success, and not especially thwarted by community taboos.' Vogt, 'Myth,' 231; Vogt, 'Entrepreneurs, Labourers, Professionals, and Farmers,' 140.

33 Vogt, 'Myth,' 232.

34 Vogt, 'Entrepreneurs, Labourers, Professionals, and Farmers,' 137. The
cartoon was a private drawing that was shown to Vogt but never published.

35 Vogt, 'Myth,' 233. Karen Dyck's unpublished paper, though limited in
scope, is a small step in this direction. She dispels the myth of the solitary
male entrepreneur, using oral history to uncover the role played by entrepreneurs' wives (and children) in Mennonite-owned businesses in Winnipeg. Dyck, 'The Invisible Labour of Survival.'

36 Epp, 'Mennonite Girls' Homes'; Esau Klippenstein, 'Doing What We
Could'; Esau Klippenstein, 'Scattered but Not Lost,' 200–32.

37 See, for example, Menno Schrag's recollections of working for H.P.
Krehbiel, founder of Herald Publishing. Schrag recalls that Krehbiel de-
fied minimum wage legislation shortly after its passage in the United
States by having employees sign over a portion of their pay cheques to
the company as 'loans' to be repaid at an unspecified future date. The
National Labour Relations Board soon put a stop to this practice. Schrag,
'H.P. Krehbiel,' 7.

38 Nisly, 'Mennonite Woman'; Thiessen, 'Business and Labour Relations.'

39 Vogt, 'Economic Questions,' 157–66; Vogt, 'Entrepreneurs, Labourers,
Professionals, and Farmers'; Vogt, 'Impact of Economic and Social Class,'
137–48; Vogt, 'Mennonite Attitudes to Property'; Vogt, 'Mennonite Studies in Economics'; Vogt, 'Myth'; Driedger, 'Canadian Mennonite Urbanism'; Driedger, *Mennonites in the Global Village*; Driedger, *Mennonites in
Winnipeg*; Driedger, 'Post-War Canadian Mennonites.'

40 Vogt, 'Impact of Economic and Social Class.'

41 The 'Anabaptist Vision' was defined by historian Harold Bender in 1943.
The Anabaptism scale developed by Kauffman and Harder was based on
this 'Vision' and included commitment to adult baptism, church discipline, pacifism, evangelism, and service, as well as refusal to swear oaths,
accept certain public offices, and take others to court. Kauffman and
Driedger, *Mennonite Mosaic*, 71. The development and consequences of
the 'Anabaptist Vision' will be discussed in chapter 1.

42 Vogt includes skilled, semi-skilled, unskilled, and service workers in this
category.

43 'It enables them to withdraw at least partially from the urban class
struggle while simultaneously permitting them to affect the appearance of
being concerned and involved because as professionals they are the judges
and evaluators of society.' Vogt, 'Impact of Economic and Social Class,'
144.

44 Ibid., 147.

45 Ibid.

46 Regehr, *Mennonites in Canada, 1939–1970*, Appendix F. The percentage
of rural Mennonites had declined to 49 per cent a decade later. Statistics
Canada, Census data, 1981.

47 The result is an identity crisis 'brought about by the fact that Mennonite
faith has not been able to cope with the technological and social changes
that have enveloped [Mennonites].' C. Redekop, 'Mennonite Identity
Crisis,' 89–97, 99, 101.

48 Winland, 'Quest for Mennonite Peoplehood,' 111.

49 Ibid., 117, 131. This identity crisis is unique to Mennonites in North
America. Mennonites in Africa and Asia tend not to be the descendants
of sixteenth-century Anabaptists and thus 'Mennonite' is primarily a religious identity for them. Most Mennonites in Central and South America
are members of Mennonite denominations that emphasize the inseparabil-
ity of religious beliefs and cultural practices (for example, through colony
life). Mennonites are also internally divided by numerous church and conference splits. To speak of a homogeneous and easily defined Mennonite
community is therefore a gross over-simplification.

50 There is a wealth of literature on this understanding of identity. See, for
example, Anderson, *Imagined Communities*; Conzen et al., 'Invention
of Ethnicity'; Gans, 'Symbolic Ethnicity: The Future'; Gans, 'Symbolic
Ethnicity and Symbolic Religiosity'; Geertz, 'Deep Play'; Geertz, 'Thick
Description'; and Sollors, Introduction.

51 Vogt, 'Mennonite Studies in Economics,' 64–5.

52 P.J. Klassen, *Economics of Anabaptism*, 28.

53 'Nothing is so strikingly basic to their attitudes toward economic factors
as the firm conviction that all facets of life constituted an indivisible unity
that must be permeated by the spirit of Christ … Faith could never be di-
vorced from practical life. Where this seemed to be the case, the Anabaptist could only conclude that the professed faith was dead.' Ibid., 114.

54 Though property remained in the hands of individuals, its use was to
conform to the needs and standards of the community. Vogt, 'Mennonite
Studies in Economics,' 66.

55 Mary Sprunger is one historian working in this field, though her focus is
on seventeenth-century Dutch Mennonites. See her doctoral dissertation,
'Rich Mennonites, Poor Mennonites.'

56 Sprunger, 'Dutch Mennonites,' 20.

57 Ibid., 25–9.

58 Ibid., 30.

59 Ibid., 40.

60 For ease of identification, I will be using these names throughout the manuscript, although the companies were known in 2010 as Friesens Corporation, Loewen, and Palliser Furniture.

61 Friesens Corporation , 'Our Past,' http://www.friesens.com/Corporate/History.asp (retrieved 15 October 2003).

62 Loewen, 'About Us,' http://www.loewen.com/site.nsf/about/more (retrieved 15 October 2003; website has changed, page removed).

63 Palliser Furniture, 'Company Info,' http://www.palliser.com/companyinfo.html (retrieved 15 October 2003; website has changed, page removed).

64 All interview participants were given the choice of using their real names or remaining anonymous; those who preferred anonymity have been given a pseudonym of my choosing.

65 Marlene Epp, for example, notes in her study of Mennonite refugee women: 'Rather than setting up a dichotomy between the "true" or "false" aspects of memory, I think it more helpful to examine the societal and cultural constraints that shape particular memories and to recognize that "we are what we remember."' Epp, *Women without Men*, 14.

66 Portelli, *Death of Luigi Trastulli*; Portelli, *The Battle of Valle Giulia*.

67 Yow, *Recording Oral History*, 57.

68 Ibid., 53.

69 M. Epp, *Women without Men*, 14.

70 'By analyzing how historical actors make sense of the events they experienced, we can gain a fuller portrait of how history is shaped both by events and emotions.' Freund and Quilici, 'Exploring Myths,' 159.

71 Access to documents at Palliser Furniture, though initially full and open, was curtailed after the company president, Art DeFehr, read my MA thesis (a social history of Friesens Corporation) and decided that his vision for my research differed from my own.

72 Thompson said of the religious dissenting tradition: 'One feels often that the dormant seeds of political Radicalism lie within it, ready to germinate whenever planted in a beneficent and hopeful social context.' Thompson, *Making of the English Working Class*, 39.

73 Lipartito, 'Culture,' 33.

1. The Mennonite Intellectual Elite: Yieldedness, Non-resistance, and Neighbourly Love

1 Garrett, 'Popular Religion,' 86.
2 Examples include P.E. Johnson, *Shopkeeper's Millennium*; Murphy, *Ten Hours' Labor*; Lazerow, *Religion and the Working Class*.
3 See, for example, Pasture, 'Role of Religion.'
4 Stout and Taylor, 'Studies of Religion,' 25; K'Meyer, 'I Just Felt Called,' 725. See also Marshall's *Secularizing the Faith*, as well as his 'Canadian Historians.'
5 See Martin, *General Theory of Secularization*; H.R. Niebuhr, *Social Sources of Denominationalism*; Herberg, *Protestant – Catholic – Jew*; Williams, *Popular Religion*; Vrijhof and Waardenburg, *Official and Popular Religion*; Wuthnow, *Restructuring of American Religion*; Marsden, *Fundamentalism*.
    For a discussion of this historiographical shift, see Stout and Taylor, 'Studies of Religion'; as well as Fox, 'Experience.'
6 New classics in this field include Hall, *Lived Religion*; Alexander, *Jazz Age Jews*; Orsi, *Madonna*; Orsi, *Thank You, St. Jude*; McDannell, *Material Christianity*; Taves, *Fits, Trances, and Visions*.
7 Orsi, 'Everyday Miracles,' 7.
8 Ibid., 9–10.
9 L. Weaver, 'Mennonite,' 116.
10 Theologian C. Norman Kraus identifies both *Gelassenheit* and discipleship with non-violence and meekness. Kraus, 'Anabaptist Spirituality,' 26–7.
11 Robert Friedmann, 'Gelassenheit,' *GAMEO*, 1955, http://www.gameo.org/encyclopedia/contents/G448.html (retrieved 13 January 2008).
12 NRSV.
13 Donovan E. Smucker and John J. Friesen, 'Love,' *GAMEO*, 1989, http://www.gameo.org/encyclopedia/contents/L675ME.html (retrieved 13 January 2008).
14 Of course, those seemingly repressed by a particular religious doctrine still may exercise their agency and redefine it on their own terms. Thus Marie Griffith notes that members of the conservative Christian group Women's Aglow Fellowship could recharacterize the doctrine of submission as 'a means of having power over bad situations, including

circumstances over which they otherwise may have no control.' Griffith, 'Submissive Wives,' 172.

15 Theologians in the United States had similar influence on Canadian scholars who were part of mainline Protestant denominations. Stackhouse, 'Protestant Experience,' 215.

16 Other American Mennonite colleges include Bluffton College in Ohio (founded in 1899) and the Kansas institutions of Tabor College (1908) and Hesston College (1909). Melvin Gingerich, 'Colleges and Universities, Mennonite,' *GAMEO*, 1953, http://www.gameo.org/encyclopedia/contents/colleges_and_universities_mennonite (retrieved 11 February 2010).

17 The 'Foundation Series' Sunday School curriculum was used extensively in the 1970s and 1980s by North American congregations of the General Conference Mennonite Church, the (Old) Mennonite Church, the Brethren in Christ, and the Church of the Brethren. The curriculum emphasized discipleship as articulated by Bender's 'Anabaptist Vision.' Harold S. Bender, Cornelius Krahn, Nanne van der Zijpp, and Marlene Kropf, 'Sunday School,' *GAMEO*, 1989, http://www.gameo.org/encyclopedia/contents/S8437ME.html (retrieved 12 February 2010); Harder, *Obedience*, 26–7.

18 Keim, 'Anabaptist Vision,' 253.

19 MBBC was owned and operated by the Canadian Conference of the Mennonite Brethren Church; CMBC by the Conference of Mennonites in Canada, later known as the General Conference (GC).

20 J.J. Friesen, *Building Communities*, 83.

21 For example, MBBC president John B. Toews was born in Russia, studied at Tabor College (Kansas), and ended his career as president of the Mennonite Brethren seminary in Fresno, California. CMBC's first president, Arnold Regier, was born in Kansas and was a graduate of both Bethel College (Kansas) and Mennonite Biblical Seminary (Chicago), and was a former professor at Bethel College. CMBC's third president, Henry Poettcker, resigned in 1978 to become president of Associated Mennonite Biblical Seminary (Kansas). Marvin Hein, 'Toews, John B. (1906–1998),' *GAMEO*, 1990, www.gameo.org/encyclopedia/contents/T6492ME.html (retrieved 10 February 2010); Ens, *Becoming a National Church*, 73; B. Dyck, 'Canadian Mennonite Bible College,' 222n89.

22 The Mennonite Church and the General Conference Mennonite Church/Conference of Mennonites in Canada were integrated in 2000. The re-

sultant national bodies are now known as Mennonite Church Canada and Mennonite Church USA. Mennonite Church Canada, 'History and Identity,' http://www.mennonitechurch.ca/about/histident.htm (retrieved 29 October 2003). The 1972 survey involved 3591 respondents; the 1989 survey included 3083 respondents. The results of the 1972 survey were published by Kauffman and Harder in *Anabaptists Four Centuries Later*. The 1989 survey's results were published in Kauffman and Driedger, *Mennonite Mosaic*. This second survey made comparisons with the data from 1972.

23 The 'Anabaptism scale' in the table was the result of a series of questions that assessed individuals' level of commitment to Anabaptism, using Bender's criteria: commitment to discipleship, suffering for the cause of Christ, adult baptism, church discipline, oath refusal, non-resistance, separation from the world, and refusal to litigate. Dueck, 'Canadian Mennonites,' 83.

24 Keim, 254.

25 Loewen, 'An Imagined Biblical Paraphrase.'

26 Mennonites were not alone in this need to redefine their beliefs in light of new social realities; mainline Protestant denominations in Canada underwent similar efforts to transform themselves. Stackhouse, 211–13.

27 Abe Dueck unconvincingly asserts the opposite. He claims that, unlike among U.S. Mennonites, the alternative to Bender's 'Vision' for Canadian Mennonites was 'not usually dispensationalist fundamentalism or other forms of North American evangelicalism' but 'a different understanding of Mennonite peoplehood.' This understanding was supposedly less dogmatic, more ecumenical, more politically activist, 'less separatistic and more individualistic.' Dueck, 80, 82.

28 Regehr, *Mennonites*, 209–10; J.J. Friesen, 132. Kee describes such revival meetings as part of the 'commodification of religion.' Revivals emphasized a consumerist individual choice (a personal decision to follow Christ) rather than commitment and accountability to, and discipleship within, the church. Kee, *Revivalists*, 178–9, 185, 191. See also Marks, *Revivals*; and Harold S. Bender, Ernst Crous, Nanne van der Zijpp, and Beulah Stauffer Hostetler, 'Revivalism,' *GAMEO*, 1989, http://www.gameo.org/encyclopedia/contents/R523ME.html (retrieved 13 February 2010).

29 R. Loewen, *Diaspora*, 82–3; J.J. Friesen, 133; Regehr, *Mennonites*, 212.

30 Wiebe, 'A Different Kind of Station,' 88. Not all Mennonites appreciated this evangelical bent; two of the founding shareholders sold their shares in CFAM as a result of their objections. These men were two of the three

brothers that were the second-generation owners of Friesens, the Altona printing firm examined in this manuscript. Ibid., 90.

31 At the same time, the radio station encouraged Mennonite involvement in the political system. Wiebe, 91, 96.

32 Goshen College, established 1894 as the Elkhart Institute by General Conference Mennonites (now Mennonite Church USA), is a Mennonite liberal arts college located in Goshen, Illinois.

33 The Schleitheim Confession, written by a Swiss Mennonite, was only one of many Anabaptist confessions of faith.

34 The full text of the Schleitheim Confession is available in a number of sources. See, for example, Baylor, *The Radical Reformation*. A number of online sources also are available, including the UK Anabaptist Network, http://www.anabaptistnetwork.com/SchleitheimConfession.htm (retrieved 28 October 2003).

35 New Testament support for this portion of the Article included Christ's rejection of the temptation offered by Peter to spurn the cross (Matthew 16:24), Christ's rebuke of the sons of Zebedee (Matthew 20:25), and 1 Peter 2:21, NRSV: 'For to this you have been called, because Christ also suffered for you, leaving you an example, so that you should follow in his steps.'

36 'But our citizenship is in heaven, and it is from there that we are expecting a Saviour, the Lord Jesus Christ.' Philippians 3:20, NRSV.

37 The ban was the subject of Article 2 of the Confession, based on the model of congregational discipline outlined by Christ in Matthew 18:15–17, NRSV: 'If another member of the church sins against you, go and point out the fault when the two of you are alone. If the member listens to you, you have regained that one. But if you are not listened to, take one or two others along with you, so that every word may be confirmed by the evidence of two or three witnesses. if the member refuses to listen to them, tell it to the church; and if the offender refuses to listen even to the church, let such a one be to you as a Gentile and a tax collector.'

38 2 Corinthians 6:17, NRSV. Revelation 18:4 is also referenced: 'Then I heard another voice from heaven saying, "Come out of her, my people, so that you do not take part in her sins."'

39 'Everything which has not been united with our God in Christ is nothing but an abomination which we should shun. By this are meant all popish and repopish works and idolatry, gatherings, church attendance, winehouses, guarantees and commitments of unbelief, and other things of the

kind, which the world regards highly, and yet which are carnal or flatly counter to the command of God, after the pattern of all the iniquity which is in the world.' 'Schleitheim Confession (Anabaptist, 1527),' *GAMEO*, 1527, http://www.gameo.org/encyclopedia/contents/S345.html (retrieved 3 January 2012).

40 Not all sixteenth-century Anabaptists accepted the Schleitheim Confession, or were committed to pacifism. James Stayer has shown that, since their origins, Anabaptists have struggled with the question of pacifism versus militance. See his *Anabaptism and the Sword*.

41 Bender made this intention clear in the inaugural issue of the *Mennonite Quarterly Review* in January 1927. Toews, *Mennonites*, 37.

42 Gross, 'Locus,' 275.

43 W. Klaassen, 'They Were Giants,' 235; Keim, 241.

44 It was not only Bender who was criticized for organizing such meetings independent of church authorities. A meeting of lay Mennonites in Clermont, France, in June 1919 to discuss post-war reconstruction of Europe was similarly viewed with uneasiness by church leaders. N. Yoder, 'J. Gresham Machen,' 257–8.

45 Keim, 241.

46 Keim, 249. Canadian statistics are difficult to obtain, in part because federal records regarding alternative service have been destroyed. The 1941 Canada census records 16,913 Mennonite men between the ages of fifteen and thirty-five. Historian Frank Epp searched records of Canadian military personnel and discovered 4453 ethnic Mennonite names. The Mennonite Heritage Centre archives has created a website, which records that, of the 10,851 Canadian conscientious objectors in the Second World War, 7543 were Mennonites. Regehr, 'Influence,' 76; MHC, 'Alternative Service in the Second World War: Farm Service,' 2004, http://www.alternativeservice.ca/service/farm/ (retrieved 17 November 2004).

47 Biesecker-Mast, 'Towards a Radical Postmodern-Anabaptist Vision,' 64.

48 The content of the 'Anabaptist Vision' was also promoted through the Herald Press Uniform Series, which were Sunday school materials used in many North American Mennonite churches. Many of the authors of these materials were Goshen graduates and former students of Harold Bender. Keim, 253.

49 Toews, *Mennonites*, 84.

50 Loewen, 'Imagined Biblical Paraphrase.'

51 Bender, *Anabaptist Vision*, 13.

52 Bender asserted that Anabaptism began in Zurich, Switzerland, in 1525
    with the adult rebaptism of Georg Blaurock by Conrad Grebel. Bender,
    Anabaptist Vision, 3–5. This 'monogenetic' view was challenged twenty
    years later by James M. Stayer, Werner Packull, and Klaus Deppermann,
    who replaced Bender's Swiss origins of Anabaptism with three streams:
    Swiss, South German/Austrian, and North German/Dutch. 'From Mono-
    genesis to Polygenesis.'

53 Bender, *Anabaptist Vision*, 20.

54 Ibid., 26–7.

55 Ibid., 28. Bethel College religion professor Duane K. Friesen argues,
    however, that the invocation of the Schleitheim Confession as support for
    a doctrine of separatism is a distortion of sixteenth-century Anabaptists'
    engagement with and confrontation of 'the dominant cultural institutions
    of their time.' D.K. Friesen, 'Anabaptist Theology,' 37.

56 Bender, *Anabaptist Vision*, 31.

57 Ibid., 34.

58 Ibid.

59 Ibid., 28.

60 'The Christian may in no circumstance participate in any conduct in the
    existing social order which is contrary to the spirit and teaching of Christ
    and the apostolic practice. He must consequently withdraw from the
    worldly system and create a Christian social order within the fellowship
    of the church brotherhood. Extension of this Christian order by the con-
    version of individuals and their transfer out of the world into the church is
    the only way by which progress can be made in Christianizing the social
    order.' Ibid., 34–5.

61 Engels, 'Socialism,' 684–5.

62 Toews, *Mennonites*, 37, 339.

63 Ibid., 38.

64 Ibid., 105.

65 Ibid., 341.

66 An exhaustive treatment of Hershberger's life and thought is Schlabach,
    War, Peace, and Social Conscience.

67 Guy F. Hershberger, Ernst Crous, and John R. Burkholder, 'Nonresis-
    tance,' *GAMEO*, 1989, http://www.gameo.org/encyclopedia/contents/
    N656ME.html (retrieved 8 March 2010).

68 Harder, 'Power and Authority,' 84.

69 Hershberger, 'Nonresistance,' 147.

70 Hershberger, *Way of the Cross*, 213, 215.
71 Schlabach, 'To Focus a Mennonite Vision,' 30; Hershberger, 'Nonresistance,' 143.
72 J.L. Burkholder, *Problem of Social Responsibility*, 25.
73 J.L. Burkholder, 'Nonresistance,' 134.
74 Ibid., 136.
75 J.L. Burkholder, 'Autobiographical Reflections,' 48–9.
76 Overwhelmed by refugees attempting to flee Shenyang, Burkholder and a pilot had to force people off a plane too overloaded to take off, knowing that they would be abandoned to the advancing People's Liberation Army. J.L. Burkholder, 'Autobiographical Reflections,' 11–20.
77 Scott Holland, 'Introduction,' in Sawatsky and Holland, eds., *The Limits of Perfection*, iii.
78 J.L. Burkholder, *Problem of Social Responsibility*, 41, 60.
79 Ibid., 61.
80 Ibid., 64.
81 Burkholder's argument is similar to that of German Evangelical theologian Reinhold Niebuhr a quarter century earlier in *Moral Man and Immoral Society*. Niebuhr claimed that coercion was a necessary aspect of human society. While *agape* love is the Christian ideal, it is unachievable by sinful humanity. Instead of aiming for an unattainable society of 'uncoerced and perfect peace and justice,' Christians (and others) should strive for a society of justice, achieved through a minimum amount of coercion. To do otherwise was to live irresponsibly in the face of social problems. Niebuhr, *Moral Man*, 22. See also Niebuhr's 1932 article, 'Must We Do Nothing?'
82 J.L. Burkholder, *Problem of Social Responsibility*, 64.
83 Ibid. Burkholder's views were shared by Mennonite professor of religion Gordon Kaufman. In 1958, Kaufman wrote an essay in which he argued that social responsibility is the necessary outcome of Christian (agape) love. 'Love means accepting the neighbor where he is "in hope that the neighbor may be transformed and the situation may be redeemed."' J. Lawrence Burkholder, 'Concern Pamphlets Movement,' *GAMEO*, 1989, http://www.gameo.org/encyclopedia/contents/C6616ME.html (retrieved 11 February 2010).
84 J.D. Weaver, 'Socially Active Community,' 78. Burkholder asserted that a socially responsible Christianity necessitated voting, political party membership, acceptance of 'the essential validity of the political office,' as well

as participation in community and service organizations. He criticized Mennonites for what he perceived to be their preference for social service 'as an alternative to political action.' J.L. Burkholder, *Problem of Social Responsibility*, 16–17, 161.

85 Theologian John Howard Yoder was the most significant voice in the Mennonite intellectual community's condemnatory discussion of Constantinianism. Chris Huebner, professor of theology at Winnipeg's Canadian Mennonite University, defines Yoder's understanding of Constantinianism thusly: 'Whereas pre-Constantinian Christianity was that of a minority church existing in a world that was largely hostile toward it, Yoder claims that the Constantinian shift [as a consequence of the Emperor Constantine's issue of the Edict of Milan and his convention of the Council of Nicea in the fourth century CE] resulted in an alignment of the church with the ruling political regime of the day. In other words, Constantinianism represents a fusion of church and state, clergy and emperor, Bible and sword, God and civil authorities, or the general continuity of Christianity with the wider world.' Yoder and others argued that such an unholy alignment occurs, even in societies that have an official separation of church and state, whenever and wherever the church identifies its aims with those of the state. Huebner, *Precarious Peace*, 57–8.

86 Weaver, 'Socially Active Community,' 78.

87 Yoder taught briefly at Goshen College before his long career at Notre Dame. Grimsrud, 'Yoder,' http://www.mcusa-archives.org/MennObits/tm98/mar98.html (retrieved 16 February 2010).

88 Harder, 'Power and Authority,' 86.

89 Ibid.

90 Ibid., 157. Yoder's views find a new incarnation today in the writings of Duke University ethics professor Stanley Hauerwas; see, for example, *The Peaceable Kingdom*.

91 Yoder, *Politics of Jesus*, 213. This book became the best known of Yoder's works, receiving a wide reading even outside of Mennonite circles.

92 Ibid., 214.

93 Ibid., 241.

94 Ibid., 97. Yoder was not saying that Christians are to abandon responsibility for the world; rather, Christians are called to be non-violent, for example, even when acts of violence appear to provide short-term solutions to problems. Christians are to trust that their individual and collective efforts are part of the divine plan and therefore need not despair that effec-

tive solutions to global problems may take longer than their lifespans to
be made manifest. Of course, this position can be (and too frequently
is) distorted into a commitment to eschatology at the expense of the
present.

95 Toews, *Mennonites*, 335–6.

96 Harold S. Bender and Harry Huebner, 'Discipleship,' *GAMEO*, 1989,
http://www.gameo.org/encyclopedia/contents/D5788ME.html (retrieved
28 October 2003).

97 Neither Bender, Burkholder, nor Yoder offered a completely satisfactory
solution to the quandary of how to love your neighbour, though Burkholder proffered an ethic that is, in many ways, more compelling. If one
examines the Christian scripture as a whole, for example, one finds an emphasis on social justice on the part of Old Testament prophets like Amos,
which offers an important counterpoint to Bender and Yoder's emphasis
on the normativity of the non-violent ethic derived from the New Testament example of Christ.

98 Dueck, 72.

2. The Mennonite Workplace: Loewen Windows, Friesen Printers, and Palliser Furniture

1 It was the largest private employer until the privatization of Manitoba
Telecom Systems in 1997.

2 Armstrong, 'Canadian Business History,' 267–8.

3 Ibid., 279.

4 See, for example, Parr, *Gender of Breadwinners*; Frager, *Sweatshop Strife*;
and Sangster, *Earning Respect*.

5 Morton, 'Millennial Reflections,' 34.

6 McCalla, *Development of Canadian Capitalism*, 220. See also Zahavi,
Workers; Heron and Storey, 'Work and Struggle,' 237–8.

7 Heron and Storey, *On the Job*, 13.

8 Ibid., 14–15.

9 Ibid., 19–20.

10 Chandler, *Visible Hand*.

11 John, 'Elaborations,' 168.

12 Nationally, these figures were 832,000 in 1946 (or 27.9 per cent of non-
agricultural paid workers) and 2,173,000 in 1970 (33.6 per cent). Black
and Silver, *Hard Bargains*, 2, table 2.

13 Phillips, 'Spinning a Web,' 118. For discussion of the Winnipeg General Strike, see Masters, *Winnipeg General Strike*; Rea, *Winnipeg General Strike*; McNaught, *Winnipeg Strike*; Winnipeg Defense Committee, *Winnipeg 1919*; Bercuson, *Confrontation at Winnipeg*; and Mitchell, 'Legal Gentlemen.'

14 The Rand Formula was a decision made by Supreme Court Justice Ivan Rand in the aftermath of a strike at the Windsor, Ontario, Ford plant in 1945. Rand ruled that deduction of union dues from all workers should be automatic. While the Rand Formula prevented workers from benefitting from unions without supporting them, it also distanced union leaders from their rank and file. Wells, 'Impact,' 149–50.

15 Black and Silver, 10.

16 Phillips, 123.

17 Black and Silver, 5. Historian Craig Heron observes that 'Italy was allegedly the only country in the Western World to match Canada in terms of militancy.' Heron, *Canadian Labour Movement*, 94.

18 Black and Silver, 16; Black and Silver, 50.

19 Black and Silver, 51, table 1.

20 Coates and McGuinness, *Keystone Province*, 96–7.

21 McGuire and Swan, 'Structure of Manufacturing,' 166.

22 Ibid., 180; Coates and McGuinness, 101.

23 Loewen Windows, *A World of Opportunity: Loewen Careers*, brochure, n.d. (ca 1990s); Statistics Canada, Steinbach, MB, Census data, 2001.

24 R.K. Loewen, *Family*, 156–7.

25 Ibid., 151.

26 Wright, *Steinbach*, 1. The prevalence of car dealerships in the city is perhaps a reaction against the stance of the *Kleine Gemeinde* church against car ownership from 1910 (when the first car was purchased by a church member) to 1919 (when the church's *Aeltester* Peter Dueck died). The Aeltester (elder or bishop) was the head of the *Lehrdienst* (the ministerial leadership). Royden Loewen observes that, during this period, 'owners of cars were called upon to repent, requested to avoid communion services, warned against riding in the cars owned by members of other churches, berated for registering cars in the names of their unbaptized children, and cautioned that ownership of gasoline-powered tractors could serve to weaken the resolve of members not to purchase cars.' R.K. Loewen, *Family*, 11, 238, 250.

27 The first Russian Mennonite immigrants to Canada were the *Kanadier*

(Canadians), arriving in the 1870s. A second migration of Russian Mennonites to Canada occurred after the 1917 Revolution. These Mennonites were called *Russlaender* (Russians). A third wave of immigration from Russia took place after the Second World War. F. Epp, *Mennonites*, 242–6.

28 Loewen, *Loewen Windows: From Family Farm to International Marketer*, photocopy, n.d., courtesy of Loewen Advertising and Corporate Communications.

29 M.J. Loewen, *The Descendants*.

30 'Serving Each New Generation: C.T. Loewen & Sons Ltd., Steinbach, Our 50th Anniversary, 1955,' advertisement, *Steinbach Carillon News* (29 April 1955): 44–5.

31 R.K. Loewen, *Family*, 152, 160. The *Kleine Gemeinde* were renamed the Evangelical Mennonite Conference in 1960.

32 *Bruderschaft* ('brotherhood') meetings were congregational meetings held to discuss church business. Until the early or mid-twentieth century (depending on the particular Mennonite congregation), only male church members were allowed to vote at these meetings.

33 Mills, 'Gender, Ethnicity, and Religion,' 136.

34 R.K. Loewen, *Family*, 246, 250–2. See also R.K. Loewen, 'Cars, Commerce, Church.' Steinbach's first car dealership was opened in 1912 by J.R. Friesen, who sold his first car to Loewen. Unlike Loewen, Friesen was asked to withdraw his church membership or he would be excommunicated and banned. Presentation made to tour group by the director of human resources, Loewen, Steinbach, MB, 12 May 2000.

35 Mills, 137.

36 Loewen Windows, *Seventy-Five Years of Traditional Craftsmanship:Enterprise with Integrity and Friendship*, brochure, spring 1980; 'Serving Each New Generation: C.T. Loewen & Sons Ltd., Steinbach, Our 50th Anniversary, 1955,' advertisement, *Steinbach Carillon News* (20 April 1955): 44–5.

37 'Serving Each New Generation,' advertisement; 'Catalogue and Price List of Beekeepers' Supplies, Manufactured by C.T. Loewen, Steinbach, Manitoba , 1936,' courtesy of Loewen Advertising and Corporate Communications; MHC, CTL, *C.T. Loewen & Sons 75th Anniversary* (1980): 11, 15; Loewen, *From Family Farm*; 'Serving Each New Generation,' 44–5; Church pews pamphlet, 1 November 1957, courtesy of Loewen Advertising and Corporate Communications.

38 MHC, CTL, *C.T. Loewen & Sons 75th Anniversary* (1980): 15.

39 Ibid.

40 Abram J. Thiessen was a conscientious objector assigned to a logging camp. He observed, 'Before the war this work had been done by experienced loggers or fellers but most of them had either joined the armed forces or found other better paying employment. All the work had been on a piecework basis ... We COs earned 50 cents per day plus food and lodging. The pieceworkers by dint of hard work and long days had earned as much as twelve to fifteen dollars per day. We heard of some that had up to twenty [dollars] in one day. Now we laugh at that sum but in the late thirties and early forties it was a very high income.' MHC, 'Alternative Service in the Second World War: Work: Logging,' 2004, http://www.alternativeservice.ca/service/camps/work/logging3.htm (retrieved 21 November 2004). For more information on these camps, see Nickel, 'Canadian Conscientious Objector'; Melvin Gingerich, 'Alternative Service Work Camps (Canada),' *GAMEO*, March 2009, http://www.gameo.org/encyclopedia/contents/A4541ME.html (retrieved 8 March 2010); and MHC, 'Alternative Service in the Second World War: Conscientious Objectors in Canada, 1939–1945,' 2004, http://www.alternativeservice.ca (retrieved 8 March 2010).

41 His daughter, Elvira, was seemingly never involved in the business, even as a shareholder.

42 Strong-Boag, 'Home Dreams,' 381.

43 Ibid., 386, quoting Canada Mortgage and Housing, *Housing in Canada, 1945–1986: An Overview and Lessons Learned* (Ottawa, 1987), 6.

44 Strong-Boag, 388.

45 Bain, 'Strong Corporate Roots.'

46 Andersen was the world's largest window manufacturer in 2000, and was the first to produce prefabricated windows. Prior to their intitiative, windows were prepared on-site by carpenters from individual components. Presentation made to tour group by the director of human resources, Loewen, Steinbach, MB, 12 May 2000.

47 Loewen Windows, 'C.T. Loewen & Sons: 60 Years of Progress, 1905–1965,' brochure, 1965.

48 MHC, *C.T. Loewen & Sons 75th Anniversary*, 13.

49 Ibid.

50 Bain, 'Strong Corporate Roots,' 21.

51 Loewen Millwork, *Seventy-Five Years*.

52 'Loewen-Bilt Wood Window Units,' catalogue, 15 March 1958, courtesy of Loewen Advertising and Corporate Communications.
53 Dave Loewen, interview.
54 A publication of Friesens Corporation, incidentally.
55 Dave Loewen, interview.
56 Loewen, *From Family Farm*.
57 'The Loewen Millwork Plant Is Western Canada's Largest,' *Steinbach Carillon News* (30 June 1961): 1.
58 Ibid.
59 'A Tour of the Loewen Plant,' *Steinbach Carillon News* (30 June 1961): 1.
60 Ownership of the lumberyard devolved to George's sons, Gary, Roger, and Curt. This portion of the business retained the name of C.T. Loewen & Sons until 1993, when it was renamed C.T. Loewen Do-It Centres. C.T.'s son Edward left the family business completely due to heart problems, selling his interest to his brothers. CCA, MCO, Loewen, File #1556037, Certificate of Registration, 29 April 1985; MCO, Loewen Mill-work, File #1144278, Certificate of Registration; MCO, C.P. Loewen Enterprises, File #2527405, Annual Returns of Information and Particulars; MCO, C.T. Loewen & Sons, File #1141121, Certificate of Registration.
61 Loewen, *From Family Farm*; Loewen, 'Loewen Windows Launches 20 Million-Dollar Expansion,' press release, 2 May 2000; Loewen, 'Directory,' http://www.loewen.com/directory.html (retrieved 16 August 1999; website has changed, page removed); Loewen, *A World of Opportunity*.
62 Loewen has not maintained records on the gender composition of staff. This comment is based on interviews with long-time and retired employees.
63 Loewen Millwork, *Seventy-Five Years*.
64 Mills, 170–1.
65 Presentation made by the director of human resources, Loewen, Steinbach, MB, 12 May 2000.
66 Winson and Leach, *Contingent Work*, 38–9.
67 Single-industry towns (also known as company towns) are towns created to service the needs of one particular business. Dominant industry towns are towns that existed prior to the creation of the industry that now employs the majority of its inhabitants and/or dominates the political and social life of the community.
68 Lucas, *Minetown*, 171.
69 Ibid., 177.

70 At a meeting of the board of directors in 1989, Charles Loewen suggested
   that Loewen was 'at a crossroads in its competitive place. It has been a
   western Canadian producer. Its future may be that of a north-central North
   American premium producer.' A decision was made to 'explore this strategy.' Loewen, Board of Directors meeting minutes, 26 May 1989. The
   possibility of entering the PVC window market was discussed on three
   occasions in the 1990s. The directors decided in 1990 that they had 'cur-
   rently little interest in using our present distribution channels to market
   a PVC window line.' The Loewen family agreed at the end of that year
   that 'PVC is still an issue but with no specific acquisition opportunities
   being seriously pursued at this time.' While Paul Loewen presented an
   opportunity to invest in a PVC window company to the family in 1994, no
   action was taken. Loewen, Board of Directors meeting minutes, 12 January 1990; Loewen, Shareholders meeting minutes, 21 December 1993, 28
   February 1994. Loewen's chief financial officer, Gary Timlick, explained
   why management did not act on Paul Loewen's suggestion. 'Vinyl is easy
   to make and the equipment to make it is extremely cheap, so it's got low
   barriers of entry. So it's highly competitive, with new players entering
   the marketplace on a regular basis, along with some pre-existing large,
   large U.S. companies that have high economies of scale.' The decision by
   Loewen's management to specialize in wood windows, 'targeting a specific niche within a segment of the marketplace allows us to be successful and to compete against the larger players. And that market segment,
   there's greater barriers of entry because it's more costly for the development of the type of window that we make. And the equipment to make it
   is very expensive ... Vinyl. It was just too easy for the price. The gross
   margin or the price per unit declined as more and more players got into
   the industry. They got cheaper to make. Either had to go big or go home
   on the vinyl.' Gary Timlick, interview.
71 Loewen Windows, 'Loewen Windows Launches 20 Million-Dollar
   Expansion,' press release, 2 May 2000.
72 A more detailed social history of Friesens Corporation is Thiessen,
   'Friesens Corporation.'
73 Epp-Tiessen, *Altona*, 19, 50–5; 'Altona,' MSS 24, no. 181, Winnipeg
   Tribune Collection, UMA; Funk, 'A Brief History of Altona.' Esther Epp-
   Tiessen is a daughter of Frank H. Epp who, as editor of the *Canadian
   Mennonite*, was a Friesens Corporation employee.
74 Such businesses included Co-op Vegetable Oils (later Canamera Foods),

Loewen Manufacturing (which produced farm machinery parts – unrelat-
ed to Loewen of Steinbach), Altona Feed Service, the Altona Cooperative,
Altona Pool Elevators and the Rhineland Farmers Co-op Machine Shop.
Epp-Tiessen, 206–12, 215–16, 244–5, 297, 304, 359–60.

75 Ibid., 65.

76 'But now I am coming to you, and I speak these things in the world so
that they may have my joy made complete in themselves. I have given
them your word, and the world has hated them because they do not belong
to the world, just as I do not belong to the world. I am not asking you to
take them out of the world, but I ask you to protect them from the evil
one. They do not belong to the world, just as I do not belong to the world'
(John 17:13–16, NRSV). 'Do not be conformed to this world but be transformed by the renewing of your minds, so that you may discern what is
the will of God – what is good and acceptable and perfect' (Romans 12:2,
NRSV).

77 MHC, Vertical File, Industry, 'Legend: How It All Began,' unpublished
manuscript, 1982, 1. This reference gives the town name as Litchfield,
which I have assumed is an Anglicism of Lichtfeld, a village southwest of
Altona. Schroeder and Huebert, *Mennonite Historical Atlas*, 62.

78 Epp-Tiessen, 64; F. Epp, 'D.W. Friesen.' Jacob Schwartz had established
this confectionery store in 1897. MHC, D.W.Friesen, 'Legend,' 1, 2;
'Brief History,' UMA

79 The Bergthaler Mennonite Church traced its origins to the Bergthal
colony in South Russia. Schroeder, *The Bergthal Colony*, 9–11, 17–19.
Bishops, elected ministers, and deacons formed a central *Lehrdienst* (ministerial group). Bishops were ordained for life and had congregations in a
certain geographic area under their care. Each congregation elected their
own ministers to preach, baptize, and serve communion. Congregations
also chose individuals to serve as deacons whose function was to assist
ministers with baptism and communion services, visit church members
in need, arbitrate conflicts among members, and aid in church discipline.
A move to congregational autonomy and the use of the English language
in the 1950s and 1960s led ultimately to the dissolution of the Bergthaler
Mennonite Church in 1971. Epp-Tiessen, 136–7, 274–5, 337–8, 341–2.
See also Gerbrandt, *Adventure in Faith*, and *Postscript to Adventure in
Faith*.

80 T.E. Friesen, interview.

81 Epp-Tiessen, 154.

82 A similar situation arose at Brigden's, a printing and engraving firm founded in Toronto in the 1870s. In 1894, founder Frederick Brigden 'tried to persuade his younger son to give up his hopes of becoming an artist and to settle, instead, for being an "art-workman" as he had done.' Davis, 'Business, Art and Labour,' 66–7.

83 The Chandler & Price Gordon, developed by George A. Gordon in the 1850s, was the most successful model of the platen press. Tremaine, *Canadian Book of Printing*, 93; Epp-Tiessen, 155.

84 D.G. Friesen, interview.

85 MHC, 'Legend,' 2, 4; T.E. Friesen, *History of D.W. Friesen*, 18, 21; Epp-Tiessen, 154–5; 'D.W. Friesen & Sons Ltd.,' promotional booklet, n.d., MSS 24, no. 3170, Winnipeg Tribune Collection, UMA; Friesens Corporation, *1990 Staff Book*, 6–7; Toews and Klippenstein, 211; Friesens Corporation, *D.W. Friesen and Sons Ltd. Seventy-Fifth Anniversary*.

86 The Linotype was invented in the 1880s by Ottmar Mergenthaler. Giebel, 'Alienation from Freedom,' 75; Dewalt, *Technology*, 125; Tremaine, 80.

87 Kealey, 'Work Control,' 74–101.

88 Peter Wolfe, interview.

89 A 'widow' occurs when a single line of type at the end of a paragraph is carried over to the next page. Peter Wolfe, interview.

90 Epp-Tiessen, 226; Toews and Klippenstein, *Manitoba Mennonite Memories*, 212.

91 John was never involved in the business. He became director of extension at the University of British Columbia.

92 Elizabeth Bergen, interview.

93 Peter Wolfe, interview.

94 Letters Patent, 23 December 1950, courtesy of David Glenn Friesen.

95 A logo was created in 1976 that highlighted the company's foray into offset printing: a stylized letter 'F' formed by a strip of paper around a press cylinder. The logo was changed in 1995 to reflect the company's specialization in book production: the word 'Friesens' in blue with a yellow book forming the dot on the letter 'i.' Friesens Corporation, Board of Directors meeting minutes, 25 May 1994, 23 November 1994; Glenn Fretz, Toronto, to David Glenn Friesen, Altona, 24 May 1994, courtesy of David Glenn Friesen; Friesens Corporation, employee newsletter, 30 December 1976, December 1994; Friesens Corporation, Shareholders meeting minutes, 8 April 1995.

96 Friesens Corporation, *1990 Staff Book*, 7.

97 David Glenn Friesen, president, Friesens Corporation, personal communication, Altona, MB, 2 April 1997.

98 Friesens Corporation, *1990 Staff Book*, 7.

99 The other two Canadian yearbook publishers were Inter-Collegiate Press of Canada and National School Services Ltd., both of Winnipeg. 'Manitoba Firms Win First Round over "Dumping,"' unnamed newspaper article, 28 May 1976, MSS 24, no. 3170, UMA. Friesens Corporation consists of five divisions: Book, Yearbook, Fastprint and Packaging, Web, and Retail. The retail division includes stationery and business machine sales, as well as a photo studio and bookstore in the Altona Mall. Friesens Corporation, http://www.friesens.com/ (retrieved 5 February 2004).

100 David Glenn Friesen, personal communication, 2 April 1997.

101 T.E. Friesen, *History*, 29–32; Altona and District Heritage Centre Archive, Friesens Corporation collection, box 5, file 3, speech by Ted Friesen to Mennonite Economic Development Associates, Newton, KS, 15 October 1987. The method of offset printing combines photography and a chemical printing process. A thin metal plate of zinc or aluminum is etched so that water will adhere to it, then made photosensitive by coating with a bichromate emulsion. A photographic negative is placed in contact with the plate and an arc lamp transfers the design. Ink adheres to the design on the plate as a positive image, and is printed onto a rubber cylinder from which it is offset onto the paper. Kelber and Schlesinger, *Union Printers*, 2; Dewalt, 98–9, 119.

102 D.G. Friesen, interview.

103 Ibid.

104 T.E. Friesen, *History*, 33; *Friesens Informer*, employee newsletter (February 1971); Friesens Corporation, Board of Directors meeting minutes, 19 November 1970.

105 Memo to staff from D.K. Friesen, October 1976; Friesens Corporation, 'A Corporate Profile,' brochure, n.d.; Friesens Corporation, employee newsletter (30 December 1976).

106 Friesens Corporation, employee newsletter (13 November 1973); Report to Board of Directors by Manufacturing Division, 19 August 1986; T.E. Friesen, personal communication.

107 Friesens Corporation, *Publishing Your Own Book* (1982), 21.

108 Friesens Corporation, 'A Corporate Profile'; Friesens Corporation, 'Ordering Colour Separations,' brochure, n.d., 4; Friesens Corporation, 'Pre-

paring Electronic Files,' brochure, January 1994; Friesen Printers, Goals
and Objectives, 1983.

109 Friesens Corporation, 'Preparing Electronic Files.'

110 Friesens Corporation, 'Ordering Colour Separations,' 8.

111 Friesen Printers, Goals and Objectives, January 1982; Bain, 'Printing
Professionals.'

112 Friesen Printers, Goals and Objectives, 1987; Friesens Corporation,
'Educational Books,' brochure, n.d.; Reimer, 'Friesen CEO'; Gordon
Sinclair, Jr., 'Printer's Story.'

113 Friesens Corporation, employee newsletter (14 August 1974); T.E. Friesen, *History*, 45, 49; Board of Directors meeting minutes, 30 March
1989. Tim Friesen and John Victor Friesen had left the board of directors
by 1989.

114 David Glenn Friesen, personal communication, 2 April 1997.

115 Kirbyson, 'Pride.'

116 See the July/August issues of *Manitoba Business.*

117 J. Friesen, 'Manitoba Mennonites,' 153.

118 Enns, *Mia*, 17.

119 Palliser Furniture, employee newsletter 11, no. 13 (Fall 1992): 9.

120 In 1992, the DeFehr family was engaged in efforts to buy back the mill.
J. Phillips, 'Never on Sunday.' The description of this effort in the corporate newsletter was somewhat melodramatic: 'A vital step ... has been
winning the confidence of the mill workers' who 'have been convinced
that capitalism is worse [than communism], and were not sure what to
expect from the DeFehrs ... During a meeting with the workers, one
old fellow spoke out with a vote of confidence. "I worked for that Mr.
DeFehr many years ago ... he was good to us" ... If the passing of time
should bring the mill back to its original owners, may the workers echo
the words of the old fellow and once again be able to say, "I work for Mr.
DeFehr ... and he is good to us!"' Palliser Furniture, employee newsletter 11, no. 13 (Fall 1992): 9.

121 Abram's brother, C.A. DeFehr, founder of the Winnipeg retailer DeFehr
Furniture and Appliances, immigrated to Winnipeg in 1925, after a year's
delay because his eyes were inflamed. Canada would not admit anyone
suspected of having trachoma. C.A. DeFehr, *Memories of My Life*,
64–5.

122 Enns, *Mia*, 161.

123 A.A. DeFehr, interview.

124 Enns, *Mia*, 125.
125 A.A. DeFehr, interview.
126 Ibid.
127 Palliser Furniture, Logic Division Communications, *A.A. DeFehr: A Legacy of Faith in Practice*, video, n.d.; Art DeFehr, president, Palliser Furniture, personal communication, Winnipeg, MB, 7 July 1997; A.A. DeFehr, interview. Abram DeFehr had given his son two lots in the Winnipeg suburb of North Kildonan, an area heavily populated by immigrant Mennonites, since they 'wanted to live near their parents, their friends and very importantly, a Mennonite church and people of their own faith.' Enns, *Mia*, 130.
128 A.A. DeFehr, interview.
129 Palliser Furniture, employee newsletter 2, no. 3 (September 1983).
130 The DeFehr family's origins are in the Mennonite Brethren community; the Friesens and Loewens are of General Conference (now Mennonite Church Canada) background.
131 This barn, located at the corner of Edison Avenue and McKay Street, was rented for twelve dollars per month. In 1974, a replica of the barn was erected as a sort of museum among the main factories of Palliser Furniture on Gateway Road in Winnipeg. Palliser Furniture, employee newsletter, 'Reflection & Celebration: Palliser Furniture 50th Anniversary Issue,' 14, no. 21 (Fall 1994): 2.
132 Enns, *Mia*, 133.
133 'The Dilly Manufacturing Co., Winnipeg, Owned by A.A. DeFehr,' advertisement, Hudson's Bay Company catalogue, 30 January 1948, courtesy of Palliser Furniture Logic Division.
134 Palliser Furniture employee newsletter, 'Reflection & Celebration: Palliser Furniture 50th Anniversary Issue,' 14, no. 21 (Fall 1994): 2.
135 DeFehr Furniture catalogues, June 1955, 1960, 1963, courtesy of Palliser Furniture Logic Division.
136 DeFehr Furniture catalogues, 1968, 1970, 1973, 1975, Spring/Summer 1979, ca 1990, courtesy of Palliser Furniture Logic Division.
137 MCO, A.A. DeFehr Furniture Manufacturing Ltd., File #4786662, Application for Incorporation , 9 November 1955, Articles of Continuance, 11 December 1979.
138 Palliser Furniture, employee newsletter 2, no. 3 (September 1983).
139 'A.A. DeFehr Furniture Manufacturing Ltd. Review of Operation,' report prepared by Dufresne, McLagan, Daignault Inc. for the Manitoba De-

partment of Industry and Commerce as part of a productivity audit program carried out in cooperation with the furniture industry, of Manitoba, 1971, 3, courtesy of Palliser Furniture Head Office.

140 Ibid.

141 Ibid., 5.

142 Ibid., 4.

143 Ibid., 10.

144 Ibid., 6.

145 'A Master Plan of Mass Production: DeFehr Furniture,' *Manitoba Business Journal* (April–May 1968): 20.

146 Letter from Art DeFehr to Lorne Kendall, Department of Regional Economic Expansion (DREE), 23 December 1975, courtesy of Palliser Furniture Head Office.

147 'DeFehr Furniture: Exploiting Special Situations Pays Off,' *Winnipeg Tribune* (17 June 1969), courtesy of Palliser Furniture Head Office.

148 East Kildonan is a suburb of Winnipeg with a sizeable Mennonite population.

149 Love, 'Major Furniture Firm Born'; Palliser Furniture, employee newsletter, 'Reflection and Celebration: Palliser Furniture 50th Anniversary Issue,' 14, no. 21 (Fall 1994).

150 Palliser Furniture, employee newsletter 1, no. 1 (December 1981).

151 'DeFehr Furniture – Expansion for 1971–73,' n.d., courtesy of Palliser Furniture Head Office.

152 This plant is in operation twenty-four hours a day, seven days a week. George Klassen, Palliser Furniture central recruitment office, employee orientation session, Winnipeg, MB, 19 August 1997.

153 Palliser Furniture, employee newsletter 8, no. 2 (July 1989).

154 James, 'Palliser Purchases Former LADD Plant'; Palliser Furniture, employee newsletter 16, no. 28 (Winter 1996); Palliser Furniture, employee newsletter, 'Reflection and Celebration: Palliser Furniture 50th Anniversary Issue,' 14, no. 21 (Fall 1994).

155 MCO, A.A. DeFehr Furniture Manufacturing Ltd., File #4786662, Articles of Amalgamation, 11 December 1979.

156 Douloff, 'Family Affair.' The name was taken from the nineteenth-century explorer of western Canada, John Palliser.

157 Many Canadian Mennonites sponsored Indo-Chinese refugees through their churches from 1979 through the early 1980s. A history conference on this subject, 'Mennonites Meet the Refugee: A 25 Year Retrospective,'

organized by the Chair in Mennonite Studies at the University of Winnipeg and Mennonite Central Committee Canada, was held in 2005.

158 S. Long, 'DeFehr Buys'; Memo from Roger Friesen, 15 February 1995, courtesy of Palliser Furniture Corporate Human Resources.

159 Memo from David DeFehr, 22 February 1996, courtesy of Palliser Furniture Corporate Human Resources.

160 Cash, 'Palliser Jobs Ebb'; McNeill, 'DeFehr Empire,' http://www.cme-mec.ca/mb/media.asp?id=157 (retrieved 27 November 2004; website has changed, page removed).

161 Art DeFehr, 'World without Pity,' speech delivered at the Mennonite Economic Development Associates (MEDA) convention, Dallas TX, 12–15 November 1998. DeFehr has been a frequent contributor to MEDA's magazine, *The Marketplace*, and for years spent half his time on humanitarian and charitable work. His activities resulted in his appointment as an officer of the Order of Canada in 2004. Office of the Secretary to the Governor General, 'Governor General announces new appointments to the Order of Canada,' 27 January 2004, http://www.news.gc.ca/cfmx/CCP/view/en/index.cfm?articleid=75919& (retrieved 2 August 2004; page removed).

162 A. DeFehr, 'World without Pity.'

163 Ibid.

164 Ibid.

165 *Maquiladoras* or *maquilas* are foreign-owned factories along the U.S.-Mexico border where products are assembled for duty-free export. Labour conditions in these factories are the subject of much criticism; see, for example, the Maquila Solidarity Network website, http://en.maquilasolidarity.org/ (retrieved 30 August 2006).

166 A. DeFehr, 'World without Pity.'

167 Ibid.

168 The Palliser factory is in Saltillo, in the province of Coahuila. Coahuila is bordered to the west by the province of Chihuahua, where most of the Mexican Mennonite colonies are located.

169 Crisis conversion is the individual decision to have a personal, salvific relationship with Christ – to be 'born again.' Often those who undergo such conversion are able to recite the exact date of their decision. More conservative Mennonites emphasize faith as a lifelong journey conducted within the ecclesial community. Salvation is a hoped-for end; to express

certainty about salvation is considered spiritual pride. Evangelism is through personal conduct rather than words.

In addition to his interest in the situation of Mexican Mennonites, DeFehr declared that Palliser's commitment to Mexico was evidenced by his personal effort to inform himself about the Zapatistas and by the DeFehr Foundation's funding of projects in the Mennonite colonies.

170 As a student at a Mennonite college in the United States, DeFehr participated in civil rights marches and Vietnam War protests.

171 A. DeFehr, 'World without Pity.'

172 Palliser was the largest private company in Winnipeg until 1997.

173 Friesens Corporation, *1990 Staff Book*, 6; 'A.A. DeFehr Furniture Manufacturing Ltd. Review of Operation,' 3; *Loewen Behold*, employee newsletter 2, no. 1 (March 1976): 1; *Loewen Behold*, employee newsletter 6, no. 4 (December 1980): 3.

174 Davis, 'Business, Art and Labour,' 194–5.

175 John Loewen, interview.

176 T.E. Friesen, interview.

177 T.E. Friesen, former director, Friesens Corporation, personal communication, Altona, MB, 20 January 1996.

178 When I was doing research at Palliser Furniture in 1996, shortly after Art DeFehr gained majority control of the company, this acquisition and the company's financial history were the only topics about which I was asked not to enquire.

179 John Loewen, interview.

180 Loewen, Shareholders meeting minutes, 30 September 1988.

181 Loewen, Board of Directors meeting minutes, 26 May 1989. 'The top level of the organizational structure was addressed ... Paul is not satisfied with the status quo in the organization. [Brother] Clyde [Loewen] will proceed with the review.' Loewen, Shareholders meeting minutes, 11 October 1994.

182 Stuart Loewen and John Loewen remained as shareholders, however.

183 T.E. Friesen, interview.

184 David Glenn Friesen, personal communication, 2 April 1997.

185 MCO, Friesens Corporation, File #8253, Annual Returns of Information and Particulars.

186 MCO, A.A. DeFehr Furniture Manufacturing Ltd., File #4786662, Annual Returns of Information and Particulars; MCO, Palliser Furniture, File #0504262, Annual Returns of Information and Particulars.

187 MCO, C.P. Loewen Enterprises, File #2527405, Annual Returns of Information and Particulars.

188 Other Manitoba companies who publicize their humble origins include
Guertin Brothers, a paint manufacturer, which originated in a two-car
garage in 1947. Similarly, Prolific Group, an offset printing company,
began in the basement of Al Alexandruk in 1975. An example of a
Manitoba business that has expanded beyond the local market is Arnold
Brothers Transport, which began in Winnipeg in 1958 and now serves
all of North America. Transport truckers Reimer Express trace their
origins to a Mennonite in Steinbach who operated both a general
store and animal-feed business in 1952. Reimer Express now operates
worldwide. While many Mennonites assert the significance of personal
religious commitments for the operation of their businesses, they are
not alone in doing so. Reimer Express employed a full-time chaplain
to minister to their employees in the 1990s. The Russian Mennonite
founder of Kitchen Craft, a cabinet manufacturing firm founded in
1971, asserts that his business philosophy is to 'glorify God ... by applying Biblical principles in everything' he does. The non-Mennonite
Dutch management of Premier Printing, offset printers founded in 1962,
notes that they acknowledge 'the Creator who provides for us so generously.' Buller and Buller, 'Leadership'; Cash et al., *Winnipeg*, 166–73,
176.

3. Mennonite Corporate Mythology: The 'Reflections' Campaign

1 See Barthes, 'Myth Today,' 93–149.

2 Lipartito, 'Culture,' 36.

3 Ibid., 5, 11.

4 John, 169–70, 188–9. See Cochran, *Challenges*; Sklar, *Corporate Reconstruction*; Livingston, 'Social Analysis,' 69–95; and Zunz, *Making
America Corporate*.

5 John, 199–200.

6 Nafziger, 'Mennonite Ethic,' 262–3.

7 Ibid., 266–8.

8 Sangster, *Earning Respect*; Sangster, 'Softball Solution.'

9 Sangster, 'Softball Solution,' 169.

10 Gramsci defines hegemony as the spontaneous consent given by subordinate groups to the means by which they are subordinated. Gramsci,
Prison Notebooks, 200–1.

11 Sangster, *Earning Respect*, 163–4.
12 Ibid., 148.
13 Sangster, 'Softball Solution,' 172.
14 Ibid., 197. See also Sangster, *Earning Respect*, 163.
15 Sangster, 'Softball Solution,' 198.
16 Ibid.
17 Joyce, *Work, Society, and Politics*, xvii, 93.
18 Joyce, *Work, Society, and Politics*; Sangster, *Earning Respect* and 'Softball Solution'; Barthes, 'Myth Today' and *Mythologies*.
19 Marks, *Revivals*; Hall, *Lived Religion in America*.
20 T.E. Friesen, 'Philosophy, Policy and Practices,' 2; MHC, Vertical File, 'D.W. Friesen Employee Handbook' (1981): 3.
21 T.E. Friesen, 'Philosophy,' 2.
22 MHC, Vertical File, Industry, 'D.W. Friesen Employee Handbook' (1981): 3.
23 Friesens Corporation, Shareholders meeting minutes, 25 April 1955.
24 Friesens Corporation, Memo to staff from D.K. Friesen, August 1957.
25 Friesens Corporation, Memo to staff from D.K. Friesen, August 1957.
26 Friesens Corporation, Performance appraisal form, staff newsletters, ca 1960s.
27 The tendency to capitalize the 'Company' or the 'Firm' surely also sent a message to employees about priorities.
28 T.E. Friesen, 'Philosophy,' 3.
29 MHC, Vertical File, Industry, 'D.W. Friesen Employee Handbook' (1981): 3.
30 D.G. Friesen, interview.
31 Palliser, 'Company Info,' http://www.palliser.com/CompanyInfo.php (retrieved 1 January 2008; website has changed, page removed).
32 Ibid.
33 Palliser, 'Message from the President and CEO,' http://www.palliser.com/Message.php (retrieved 1 January 2008; website has changed, page removed).
34 Art DeFehr, personal communication, 2 September 1997.
35 Enns, *Mia*, 148–9.
36 David (Dave) DeFehr, interview.
37 Regehr, *Mennonites*, 158; McArthur, 'Our Father.' Attendance at the turn of the millennium was voluntary and employee time was paid.
38 Charles Loewen, interview.
39 See Sangster, 'Softball Solution' and *Earning Respect*; Parr, *Gender*;

Tone, *Business of Benevolence*; Mandell, *Corporation as Family*; Zahavi, *Workers*.

40 T.E. Friesen, *History*, 74; Memos to staff from D.K. Friesen, 17 June 1970, 3 December 1970; Palliser Furniture, *Palliser Furniture: Company Profile*, n.d. [1980s], 8; Palliser Furniture, employee newsletter 1, no. 1 (December 1981); 2, no. 5 (December 1983); 11, no. 12 (Summer 1992): 12; 17, no. 3 (Summer 1997).

41 Palliser Furniture president Art DeFehr, for example, has served as United Nations high commissioner for refugees in Somalia, was Mennonite Central Committee program director in Bangladesh, founded the Lithuanian Christian College in Klaipeda, Lithuania, and was a founding member of the Canadian Foodgrains Bank, among other involvements.

42 The advertising campaign was replaced in 2004. A press release from the company explained, 'The new "Design. Create. Inspire." [campaign] carries a compelling message and while it is perhaps not as arresting as "Reflections," it is visually appealing and makes the product – not the ad concept – the hero of the piece. Unlike "Reflections," it does not tie us as strongly to tradition and the unintended suggestion that Loewen is best suited to a particular style of architecture.' Loewen, 'Loewen Launches New Ad Campaign,' August 2004, http://www.loewen.com/home.nsf/about/pressroom/archive/PLEE-633PFT (retrieved 30 August 2006).

43 Loewen, 'Pressroom: Advertising,' http://www.loewen.com/site.nsf/about/pressroom_advertising (retrieved 29 January 2004; website has changed, page removed).

44 Matthew 5:13–16, NRSV.

45 Clyde Loewen, interview.

46 The quotations are from the 'Soul' brochure, December 2002.

47 At the same time, the equation of industrial production with the Creation points subtly to the environmental stewardship of the company.

48 'Soul' brochure, December 2002.

49 Ibid.

50 Mitch Toews, interview.

51 Ibid.

52 Prior to these two campaigns, product advertising in local newspapers tended to consist of a simple photo or sketch of the product, together with a listing of its dimensions, composition, and price.

53 *Porte* is French for door; *Fenster* is the German word for window, from which the English word 'defenestrate' is derived. Windows and doors are the company's sole products.

54 Two employees costumed as Fenster guided dignitaries on plant tours as part of the seventy-fifth anniversary celebrations in 1980.
55 Clyde Loewen, interview.
56 Loewen, 'Loewen captures brand essence with new Reflections campaign,' 8 January 2003, http://www.loewen.com/site.nsf/about/pressroom_news_archive/DLEN-5L6U4V (retrieved 29 January 2004; website has changed, page removed).
57 Mitch Toews, interview.
58 Clyde Loewen, interview.
59 Mitch Toews, interview.
60 Ibid.
61 Barthes, 'Myth Today,' 133.
62 Marchand, *Creating the Corporate Soul.*
63 McMurtry, *Marx's World-View*, 152–3.
64 Charles Loewen, interview.
65 Clyde Loewen, interview.
66 John Loewen, interview.
67 Ibid.
68 Charles Loewen, interview.
69 Ibid.
70 Ken Friesen, interview. The quotation is from Matthew 6:3, NRSV: 'But when you give alms, do not let your left hand know what your right hand is doing.'
71 Ibid.
72 Ibid.
73 Charles Loewen, interview.
74 John Loewen, interview.
75 Charles Loewen, interview.
76 Ibid.
77 Barthes, 'Myth Today,' 117.
78 Miller, *Bon Marché*, 15.
79 Tilly, 'Citizenship.'

4. 'You Had to Know Everything; Otherwise, You Weren't Fit': Worker Experience and Identity

1 Friesens Corporation, 'Friesens Graphic Arts Book Manufacturing Course,' http://www.friesens.com/Corporate/GraphicArts.asp (retrieved 29 March 2010).

2 J.J. Friesen, *Building Communities*, map 7, 'Location of Mennonite Churches on Reserves,' 127.

3 Manitoba Community Profiles, 'Pembina Valley Census Division Profile: Welcome,' http://www.communityprofiles.mb.ca/cgi-bin/cd/index .cgi?id=4603 (retrieved 29 March 2010; website has changed, page removed). The Pembina Valley census division includes the municipalities of Dufferin, Thompson, Roland, Morris, Montcalm, Rhineland (where Altona is located), and Stanley. More than half of residents gave their ethnic origin as German in the 1990s; another 18–25 per cent were Dutch; just over 7 per cent were French and from 1–7 per cent were Russian. Manitoba Community Profiles, 'Pembina Valley,' http://www .communityprofiles.mb.ca/maps/census/cd3.html (retrieved 29 March 2010; website has changed, page removed).

4 Loewen, 'Loewen Celebrates 100 Years of Community Involvement,' Loewen Press Room, 6 June 2005, http://www.loewen.com/home .nsf/about/pressroom/archive/PLEE-6D4L44 (retrieved 29 March 2010).

5 J.J. Friesen, *Building Communities*, map 7, 127.

6 Loewen, 'Loewen Featured in CBC Documentary,' Loewen Press Room, 17 November 2004, http://www.loewen.com/home.nsf/about/pressroom/ archive/PLEE-66TN6N (retrieved 29 March 2010); Centre for Canadian Language Benchmarks, 'Section 4.9: Loewen Windows Pilot Project: New Employees English Language Training Program,' *Work Ready, Section IV: Case Studies*, http://www.language.ca/display_page.asp?page_ id=850 (retrieved 29 March 2010). The Steinbach area census division includes the rural municipalities of Ritchot, Taché, Ste Anne, De Salaberry, Hanover, La Broquerie, and Franklin. The ethnic origins of those living in the region in the 1990s included German (39–41%), Dutch (12–15%), and French (24–9%). Manitoba Community Profiles, 'Steinbach Area,' http://www.communityprofiles.mb.ca/maps/census/cd2.html (retrieved 29 March 2010; website has changed, page removed); Manitoba Community Profiles, 'Steinbach Area Census Division Profile: Demographic Characteristics,' http://www.communityprofiles.mb.ca/cgi-bin/cd/demographics. cgi?id=4602 (retrieved 29 March 2010; website has changed, page removed).

7 Manitoba Community Profiles, 'Winnipeg Census Division Profile: Demographics Characteristics,' http://www.communityprofiles.mb.ca/cgi-bin/cd/demographics.cgi?id=4611 (retrieved 29 March 2010; website has changed, page removed).

8 Friesen, *Building Communities*, map 8, 'Location of Mennonite Churches in Winnipeg, ca 2005,' 128.

9 Art DeFehr, 'Message from the President and CEO,' Palliser Furniture, http://www.palliser.com/Message.php (retrieved 29 March 2010; website has changed, page removed); Canadian Manufacturers & Exporters (Ontario Division), 'Take a Look at What's Working,' http://www.cme-mec .ca/shared/upload/on/reference_piece.pdf, 8 (retrieved 29 March 2010; website has changed, page removed).

10 Jakob Pries, interview.

11 Peter Reimer, interview.

12 Ibid.

13 Jakob Pries, interview.

14 Peter Reimer, interview.

15 See Portelli's *Death of Luigi Trastulli*.

16 Frisch, 'Oral History,' 36.

17 Portelli, 'Uchronic Dreams: Working-Class Memory and Possible Worlds,' in *The Death of Luigi Trastulli*, 113.

18 Joyce, 98.

19 D.G. Friesen, interview.

20 John Geddert, interview.

21 Ian McKay, quoted in Moore and Morrison, *Work, Ethnicity, and Oral History*, 91.

22 Ernie Dyck, interview.

23 Ibid.

24 Ibid. For further discussion of the share ownership plan at Friesens, see Thiessen, 'Friesens Corporation.'

25 Ernie Dyck, interview.

26 Ibid.

27 Henry Froese, interview.

28 Henry Wallman, interview.

29 Henry Thiessen, interview.

30 Hawaleshka, 'Mennonite Millionaires.'

31 Susan Enns, interview.

32 Henry Wallman, interview.

33 Jakob Pries, interview.

34 Dave Hiebert, interview.

35 Bill Unrau, interview.

36 In the late 1990s, Friesens Corporation was certified under ISO 9002 and Palliser Furniture was certified under ISO 9001.

37 For some products sold in the European community, ISO certification is mandated. P.L. Johnson, *ISO 9000*, 8–9. For further discussion of the effects of ISO certification on the labour process at Friesens Corporation, see Thiessen, 'Friesens Corporation.'

38 Ben Funk, interview.

39 Henry Thiessen, interview.

40 Henry Wallman, interview.

41 Ibid.

42 Jake Ginter, interview.

43 Moody, *Workers*, 88–9.

44 Bruce MacDonald, interview.

45 Ibid.

46 Peter Reimer, interview.

47 Susan Enns, interview.

48 Anna Simon, interview.

49 Ibid.

50 Grant and Rosenstock, 'Do Mennonites Earn Less,' 73.

51 Ibid., 87.

52 For example, Okbazgi Gebreab, a carpentry apprentice from Eritrea who found work at Palliser Furniture as an upholsterer/framer, notes that he was paid only minimum wage there in 2004–5. He left the job after five months to do similar work at A&K Millwork largely because the wages were better. Career Destination Manitoba for Newcomers, 'Okbazgi Gebreab, Apprentice Cabinetmaker,' http://www.immigrantsandcareers. mb.ca/cdmb-newcomers/121_130/125_okbazgi_g/__story__/story__ combined.html (retrieved 30 March 2010; website has changed, page removed).

53 JoAnna Guerra, acting assistant deputy minister, Manitoba Workplace Safety and Health, letter to the author, Winnipeg, MB, 20 February 2004, in response to FIPPA request #2004.631.

54 JoAnna Guerra, acting assistant deputy minister, letter to the author, Winnipeg, MB, 19 February 2004, in response to FIPPA #2004.632; JoAnna Guerra, acting assistant deputy minister, letter to the author, Winnipeg, MB, 19 March 2004, in response to FIPPA request #2004.630.

55 Workplace Safety and Health Branch, incident investigation summary reports, prepared by Daniel A. Bartlette, assignment #991230, n.d. [November 1999]; prepared by Dan Bartlette, n.d. [August 2000].

56 Workplace Safety and Health Branch, incident investigation summary

reports, prepared by Dan Bartlette, n.d. [July 2000]; prepared by Dan Bartlette, n.d. [October and December 2000]; prepared by Dan Bartlette, n.d. [October 2002] (the quotation is from this report).

57 Of the ten incidents that occurred between 1990 and 2001, seven resulted in improvement orders – two of them stop-work orders. In two other cases, orders were not issued but the investigator offered specific criticism. The injured workers in all cases were males, with from six weeks' to fifteen years' experience. Workplace Safety and Health Branch, incident investigation reports and summary reports, no author, n.d. [February 1990]; prepared by Elmer Derksen, n.d. [September 1992]; prepared by Elmer Derksen, 31 May 1993; prepared by Elmer Derksen, 2 February 1995; prepared by Elmer Derksen, 8 March 1995; prepared by J.P. Duthie, assignment #990602, 7 September 1999; prepared by Jim Duthie, n.d. [November 1999]; prepared by Giselle Stuve, n.d. [April 2000]; prepared by Giselle Stuve and Daf Francisco, n.d. [May 2001]; prepared by Giselle Stuve, 22 August 2001.

58 Workplace Safety and Health Branch, incident investigation report, prepared by Elmer Derksen, 31 May 1993.

59 Ibid. Management was criticized again after an accident in 1995, when an investigator noted his suspicion that missing safety equipment was replaced before the investigating police officer arrived. Workplace Safety and Health Branch, incident investigation report, prepared by Elmer Derksen, 2 February 1995.

60 Workplace Safety and Health Branch, incident investigation report, prepared by J.P. Duthie, assignment #990602, 7 September 1999.

61 Workplace Safety and Health Branch, incident investigation report, prepared by Jim Duthie, n.d. [November 1999].

62 Palliser and Loewen were not the only companies with a culture where workers believed the demands of production required them to take shortcuts with their personal safety. Such was also the case at Buhler Industries, a collection of companies owned by Manitoban Mennonite John Buhler. Buhler's Allied Division, manufacturers of farm equipment, employed six hundred workers in Winnipeg in the 1990s. Improvement orders were issued at the company in September 1994 and January 1997. In the first incident, a newly employed worker had to have his thumb reattached after bypassing machine safeguards to increase production. Though he claimed that supervisors were aware that he did so regularly, co-workers and managers disagreed. In the second incident, a worker with

four months' experience broke his pelvis and leg and sustained internal injuries while removing a jam from powered equipment. The report noted that while Allied workers received only ten minutes of on-the-job training, this was standard practice in metalwork shops! The report also noted that workers regularly bypassed safety systems in order to maintain the pace of production, though management claimed not to be aware of the practice. The authors of the reports of incidents at Buhler's Allied Division, however, do not criticize management practice – unlike the authors of reports on similar incidents at Palliser. Workplace Safety and Health Branch, incident investigation reports, prepared by Stanley Wolf, 8 September 1994; prepared by Gene Fontaine, 6 January 1997.

63 Ernie Dyck, interview.
64 Dan Klassen, interview.
65 John Geddert, interview.
66 Henry Wallman, interview.
67 Ibid.
68 Ibid.
69 Conrad Stoesz, interview.
70 Henry Kroeker, interview.
71 Henry Thiessen, interview.
72 Government of Manitoba, The Workplace Safety and Health Act, C.C.S.M. c. W210.
73 Henry Wallman, interview.
74 Jakob Pries, interview.
75 Dan Paetkau, interview.
76 Ibid.
77 Ben Funk, interview, 24 August 1999.
78 John Geddert, interview.
79 Peter Reimer, interview.
80 Henry Froese, interview.
81 Abe Toews, interview.
82 Ernie Dyck, a former Loewen employee, shared Abe Toews's attitude towards the job. Dyck left Loewen to work as a folder operator at Friesens Corporation. He said he had been 'very dissatisfied' with his job at Loewen. 'The only challenge it held was keeping my sanity.' Ernie Dyck, interview.
83 Rempel-Burkholder, 'Little United Nations.'
84 M.L. Driedger, 'From Generation to Generation.'

85 Mitch Toews, interview.
86 Ibid.
87 Dan Paetkau, interview.
88 David Strempler, interview.
89 Joyce, xvii, xxi–xxii, 53.
90 Ibid., 124–5.
91 Ibid., 92.
92 Ibid.
93 Ibid., 93.
94 Ibid., 93–4.
95 Vogt, 'Entrepreneurs,' 137.
96 For descriptions of Mennonite settlement in Mexico and Paraguay, see
    Sawatzky, *They Sought a Country*; Quiring, *Mennonite Old Colony Vision*;
    Stoesz and Stackley, *Garden*; Stoesz, *Mustard Seed*.

5. Unequally Yoked: Manitoba Mennonites and the Schreyer Government

1 McAllister, *Edward Schreyer*, 108; Manitoba Labour and Immigration,
   'A History of Manitoba Labour and Immigration,' http://www.gov.mb.ca/
   labour/labmgt/history.html (retrieved 20 July 2004); Sprague, *Post-
   Confederation Canada*, 311; Hobsbawm, *Age of Extremes*. There were a
   record 1218 strikes in Canada in 1974; the highest number of strikers was
   1.5 million in 1976. Black and Silver, 'Labour in Manitoba: Facing the
   1990s,' in *Hard Bargains*, 6–7.
2 Stinson, *Political Warriors*, 245.
3 Ibid., 223–4.
4 Urry, *Mennonites*, 224.
5 The results provincially were: 28 NDP, 22 PC, 5 Liberal, 1 Social Credit,
   and 1 Independent.
6 McAllister's assertion that the 'main opposition' to the NDP in Manitoba
   in 1973 came from Protestants, including Mennonites, ignores the differences between rural and urban Mennonites. McAllister, 121.
7 Joe Friesen, 'Politics and Mennonites in Winnipeg,' 181.
8 Ibid., 186–8.
9 Percentage of Mennonites supporting unions: blue-collar, 58%; business,
   61%; students, 51%; housewives, 40%; professionals, 65%; farmers, 37%.
   Driedger, *Mennonites in the Global Village*, 45, table 2.6.

10 In 1970, 31.6 per cent of Canadians were unionized; this number increased to 34.7 per cent by 1984. In the United States, 23.5 per cent were unionized in 1973, and this number decreased to 19.5 per cent in 1983. Kauffman and Harder, *Anabaptists*, 146; Kauffman and Driedger, *Mennonite Mosaic*, 92, 207–8; Visser, 'Union Membership,' 45, table 3.

11 These groups included the Mennonite Church; the General Conference Mennonite Church; the Lancaster Mennonite Conference; the Brethren in Christ; the Church of God in Christ, Mennonite; the Mennonite Brethren; and Mennonite Central Committee.

12 Mennonite churches tend to be democratic rather than hierarchical. Annual meetings of various Mennonite denominations are known as conferences, as are certain Mennonite denominations themselves (e.g., the former General Conference Mennonite Church, now known as Mennonite Church Canada and Mennonite Church USA). Delegates to annual conferences are chosen by their individual congregations. Resolutions are drafted and voted on by these delegates at these conferences.

13 'General Conference Western District, "Mennonites and Russian Communism," 46th session, 20–22 October 1937, McPherson, KS,' in Peachey, *Mennonite Statements*, 19–20.

14 'Mennonite Central Committee, "Report on Communism," International Mennonite Peace Conference, 9–11 June 1952, Heerewegen, Zeist, Netherlands,' in Peachey, 20.

15 'Mennonite Church, "Resolution on Communism and Anti-Communism," 32nd session, 23 August 1961, Johnstown, PA'; and 'General Conference Mennonite Church, "A Christian Declaration on Communism and Anti-Communism," 36th session, 8–14 August 1962, Bethlehem, PA,' in Peachey, 19–21.

16 'Mennonite Church Peace Problems Committee, "Anti-Communism on the Radio and in the Press," Spring 1964,' in Peachey, 21–2.

17 Vogt, 'Mennonite Studies,' 65; Regehr, *Mennonites*, 158.

18 'Mennonite Church, "Resolution on Unionism," 20th session, 24–26 August 1937, Turner, OR,' in Peachey, 105.

19 Bible references included Isaiah 9:6, Matthew 26:61–3, Matthew 5:38–45, John 18:36, Romans 12:17–21, 2 Corinthians 10:4, Ephesians 4:31–2, and James 5:6.

20 2 Corinthians 6:14–16, King James Version. The NRSV replaces the agrarian image 'unequally yoked' with the less evocative 'mismatched.' This same passage was used by the bishops of the Lancaster Mennonite

Conference in 1941 as the rationale for their opposition to union membership. 'Mennonite Church Lancaster Conference, "Labor Unions," board
of bishops special meeting, 24 September 1941, Ephrata, PA,' in Peachey,
107. An earlier meeting of the bishops in 1933 also condemned union
membership, but did not quote from 2 Corinthians. 'Mennonite Church
Lancaster Conference, "Labor Unions," board of bishops, 18 October
1933, Lancaster, PA,' in Peachey, 107.

21 'Brethren in Christ Church, "Industrial Relations," 71st session, 4–9 June
1941, Milford, IN'; and 'Mennonite Church, "Industrial Relations," 22nd
session, 26 August 1941, Wellman, IA,' in Peachey, 102–3, 105–6.

22 The Committee on Industrial Relations was known after 1951 as the Committee on Economic and Social Relations. In 1965, it was merged with
the Peace Problems Committee to become the Committee on Peace and
Social Concerns of the Mennonite Church. Mennonite Central Committee
formed its own Peace and Social Concerns Committee in 1964. Mennonite Church, 'The Way of Christian Love in Race Relations (Mennonite
Church, 1955),' *GAMEO*, http://www.gameo.org/encyclopedia/contents/
W39.html (retrieved 20 July 2004).

23 'Mennonite Church, "Organized Labor," study conference, 24–27 June
1951, Laurelville Mennonite Camp, PA,' in Peachey, 106–7.

24 Guy F. Hershberger and John H. Redekop, 'Labor Unions,' *GAMEO*,
1989, http://www.gameo.org/encyclopedia/contents/W39.html (retrieved
2 July 2004).

25 'Church of God in Christ, Mennonite, "Labor Unions," special delegate
conference, 27 September 1953, Galva, KS,' in Peachey, 104.

26 'Church of God in Christ, Mennonite, "Labor Unions," general conference, 4–8 August 1967, Ste Anne, MB,' in Peachey, 104. This statement
also declared that membership in cooperatives would be left to 'the discretion of each local Church staff.'

27 'Mennonite Brethren Church, "The Christian and Labor Unions," 51st
session, 23–26 August 1969, Vancouver, BC,' in Peachey, 104–5.

28 The principle of local church autonomy among Mennonites, however,
allows individual congregations (to some extent) to make their own decisions on matters of doctrine. Thus the Locust Grove Mennonite Church
of Belleville, Pennsylvania, a member of the Conservative Mennonite
Conference, stated the following in their 1993 church constitution: 'We
believe that the way of love extends also to labor relations in our brotherhood to both employers and employees. We counsel employees to work

diligently, to see that their jobs give opportunities to serve Christ, and to refrain from participation in violence which may be required of members in labor unions.' Reference is made to Ephesians 6:5–9. This passage declares: 'Slaves, obey your earthly masters with fear and trembling, in singleness of heart, as you obey Christ; not only while being watched, and in order to please them, but as slaves of Christ, doing the will of God from the heart. Render service with enthusiasm, as to the Lord and not to men and women, knowing that whatever good we do, we will receive the same again from the Lord, whether we are slaves or free. And, masters. do the same to them. Stop threatening them, for you know that both of you have the same Master in heaven, and with him there is no partiality.' Locust Grove Mennonite Church, *Statement of Faith and Practice*, 1993, http://locustgrovemc.org/documents/faith.htm (retrieved 5 January 2005); Bible quotation from NRSV.

29 Mennonite Church, 'Mennonite Confession of Faith, 1963,' *GAMEO*, http://www.gameo.org/encyclopedia/contents/M4663.html (retrieved 15 March 2009).

30 Mennonite Brethren Church, 'Confession of Faith (Mennonite Brethren, 1975),' *GAMEO*, http://www.gameo.org/encyclopedia/contents/C6655.html (retrieved 15 March 2009).

31 See Urry, *Mennonites*, chapter 9; and J. Redekop, 'Decades of Transition.'

32 This section was replaced by section 76(3), which specifies that the employee must be 'a member of a religious group which has as one of its articles of faith the belief that members of the group are precluded from being members of, and financially supporting, any union or professional association' and that the employee 'has a personal belief in those articles of faith.' Government of Manitoba, 'Continuing Consolidation of the Statutes of Manitoba: The Labour Relations Act,' 9 June 2004, http://web2.gov.mb.ca/laws/statutes/ccsm/l010e.php (retrieved 20 July 2004).

33 MCC Canada press release, 10 January 1975, 'MCC Manitoba (1975–80),' Volume 3650, MHC.

34 Letter from A. Russell Paulley, minister of labour, to Peter Peters, MCC Manitoba, 27 January 1975, 'MCC Manitoba (1975–80),' Volume 3650, MHC. No mention of this meeting, or of the Manitoba Mennonites' concerns in general, is made in the Andrew Russell Paulley papers. Don Hurst, access and privacy officer, Manitoba Labour and Immigration Workplace Safety and Health Division, letter to the author, Winnipeg, MB, 16 June 2005, in response to FIPPA requests #2005.767, 2005.768, and 2005.769.

35 'Reasons for Decision' regarding the application by Henry Funk to the Manitoba Labour Board under Section 68(3) of the Labour Relations Act, with McGavin Toastmaster Ltd. as employer-respondent and Bakery and Confectionery Workers' International Union Local 389 as bargaining agent and agreement holder, 1975, 'MCC Manitoba (1974–80),' Folder 6, Volume 3636, MHC.

36 Manitoba Court of Appeals, Henry Funk v. Manitoba Labour Board, 5 January 1976, 'MCC Manitoba (1975–80),' Volume 3650, MHC; 'Labor Board Decision Overturned,' *Steinbach Carillon* (7 January 1976): 1:1. See the Schleitheim Confession's Article 6, regarding Anabaptists' earlier stance against use of the legal system to resolve disputes. Even more conservative groups such as the Hutterites have been known, in recent years, to abandon their traditional refusal to take fellow Hutterites to court. See Esau, *Courts and the Colonies*.

37 Letter from H. Klassen, Donwood Manor, to Mennonite Churches of Manitoba, 19 March 1975, 'MCC Manitoba (1975–80),' Volume 3650, MHC. The Canadian Mennonite Health Assembly was formed as the Canadian Association of Mennonite Hospitals and Homes in 1966. It changed names in 1973. Centre for Mennonite Brethren Studies, 'Canadian Mennonite Health Assembly,' 16 August 2003, http://www.mbconf .ca/home/products_and_services/resources/published_genealogies/ other_mennonite_and_mennonite_brethren_organizations/canadian_ mennonite_health_assembly/ (retrieved 20 July 2004).

38 Proceedings from the 1975 Conference of the Canadian Mennonite Health Assembly held at Donwood Manor, Winnipeg, MB, 23–25 April 1975, 'MCC Manitoba (1975–80),' Volume 3650, MHC.

39 The topic of this speech (and presumably its content) was the same as that of a presentation Redekop later made at a series of seminars on labour-management relations organized by Mennonite Central Committee Manitoba in January 1976.

40 CMHA Proceedings, 1975, Volume 3650, MHC.

41 Delegates were those who had been chosen to represent their congregations and had voting rights; guests were interested observers who had no voting rights.

42 'Mennonites Struggle with Union Membership Issue,' *Steinbach Carillon* (26 November 1975): 2:1.

43 The Canadian Union of Postal Workers, as a result of the 1975 strike, received a 71 per cent wage increase and had their work week reduced to thirty hours. Sprague, *Post-Confederation Canada*, 311.

44 Nine Mennonite nurses at this hospital had refused to join the union and requested assistance from MCC. Memo from Arthur Driedger, executive director of Peace and Social Concerns Committee, MCC Manitoba, to committee members, 13 June 1975, 'MCC Manitoba (1975–80),' Volume 3650, MHC.

45 Two hundred five people were registered: sixty-one at Steinbach, seventy-two at Winkler, and seventy-two at Winnipeg. Others may have attended without signing their names at the door. 'MCC Manitoba (1974–80),' Folder 6, Volume 3636, MHC.

46 Labour-Management Relations Seminar advertisement, 'MCC Manitoba (1974–80),' Folder 6, Volume 3636, MHC.

47 'Labor, Management, Meeting at Steinbach,' *Steinbach Carillon* (21 January 1976): 1:1.

48 Ibid.

49 Letter from Arthur Driedger, executive director of Peace and Social Concerns Committee, Mennonite Central Committee Manitoba, to Gerald Vandezande, former head of the Christian Labour Association of Canada, 22 December 1975, 'MCC Manitoba (1974–80),' Folder 6, Volume 3636, MHC.

50 The Christian Labour Association of Canada (CLAC) was formed in 1952 by individuals in the Christian Reformed religious tradition (Dutch Calvinists) as an alternative to traditional labour unions. The CLAC objects to the 'adversarial nature' of traditional unions and is opposed to the closed shop. The CLAC is not affiliated with the Canadian Labour Congress. Christian Labour Association of Canada, 'CLAC Tour,' 2004, http://www.clac.ca/Flash_Tour.asp (retrieved 20 July 2004; website has changed, video removed).

51 John H. Redekop, 'Labor-Management Relationships: A Biblical Perspective,' 1, 'MCC Manitoba (1974–80),' Volume 3636, MHC.

52 Ibid., 2.

53 Ibid., 1. Redekop noted, 'There are, of course, also some positive trends but since they are not controversial we will omit listing them. It is the negative ones that cause the problems.' Ibid., 2.

54 Ibid., 2–3.

55 Ibid., 3.

56 Ibid., 4.

57 Ibid., 10.

58 'ITEM 7: What Are Our Concerns?' 'MCC Manitoba (1974–80),' Volume 3636, MHC.

59 'Labor-Seminar Speaker: "Christians May Have to Pay High Price,"' *Steinbach Carillon* (4 February 1976): 1:1; Redekop, 10–11, MHC.

60 Letter from Egon Frech, special assistant to Premier Edward Schreyer, to Gerald Vandezande, executive director, CJL Foundation, 16 September 1974, 'MCC Manitoba (1974–80),' Volume 3636, MHC.

61 Mennonite Industry and Business Associates (MIBA), 'Report on Management/Labor Relations,' *The Marketplace* (March 1980): 9–10.

62 Ibid., 10.

63 Ibid.

64 Ibid., 11.

65 Ibid.

66 Ibid., 11–12.

6. 'No One Is Always Happy with His Environment': Union Drives and Corporate Responses

1 Ted Friesen preserved copies of the speeches D.K. Friesen delivered at company Christmas parties from 1961 to 1985.

2 Friesens Corporation, employee newsletter (July 1968).

3 D.K. Friesen, Christmas party speech, 14 December 1973.

4 Ibid., 13 December 1968.

5 Ibid., 10 December 1971.

6 Ibid., 12 December 1969.

7 Ted Friesen explained: 'We did have time clocks once, but we threw them out … We simply felt that our staff could be trusted. If anyone would be abusing it, I think that … somebody would be alerting their supervisor. It's difficult to goof off in a business like ours. Maybe in the city it's a little different, but certainly in a small town … And it was a deliberate choice on our part, not to have time clocks.' T.E. Friesen, interview.

8 D.K. Friesen, memo to staff, 16 September 1969, 21 September 1970, 6 December 1971; T.E. Friesen, interview.

9 Monthly meeting minutes, Winnipeg Typographical Union Local 191, 23 February 1962, MG 10 A29, Box 5, Folder 5, Provincial Archives of Manitoba, Winnipeg, MB.

10 D.G. Friesen, interview.

11 Elizabeth Bergen, interview. Though she declared she knew personally the person who instigated the union drive at Friesens, Ms Bergen declined to name the individual.

12 D.K. Friesen, memo to staff, draft copy, 1 April 1972. It is not known if

this memo was issued to staff in this form. It nonetheless provides insight into the thinking of management on the question.

13 Italics in original.

14 D.K. Friesen, memo to staff, draft copy, 1 April 1972.

15 D.K. Friesen, memo to board of directors, 30 August 1972.

16 Notation made on memo to board of directors from D.K. Friesen, 30 August 1972.

17 Letter to the author from Don Penner, vice-president and general manager, Yearbook Division, Friesens Corporation, Altona, MB, 21 April 1997.

18 D.K. Friesen, memo to staff, 28 November 1972.

19 Ibid.

20 Ibid.

21 Ray Rudersdorfer, interview.

22 D.K. Friesen had been president and general manager of the Altona Co-operative Store and vice-president of Cooperative Vegetable Oils; Ray Friesen had been president of the Red River Valley Mutual Insurance Company.

Management at Friesens Corporation were not alone in their assessment that unions were unnecessary. The editor of the local newspaper, the *Altona Echo*, a Friesens Corporation publication, expressed this opinion in an editorial in April of 1972. 'One wonders, however, whether many of the unions haven't outlived their usefulness by now. Many of the demands made by unions nowadays are simply schemes by union leaders to try and prove their continuing worth. Many of the disputes between labor leaders and management are little more than power struggles … The way things are going now, even the strongest labor sympathizers must know in their hearts that a better way of settling wage disputes must be found.' Penner, 'Unworthy Strikes.'

23 D.K. Friesen, Christmas party speech, 15 December 1972.

24 Italics in original.

25 D.K. Friesen again confessed and apologized for the growing distance between management and workers. 'I often catch myself preaching what I do not practice. I walk through the plant, forgetting to say "good morning," as I may be deep in thought or do not have my glasses on to recognize someone at a distance. Or I forget to congratulate someone on a job well done, on an anniversary, or an event in your family. It was much easier to do this when we had fewer employees, and I apologize for and regret

these shortcomings.' D.K. Friesen, Christmas party speech, 15 December 1972.

26 Ibid.

27 Epp-Tiessen, 299.

28 'Printing Firm's Roots Still "Small Town,"' 28 May 1976, UMA.

29 Wright, 61.

30 Patrick Martin, former business representative for UBCJA Local 343, personal communication, Winnipeg, MB, 10 July 1997.

31 Palliser Furniture, *A.A. DeFehr Mfg. Ltd. Employee Policy* (1 October 1970).

32 Palliser Furniture, employee handbook (December 1993): 29.

33 UBCJA Local 343 newsletter, 1996, courtesy of UBCJA Local 343.

34 Patrick Martin, personal communication.

35 UBCJA Local 343, *Palliser Union News* 1, no. 8 (February 1996), courtesy of UBCJA Local 343.

36 Palliser Furniture, employee handbook (December 1993): 41.

37 Ibid., 43.

38 Ibid., 66.

39 Ibid., 69.

40 UBCJA Local 343, *Palliser Union News* 1, no. 1 (31 January 1996); *Palliser Union News* 1, no. 5 (February 1996), both courtesy of UBCJA Local 343.

41 Henry Wallman, interview.

42 UBCJA Local 343, *Palliser Union News*, n.d., courtesy of UBCJA Local 343.

43 Palliser received assistance from the Industrial Development Bank (IDB) in 1963, requested $150,000 from the Manitoba Development Fund in 1968, received $298,160 from the Department for Regional Economic Expansion (DREE) in 1976, received $688,000 from DREE in 1982, and received $1.5 million from Western Economic Diversification in 1988. 'North Kildonan Firm Shows Phenomenal Growth in 25 Years,' unnamed newspaper article (1969), courtesy of Palliser Furniture; Palliser Furniture application to the Industrial Development Bank, form 58B (rev. 10/67), 11 June 1968; letter from J.D. Collinson, director-general of DREE, to A.A. DeFehr, 8 September 1976, courtesy of Palliser Furniture; 'DeFehr Plant Staff Doubled,' *Winnipeg Free Press* (26 May 1984): 44; Western Economic Diversification Canada, press release, 3 October 1988, courtesy of Palliser Furniture.

44 UBCJA Local 343, *Palliser Union News* 1, no. 1 (31 January 1996); and
    1, no. 6 (February 1996), courtesy of UBCJA Local 343.
45 Later that year, the Manitoba Labour Relations Act was amended by
    the Conservative government led by Premier Gary Filmon. Automatic
    union certification was ended; all applications for certification required
    a secret ballot vote. Applications where less than 40 per cent of workers
    signed union cards were rejected. An NDP government led by Premier
    Gary Doer was elected in 1999; in 2000, the Labour Relations Act was
    amended to reverse the changes instituted by the Filmon government. Hu-
    man Resources and Skills Development Canada, 'Labour and Workplace
    Information, 1996–1997,' http://www110.hrdc-drhc.gc.ca/psait_spila/
    eltc_dllc/1996_1997/index.cfm/doc/english#legislation_2 (retrieved 8
    March 2005); Manitoba Labour and Immigration, 'A History of Manitoba
    Labour and Immigration,' http://www.gov.mb.ca/labour/labmgt/history.
    html (retrieved 20 July 2004).
46 Patrick Martin, personal communication.
47 In November 2004, a pamphlet produced by the Manitoba Committee
    of the Communist Party of Canada, titled 'Fight for Workers' Rights at
    Palliser: It Takes a Struggle to Win,' was available at the Winnipeg office
    of Project Peacemakers. (Project Peacemakers is an affiliate of Project
    Ploughshares, an ecumenical peace centre founded by Mennonites and the
    Society of Friends [Quakers] in 1976.) The pamphlet describes 'sweat-
    ing, piece work, intense speed-up, incentives to cover up injury benefits,
    reductions in incentives and lowering of wage ceilings for piece work,'
    limited vacations, and the elimination of profit sharing in some plants, and
    advocates the formation of a union at Palliser.
48 Charles Loewen, interview.
49 None of the employees I interviewed recalled any attempts to organize.
50 Charles Loewen, interview.
51 David Glenn Friesen, personal communication, 22 September 1995; Da-
    vid Glenn Friesen, letter to the author, Steinbach, MB, 21 May 1996; T.E.
    Friesen, interview.
52 Friesens Corporation, Shareholders meeting minutes, 9 December 1960.
53 David Glenn Friesen, personal communication, 22 September 1995.
54 Friesens Corporation, Shareholders meeting minutes, 9 December 1960.
55 This requirement was later lowered to three and a half years. T.E. Friesen,
    'Philosophy, Policy and Practices,' 4; Friesens Corporation, *Seventy-Fifth
    Anniversary.*

56 Friesens Corporation, '1981 Employee Handbook,' 20–1, MHC; Friesens Corporation, Board of Directors meeting minutes, 6 August 1981.

57 David Glenn Friesen, personal communication, 2 April 1997; Friesens Corporation, Board of Directors meeting minutes, 15 April 1985.

58 Friesens Corporation, Shareholders meeting minutes, 9 December 1960.

59 David Glenn Friesen, personal communication, 2 April 1997.

60 Palliser Furniture, employee newsletter 2, no. 1 (March 1983).

61 Palliser Furniture, employee newsletter 10, no. 6 (March/April 1991): 8.

62 Palliser Furniture, employee newsletter 2, no. 1 (March 1983).

63 The validity of Palliser's claims cannot be determined, as profit-sharing statistics are not available.

64 Lloyd Plett, interview.

65 Ibid.

66 John Ferris, interview.

67 Barry Dyck, interview; 'Company Announces Profit-Sharing Payout,' *Steinbach Carillon* (18 February 2002): 14A.

68 Barry Dyck, interview.

69 Hawaleshka, 'Mennonite Millionaires.'

70 Barry Dyck, interview.

71 The profit-sharing plan replaced the company pension plan in the mid-1990s, which had been offered only to salaried employees. Lloyd Plett, interview.

72 Gary Timlick, interview.

73 Friesens, *Working with Friesens*, employee handbook (1993): 71; Palliser Furniture, employee handbook (December 1993): 61–4.

74 Lloyd Plett, interview.

75 Hawaleshka, 'Mennonite Millionaires,' 22. Despite this pay increase, it was necessary in December 2003 to make Christmas food hampers for some employees. Workers interviewed volunteered this information to the author, perceiving these hampers to be a sign of management benevolence rather than possible evidence of low wages.

76 Long, 'Incidence,' 473, 475, 477–8.

77 Ibid., 473.

78 Elizabeth Bergen, interview.

79 Friesens Corporation, Board of Directors meeting minutes, 18 September 1965.

80 Ibid., 24 May 1972.

81 Ibid., 7 September 1973.

82 David Glenn Friesen, personal communication, 2 April 1997; Friesens
    Corporation, Board of Directors meeting minutes, 23 February 1982;
    Friesens Corporation, letter to shareholders, 16 November 1982; Friesen
    Printers, Goals and Objectives, January 1983.
83 Friesens Corporation, Board of Directors meeting minutes, 7 December
    1987.
84 T.E. Friesen, letter to the author, Steinbach, MB, 30 May 1996.
85 Friesens, *Working with Friesens*, employee handbook (1993): 82.
86 Ibid., 86. The 1993 handbook stated that there are 'no plans to increase
    the share portion beyond 40%.' Richard Long's survey of 626 Canadian
    companies in 1989–90 found that only two companies offered stock
    through their profit-sharing plans. Long, 478.
87 Ninety per cent of employees kept their shares in 1995. Friesens Corpora-
    tion, Board of Directors meeting minutes, 19 July 1995.
88 Henry Froese, interview.
89 Eugene Letkeman, interview.
90 Memo from W.A. Redekopp to A.A., Frank, Art, and Dave DeFehr, n.d.
91 Ibid.
92 Ibid.
93 Ibid.
94 Palliser Furniture, Executive Committee meeting minutes, 19–20 January
    1979.
95 Palliser Furniture, employee newsletter 1, no. 5 (September 1982). Pal-
    liser had 125 shareholders in 1989 and 188 shareholders in 1991. Palliser
    Furniture, employee newsletter 8, no. 2 (July 1989); employee newsletter
    10, no. 7 (May/June 1991): 5.
96 Palliser Furniture employee newsletter 8, no. 2 (July 1989).
97 I was not granted access to share ownership information at Palliser Furni-
    ture. The December 1993 employee handbook does not list share owner-
    ship as a benefit; perhaps share ownership is restricted to those employees
    of the company who hold managerial positions.
98 Knell, 'Palliser Selling.'
99 'Shared Profits Aid Business, Meet Told,' *Winnipeg Tribune* (19 Novem-
    ber 1953); 'Profit Sharing Key to Success,' *Winnipeg Tribune* (27 June
    1967); Harry L. Mardon, 'A Radical Plan for Capitalists,' *Winnipeg Tri-
    bune* (3 October 1975); 'Profit Sharing to Security,' *Winnipeg Tribune* (24
    December 1976). All found in 'Profit Sharing,' MSS 24, no. 5508, Win-
    nipeg Tribune Collection, UMA.

Conclusion

1 Memory is essential in the ongoing formation of identity. Collective memory is memory created and shared by a group; communicative memory is a form of memory transmitted by everyday conversation (and thus exists for a shorter time span – only a few generations – than does collective memory). Maurice Halbwachs, Harold Welzer, and Jan Assmann are the forerunners of the growing field of memory studies. See, for example, Halbwachs, *On Collective Memory*; Welzer, 'Communicative Memory'; Assmann, 'Collective Memory and Cultural Identity.'

2 Thompson, 33–4, 39, 47–8.

3 Ibid., 49, 50.

4 Guy F. Hershberger and John H. Redekop, 'Labor Unions,' *GAMEO*, 1989, http://www.gameo.org/encyclopedia/contents/L205ME.html (retrieved 5 January 2005).

5 The priesthood of all believers is a theological concept popularized by Luther in 1520. In Mennonite theology, this concept refers to the absence of a separation between clergy and laity, the collective decision-making process of the church, and the responsibility of all believers to act as a conduit of God's grace to others. Harold S. Bender and Marlin E. Miller, 'Priesthood of All Believers,' *GAMEO*, 1989, http://www.gameo.org/encyclopedia/contents/P742ME.html (retrieved 5 April 2010).

6 Kauffman and Driedger, 38.

7 Sangster, 'Softball Solution,' 198.

8 Ibid., 197.

9 Orsi, 'Everyday Miracles,' 13.

Bibliography

Manuscript Sources

Altona and District Heritage Centre Archive. Friesens Corporation Collection. Altona, MB.

Archives of Manitoba. Winnipeg Typographical Union Collection, MG 10 A29. Winnipeg, MB.

Friesen, David Glenn. Private Collection. Altona, MB.

Friesen, T.E. Private Collection. Altona, MB.

Friesens Corporation. Private Collection. Altona, MB.

Loewen Windows. Private Collection. Steinbach, MB.

Mennonite Economic Development Associates. Private Collection. Winnipeg, MB.

Mennonite Heritage Centre. Mennonite Central Committee Manitoba Collection, volumes 3636, 3650. Winnipeg, MB.

Mennonite Heritage Centre. C.T. Loewen & Sons, Vertical File, 1980. Winnipeg, MB.

Mennonite Heritage Centre. D.W. Friesen, Vertical File, 1981–2. Winnipeg, MB.

Palliser Furniture. Private Collection. Winnipeg, MB.

Project Peacemakers. Private Collection. Winnipeg, MB.

United Brotherhood of Carpenters and Joiners of America. Local 343. Private Collection. Winnipeg, MB.

University of Manitoba Archives. The Winnipeg Tribune Subject Clipping Research Files, MSS 24. Winnipeg, MB.

Government Sources

Government of Canada

Human Resources and Skills Development Canada.
Labour Canada.
Statistics Canada.

Government of Manitoba

Consumer and Corporate Affairs, Manitoba Companies Office.
Labour and Immigration.
Labour and Immigration, Workplace Safety and Health Division.
Queen's Printer, Statutory Publications.

Interviews

Note: Occupation listed is the occupation at the time of the interview.

Bergen, Elizabeth (Isby). Former newspaper reporter, Friesens Corporation. Interview by author, 28 March 1996, Altona. Tape recording. MHC, Winnipeg.

Bretecher, Rhonda. Organizational development manager, Loewen Windows. Interview by author, 22 December 2003, Steinbach. Tape recording.

Bueckert, Gordon. Assembler, Floform. Interview by author, 26 August 1998, Winnipeg. Tape recording. MHC, Winnipeg.

Corbett, Mallory. Health and safety manager, Loewen Windows. Interview by author, 22 December 2003, Steinbach. Tape recording. MHC, Winnipeg.

DeFehr, A.A. Founder, Palliser Furniture. Interview by author, 1 August 1997, Winnipeg. Tape recording.

DeFehr, David (Dave). Vice-president, Carolina Division, Palliser Furniture. Interview by author, 18 July 1997, Winnipeg. Tape recording.

Dutchak, Richard. Engineering and facilities manager, Loewen Windows. Interview by author, 22 December 2003, Steinbach. Tape recording. MHC, Winnipeg.

Dyck, Barry. Compensation and benefits manager, Loewen Windows.

Interview by author, 19 December 2003, Steinbach. Tape recording. MHC, Winnipeg.

Dyck, Ernie. Former employee, Loewen Windows. Folder operator, Friesens Corporation.
Interview by author, 29 March 1999, Altona. Tape recording. MHC, Winnipeg.

Enns, Susan [pseudonym]. Human resources, Loewen Windows.
Interview by author, 29 December 2003, Steinbach. Tape recording.

Falk, Alvina [pseudonym]. Production worker, Loewen Windows.
Interview by author, 19 December 2003, Steinbach. Tape recording.

Ferris, John. Vice-president human resources, Loewen Windows.
Interview by author, 17 December 2003, Steinbach. Tape recording. MHC, Winnipeg.

Friesen, D.G. Former press operator, Friesens Corporation.
Interview by author, 27 March 1996, Altona. Tape recording. MHC, Winnipeg.

Friesen, Ken. Executive director, Loewen Foundation.
Interview by author, 17 December 2003, Steinbach. Tape recording. MHC, Winnipeg.

Friesen, Peter. Former quality advocate, Loewen Windows.
Interview by author, 29 December 2003, Steinbach. Tape recording. MHC, Winnipeg.

Friesen, T.E. Former director, Friesens Corporation.
Interview by author, 6 January 1995, Altona. Tape recording. MHC, Winnipeg.

Froese, Henry. Paper cutter, Friesens Corporation.
Interview by author, 24 June 1999, Altona. Tape recording. MHC, Winnipeg.

Funk, Ben. Former production manager, Loewen Windows.
Interview by author, 24 August 1999, Steinbach. Tape recording. MHC, Winnipeg.
Interview by author, 29 December 2003, Steinbach. Tape recording. MHC, Winnipeg.

Funk, Dave. Supervisor, Loewen Windows.
Interview by author, 18 December 2003, Steinbach. Tape recording. MHC, Winnipeg.

Goerz, John [pseudonym]. Sales, Loewen Windows.
Interview by author, 18 December 2003, Steinbach. Tape recording.

Geddert, John. Former assembler, Palliser Furniture.
    Interview by author, 11 January 1999, Winnipeg. Tape recording. MHC,
    Winnipeg.
Giesbrecht, Harry. President, Central Canadian Structures.
    Interview by author, 19 November 1998, Winnipeg. Tape recording. MHC,
    Winnipeg.
Ginter, Jake. Supervisor, Palliser Furniture.
    Interview by author, 7 January 1999, Winnipeg. Tape recording. MHC,
    Winnipeg.
Hancox, Gord. Plant manager, Loewen Windows.
    Interview by author, 22 December 2003, Steinbach. Tape recording. MHC,
    Winnipeg.
Heidebrecht, Frank [pseudonym]. Millshop team leader, Loewen Windows.
    Interview by author, 22 December 2003, Steinbach. Tape recording.
Hiebert, Anne. Food services, Loewen Windows.
    Interview by author, 18 December 2003, Steinbach. Tape recording. MHC,
    Winnipeg.
Hiebert, Dave. Customer and market support manager, Loewen Windows.
    Interview by author, 19 December 2003, Steinbach. Tape recording. MHC,
    Winnipeg.
International Typographers Union Local 191 union leader.
    Interview by author, 6 September 1995, Winnipeg. By telephone.
Klassen, Dan. Machine operator, Friesens Corporation.
    Interview by author, 20 July 1999, Altona. Tape recording. MHC, Winni-
    peg.
Klassen, Ernie. Machine operator, Friesens Corporation.
    Interview by author, 13 July 1999, Altona. Tape recording. MHC, Winni-
    peg.
Klassen, Paul [pseudonym]. Electrician, Loewen Windows.
    Interview by author, 22 December 2003, Steinbach. Tape recording.
Kroeker, Henry. Former foreman, Loewen Windows.
    Interview by author, 18 August 1998, Steinbach. Tape recording. MHC,
    Winnipeg.
Letkeman, Eugene. Graphic arts instructor, Friesens Corporation.
    Interview by author, 21 July 1999, Altona. Tape recording. MHC, Winni-
    peg.
Letkeman, John. North American sales co-ordinator, Loewen Windows.
    Interview by author, 29 December 2003, Steinbach. Tape recording.

Loewen, Charles. Chief executive officer, Loewen Windows.
  Interview by author, 18 December 2003, Steinbach. Tape recording. MHC,
  Winnipeg.
Loewen, Clyde. Vice-president of product and technical services, Loewen
  Windows.
  Interview by author, 17 December 2003, Steinbach. Tape recording. MHC,
  Winnipeg.
Loewen, Dave. Former sales manager, Loewen Windows.
  Interview by author, 29 December 2003, Steinbach. Transcript.
Loewen, John. Co-owner, Loewen Windows.
  Interview by author, 30 December 2003, Winnipeg. Tape recording. MHC,
  Winnipeg.
MacDonald, Bruce. Quality facilitator, Palliser Furniture.
  Interview by author, 1 August 1997, Winnipeg. Tape recording. MHC,
  Winnipeg.
Nickel, Joseph [pseudonym]. Team leader, Loewen Windows.
  Interview by author, 22 December 2003, Steinbach. Tape recording.
Paetkau, Dan [pseudonym]. Supervisor, Loewen Windows.
  Interview by author, 24 August 1999, Steinbach. Transcript.
Peters, Gerhard [pseudonym]. Assembler, Loewen Windows.
  Interview by author, 23 August 1999, Pansy. Transcript. MHC, Winnipeg.
Plett, Lloyd. Former vice-president finance, Loewen Windows.
  Interview by author, 29 December 2003, Steinbach. Tape recording.
Pries, Jakob. Former plant manager, Woodland Supply.
  Interview by author, 25 August 1998, Winnipeg. Tape recording. MHC,
  Winnipeg.
Rahn, Hardy. Canadian sales manager, Loewen Windows.
  Interview by author, 22 December 2003, Steinbach. Tape recording. MHC,
  Winnipeg.
Reimer, Peter. Former plant manager, Palliser Furniture.
  Interview by author, 7 September 1998, Winnipeg. Tape recording. MHC,
  Winnipeg.
Rempel, Jake. Press operator, Friesens Corporation.
  Interview by author, 20 July 1999, Altona. Tape recording. MHC, Winni-
  peg.
Rudersdorfer, Ray. Former union organizer, International Typographers
  Union, Winnipeg Local 191.
  Interview by author, 6 November 1995, Vancouver, BC. By telephone.

Schroeder, Peter. Wholesale division supervisor, Friesens Corporation.
    Interview by author, 21 July 1999, Winnipeg. Transcript. MHC, Winni-
    peg.
Simon, Anna [pseudonym]. Human resources, Loewen Windows.
    Interview by author, 22 December 2003, Steinbach. Tape recording. MHC,
    Winnipeg.
Stoesz, Conrad. Former assembler, Floform Industries.
    Interview by author, 24 August 1998, Winnipeg. Tape recording. MHC,
    Winnipeg.
Strempler, David. Assembler, Palliser Furniture.
    Interview by author, 17 August 1998, Winnipeg. Transcript. MHC, Winni-
    peg.
Thiessen, Henry. Film assembler, Friesens Corporation.
    Interview by author, 21 July 1999, Altona. Tape recording. MHC, Winni-
    peg.
Timlick, Gary. Vice-president finance, Loewen Windows.
    Interview by author, 19 December 2003, Steinbach. Tape recording.
Toews, Abe [pseudonym]. Former moulder operator, Loewen Windows.
    Interview by author, 26 August 1999, Steinbach. Tape recording. MHC,
    Winnipeg.
Toews, Anne. Buyer, Loewen Windows.
    Interview by author, 18 December 2003, Steinbach. Tape recording.
Toews, Mitch. Advertising and corporate communications manager, Loewen
    Windows.
    Interview by author, 19 December 2003, Steinbach. Tape recording. MHC,
    Winnipeg.
Unrau, Ben. Production worker, Loewen Windows.
    Interview by author, 18 December 2003, Steinbach. Tape recording. MHC,
    Winnipeg.
Unrau, Bill [pseudonym]. Production worker, Loewen Windows.
    Interview by author, 18 December 2003, Steinbach. Tape recording.
Unrau, Henry. Traffic manager, Loewen Windows.
    Interview by author, 18 December 2003, Steinbach. Tape recording. MHC,
    Winnipeg.
Wall, Anna. Bindery worker, Friesens Corporation.
    Interview by author, 16 July 1999, Altona. Transcript. MHC, Winnipeg.
Wall, Nettie. Small equipment operator, Friesens Corporation.
    Interview by author, 25 June 1999, Altona. Tape recording. MHC, Winni-
    peg.

Wallman, Henry. Former manager, Palliser Furniture.
 Interview by author, 24 August 1998, Winnipeg. Tape recording. MHC,
 Winnipeg.
Wiebe, Margaretha [pseudonym]. Former Winnipeg sewing factory worker.
 Interview by author, 13 January 1999, Winnipeg. Transcript. MHC, Win-
 nipeg.
Wiens, Hans (and Susie). Former plant manager, Loewen Windows.
 Interview by author, 17 August 1998, Steinbach. Tape recording. MHC,
 Winnipeg.
Wolfe, Peter. Former press operator, Friesens Corporation.
 Interview by Fred McGuinness, 30 August 1999, Altona. Transcript.

Speeches

DeFehr, Art. 'Creating a Successful Manitoba-based Company with International Influence.' Speech to the Winkler Chamber of Commerce, 25 June
 1997. Tape recording courtesy of Hans Werner, Winkler, MB.
– 'World without Pity.' Speech delivered at the Mennonite Economic Development Associates convention, Dallas, TX, 12–15 November 1998. Copy
 courtesy of Wally Kroeker, MEDA.
Human resources director, Loewen Windows. Speech to tour group, 12 May
 2000.
Klassen, George. Palliser Furniture central recruitment office, employee orientation session, Winnipeg, MB, 19 August 1997.
Loewen, Royden K. 'An Imagined Biblical Paraphrase: The Voice of Menno
 Simons.' Speech delivered at the Canadian Association of Mennonite
 Schools Educators Conference, Brandon, MB, 18 February 2009.
– 'Poetics of Peoplehood: Disparate Mennonite Voices Today.' Speech deliv-
 ered at the Canadian Association of Mennonite Schools Educators Confer-
 ence, Brandon, MB, 20 February 2009.

Printed Sources and Typescripts

Alexander, Michael. *Jazz Age Jews.* Princeton, NJ: Princeton University
 Press, 2001.
Amatori, Franco, and Geoffrey Jones, eds. *Business History Around the
 World.* Cambridge: Cambridge University Press, 2003.
Anderson, Benedict. *Imagined Communities: Reflections on the Origin and
 Spread of Nationalism.* Rev. ed. London: Verso, 1991.

Armstrong, Frederick H. 'Canadian Business History: Approaches and Publications to 1970.' In *Canadian Business History: Selected Studies, 1497–
1971*, ed. David S. Macmillan. Toronto: McClelland and Stewart, 1972.

Assmann, Jan. 'Collective Memory and Cultural Identity.' Translated by John
Czaplicka. *New German Critique* 65 (Spring–Summer 1995): 125–33.

Bain, Don. 'The Printing Professionals.' *Manitoba Business* 11, no. 4 (May
1989): 7.

– 'Strong Corporate Roots, Innovative Management, Keynote Firm's Success.' *Trade and Commerce* 73, no. 9 (September 1978): 21.

Bainton, Roland H. 'The Left Wing of the Reformation.' *Journal of Religion*
21 (1941): 124–34.

Barthes, Roland. *Mythologies*. Translated by Annette Lavers. New York: Hill
and Wang, 1972.

– 'Myth Today.' In *A Barthes Reader*, ed. Susan Sontag. New York: Hill and
Wang, 1982.

Baylor, Michael G., ed. and trans. *The Radical Reformation*. Cambridge Texts
in the History of Political Thought. Cambridge: Cambridge University
Press, 1991.

Bender, Harold S. *The Anabaptist Vision*. Scottdale, PA: Herald Press, 1944.

Bercuson, David J. *Confrontation at Winnipeg: Labour, Industrial Relations,
and the General Strike*. Montreal: McGill-Queen's University Press, 1990.

Black, Errol, and Jim Silver, eds. *Hard Bargains: The Manitoba Labour
Movement Confronts the 1990s*. Winnipeg, MB: Manitoba Labour Education Centre, n.d.

Biesecker-Mast, Gerald J. 'Towards a Radical Postmodern-Anabaptist Vision.'
Conrad Grebel Review 13 (1995): 55–68.

Buller, Herb, and Erna Buller. 'Leadership, Opportunity, Integrity, and Can-
cer.' *Power to Change*. http://powertochange.com/discover/faith/buller (retrieved 24 March 2010).

Burkholder, J. Lawrence. 'Autobiographical Reflections.' In *The Limits of
Perfection: A Conversation with J. Lawrence Burkholder*, ed. Rodney J.
Sawatsky and Scott Holland. Waterloo, ON: Institute of Anabaptist and
Mennonite Studies, 1993.

– 'Nonresistance, Nonviolent Resistance, and Power.' In *Kingdom, Cross and
Community: Essays on Mennonite Themes in Honor of Guy F. Hershberger*.
Scottdale, PA: Herald Press, 1976.

– *The Problem of Social Responsibility from the Perspective of the Mennonite
Church*. Elkhart, IN: Institute of Mennonite Studies, 1989.

Burkholder, John Richard, and Calvin Redekop, eds. *Kingdom, Cross, and Community: Essays on Mennonite Themes in Honor of Guy F. Hershberger.* Scottdale, PA: Herald Press, 1976.

Campbell, Peter. 'The Cult of Spontaneity: Finnish-Canadian Bushworkers and the Industrial Workers of the World in Northern Ontario, 1919–1934,' *Labour/Le Travail* 41 (1998): 117–46.

Cash, Martin. 'Palliser Jobs Ebb in Face of Chinese Challenge.' *Winnipeg Free Press* (5 September 2003): B4.

Cash, Martin, with Wendy Stephenson and Judy Waytiuk. *Winnipeg: A Prairie Portrait.* Montgomery, AL: Community Communications, 1998.

Chandler, Alfred Dupont, Jr. 'Luck and the Shaping of a Historian's Professional Education.' *The Massachusetts Historical Review* 6 (2004): 1–10.

– *The Visible Hand: The Managerial Revolution in American Business.* Cambridge, MA: Harvard Belknap, 1977.

Checole, Alemu, with Samuel Asefa, Bekithemba Dube, Doris Dube, Michael Kodzo Badasu, Erik Kumedisa, Barbara Nkala, I.U. Nsasak, Siaka Traore, and Pakisa Tshimika. *A Global Mennonite History: Africa.* Kitchener, ON, Scottdale, PA, and Waterloo, ON: Pandora Press and Herald Press, 2003.

Clark, Peter, and Michael Rowlinson. 'The Treatment of History in Organisation Studies: Towards an "Historic Turn"?' *Business History* 46, no. 3 (July 2004): 331–52.

Coates, Ken, and Fred McGuinness. *The Keystone Province: An Illustrated History of Manitoba Enterprise.* Burlington, ON: Windsor Publications, 1988.

Cochran, Thomas C. *Challenges to American Values: Society, Business, and Religion.* New York and Oxford: Oxford University Press, 1985.

Conzen, Kathleen Neils, David A. Gerber, Ewa Morawska, George E. Pozzetta, and Rudolph J. Vecoli. 'The Invention of Ethnicity: A Perspective from the U.S.A.' *Journal of American Ethnic History* 12, no. 1 (Fall 1992): 3–41.

Cuff, Robert D. 'Notes for a Panel on Entrepreneurship in Business History.' *Business History Review* 76, no. 1 (Spring 2002): 123–32.

Davis, Angela E. 'Business, Art and Labour: Brigden's and the Growth of the Canadian Graphic Arts Industry 1870–1950.' PhD diss., University of Manitoba, 1986.

DeFehr, C.A. *Memories of My Life Recalled for My Family.* Altona, MB: D.W. Friesen & Sons for C.A. DeFehr, 1967.

Dewalt, Bryan. *Technology and Canadian Printing: A History from Lead Type to Lasers*. Transformation Series. Ottawa: National Museum of Science and Technology, 1995.

Douloff, Don. 'A Family Affair.' *Canada's Furniture Magazine* (July/August 1989): 60.

Driedger, Leo. 'Canadian Mennonite Urbanism: Ethnic Villages or Metropolitan Remnant?' *Mennonite Quarterly Review* 49 (1975): 226–41.

– 'Mennonite Business in Winnipeg.' In *Anabaptist/Mennonite Faith and Economics*, ed. Calvin Redekop, Victor A. Krahn, and Samuel J. Steiner. Lanham, MD: Institute of Anabaptist and Mennonite Studies and University Press of America, 1994.

– *Mennonites in the Global Village*. Toronto: University of Toronto Press, 2000.

– *Mennonites in Winnipeg*. Winnipeg, MB: Kindred Press, 1990.

– 'Post-War Canadian Mennonites: From Rural to Urban Dominance.' *Journal of Mennonite Studies* 6 (1988): 70–88.

Driedger, Mary Lou. 'From Generation to Generation: The Loewen Brothers Pick Up the Challenge.' *Mennonite Mirror* (June 1988): 5.

Dueck, Abe. 'Canadian Mennonites and the Anabaptist Vision.' *Journal of Mennonite Studies* 13 (1995): 71–88.

Dyck, Bruno. 'Half a Century of Canadian Mennonite Bible College: A Brief Organizational History.' *Journal of Mennonite Studies* 11 (1993): 194–223.

Dyck, Cornelius J., and Dennis D. Martin, eds. *The Mennonite Encyclopedia: A Comprehensive Reference Work on the Anabaptist-Mennonite Movement.* Vol. 5. Scottdale, PA: Herald Press, 1990.

Dyck, Karen. 'The Invisible Labour of Survival: The Contributions of Mennonite Women to Their Family Businesses in North Kildonan, Winnipeg, 1930–1960.' Unpublished paper, March 2001.

Engels, Friedrich. 'Socialism: Utopian and Scientific.' In *The Marx-Engels Reader*, 2nd ed., ed. Robert C. Tucker. New York: W.W. Norton & Company, 1978.

Enns, Mary M. *Mia: The Story of a Remarkable Woman*. Winnipeg, MB: A.A. DeFehr Trust, 1982.

Ens, Adolf. *Becoming a National Church: A History of the Conference of Mennonites in Canada*. Winnipeg, MB: CMU Press, 2004.

Epp, Frank H. 'D.W. Friesen and His Life Work.' *Mennonite Life* (July 1956): 118.

– *Mennonites in Canada, 1920–1940: A People's Struggle for Survival.* Toronto: Macmillan, 1982.

Epp, Marlene. 'The Mennonite Girls' Homes of Winnipeg: A Home Away from Home.' *Journal of Mennonite Studies* 6 (1988): 100–14.

– *Women without Men: Mennonite Refugees of the Second World War*. Toronto: University of Toronto Press, 2000.

Epp-Tiessen, Esther. *Altona: The Story of a Prairie Town*. Altona, MB: D.W. Friesen & Sons, 1982.

Esau, Alvin J. *The Courts and the Colonies: The Litigation of Hutterite Church Disputes*. Vancouver: University of Brtish Columbia Press, 2004.

Esau Klippenstein, Frieda. '"Doing What We Could": Mennonite Domestic Servants in Winnipeg, 1920s to 1930s,' *Journal of Mennonite Studies* 6 (1988): 145–66.

– 'Scattered but Not Lost: Mennonite Domestic Servants in Winnipeg, 1920s–50s.' In *Telling Tales: Essays in Western Women's History*, ed. Catherine A. Cavanaugh and Randi R. Warne. Vancouver: University of British Columbia Press, 2000.

Fogel, Robert William, and Stanley L. Engerman, eds. *The Reinterpretation of American Economic History*. New York: Harper & Row, 1971.

Fox, Richard Wightman. 'Experience and Explanation in Twentieth-Century American Religious History.' In *New Directions in American Religious History*, ed. Harry S. Stout and D.G. Hart. New York and Oxford: Oxford University Press, 1997.

Frager, Ruth A. *Sweatshop Strife: Class, Ethnicity, and Gender in the Jewish Labour Movement of Toronto, 1900–1939*. Toronto: University of Toronto Press, 1992.

Freund, Alexander, and Laura Quilici. 'Exploring Myths in Women's Narratives: Italian and German Immigrant Women in Vancouver, 1947–1961.' *B.C. Studies* 105–6 (Spring/Summer 1995): 159–82.

Friesen, Duane K. 'An Anabaptist Theology of Culture for a New Century.' *Conrad Grebel Review* 13, no. 1 (Winter 1995): 33–53.

Friesen, Joe. '"It's Not That the Tories Are Closer to God, They're Furthest From the Devil": Politics and Mennonites in Winnipeg, 1945–1999.' *Journal of Mennonite Studies* 21 (2003): 175–90.

Friesen, John J. *Building Communities: The Changing Face of Manitoba Mennonites*. Winnipeg, MB: CMU Press, 2007.

– 'Manitoba Mennonites in the Rural-Urban Shift.' *Mennonite Life* 23, no. 4 (October 1968): 152–8.

Friesens Corporation. *D.W. Friesen 1990 Staff Book*. Altona, MB: D.W. Friesen, 1990.

– *D.W. Friesen and Sons Ltd. Seventy-Fifth Anniversary, 1907–1982*. Altona: D.W. Friesen, 1982.
– *Publishing Your Own Book: A Guide for the First-Time Publisher*. Altona, MB: Friesen Printers, 1982 and 1992.
Friesen, T.E. *A History of D.W. Friesen: A Unique Company, 1907–1993*. Altona, MB: D.W. Friesen, 1993.
– 'Philosophy, Policy and Practices.' Unpublished manuscript, draft copy, n.d.
Frisch, Michael. 'Oral History and *Hard Times*: A Review Essay.' In *The Oral History Reader*, ed. Robert Perks and Alistair Thomson. London: Routledge, 1998.
Funk, Peter. 'A Brief History of Altona.' Unpublished paper, 17 July 1950.
Gans, Herbert. 'Symbolic Ethnicity: The Future of Ethnic Groups and Cultures in America.' *Ethnic and Racial Studies* 2, no. 1 (January 1979): 1–20.
– 'Symbolic Ethnicity and Symbolic Religiosity: Towards a Comparison of Ethnic and Religious Acculturation.' *Ethnic and Racial Studies* 17, no. 4 (October 1994): 577–92.
Garrett, Clarke. 'Popular Religion and the Laboring Classes in Nineteenth-Century Europe.' *International Labor and Working-Class History* 34 (Fall 1988): 86–91.
Geertz, Clifford. 'Deep Play: Notes on the Balinese Cockfight.' In *The Interpretation of Cultures: Selected Essays*. New York: Basic Books, 1973.
– 'Thick Description: Toward an Interpretive Theory of Culture.' In *The Interpretation of Cultures: Selected Essays*. New York: Basic Books, 1973.
Gerbrandt, Henry J. *Adventure in Faith: The Background in Europe and the Development in Canada of the Bergthaler Mennonite Church of Manitoba*. Altona, MB: Bergthaler Mennonite Church of Manitoba, 1970.
– *Postscript to Adventure in Faith*. Winnipeg, MB: Canadian Mennonite Bible College, 1986.
Giebel, Gregory. 'Alienation from Freedom: The Effect of the Loss of Union Power upon the Relationship between Technology and Work.' PhD diss., Pennsylvania State University, 1980.
Gramsci, Antonio. *Prison Notebooks*. Vol. 2. Edited and translated by Joseph A. Buttigieg. New York: Columbia University Press, 1975.
Grant, Hugh, and Michael Rosenstock. 'Do Mennonites Earn Less than Other Canadians? The Role of Religion in the Determination of Income.' *Journal of Mennonite Studies* 24 (2006): 73–92.
Griffith, R. Marie. 'Submissive Wives, Wounded Daughters, and Female Sol-

diers: Prayer and Christian Womanhood in Women's Aglow Fellowship.'
In *Lived Religion in America: Toward a History of Practice*, ed. David D.
Hall. Princeton, NJ: Princeton University Press, 1997.

Grimsrud, Ted. 'Yoder, John Howard: A Faithful Teacher in the Church.' *The
Mennonite* 1, no. 3 (3 March 1998): 8–9.

Gross, Leonard. 'The Locus of Mennonite Spiritual Intelligence: The Anabaptist Vision as Confession.' *Conrad Grebel Review* 12, no. 3 (Fall 1994):
271–82.

Hackett, David G., Laurie F. Maffly-Kipp, R. Laurence Moore, and Leslie
Woodcock Tentler. 'Forum: American Religion and Class.' *Religion and
American Culture* 15, no. 1 (Winter 2005): 1–29.

Halbwachs, Maurice. *On Collective Memory*. Edited and translated by Lewis
A. Coser. Chicago: University of Chicago Press, 1992.

Hall, David D., ed. *Lived Religion in America: Toward a History of Practice*.
Princeton, NJ: Princeton University Press, 1997.

Harder, Lydia Neufeld. *Obedience, Suspicion, and the Gospel of Mark: A
Mennonite-Feminist Exploration of Biblical Authority*. Waterloo, ON:
Wilfrid Laurier University Press, 1998.

– 'Power and Authority in Mennonite Theological Development.' In *Power,
Authority and the Anabaptist Tradition*, ed. Calvin Redekop and Benjamin
Redekop. Baltimore, MD: Johns Hopkins University Press, 2001.

Harris, Al, ed. *The History of Trucking in Manitoba: 1900–1997*. Winnipeg,
MB: Manitoba Trucking Association, 1997.

Hauerwas, Stanley. *The Peaceable Kingdom: A Primer in Christian Ethics*.
Notre Dame, IN: University of Notre Dame Press, 1983.

Hawaleshka, Danylo. 'Mennonite Millionaires.' *Maclean's* 115, no. 2 (14
January 2002): 22.

Herberg, Will. *Protestant – Catholic – Jew: An Essay in American Religious
Sociology*. Rev. ed. Garden City, NY: Doubleday/Anchor Books, 1960.

Heron, Craig. *The Canadian Labour Movement: A Short History*. 2nd ed. Toronto: James Lorimer, 1996.

Heron, Craig, and Robert Storey. 'Work and Struggle in the Canadian Steel
Industry, 1900–1950.' In *The Development of Canadian Capitalism: Essays
in Business History*, ed. Douglas McCalla. Toronto: Copp Clark Pitman,
1990.

Heron, Craig, and Robert Storey, eds. *On the Job: Confronting the Labour
Process in Canada*. Kingston and Montreal: McGill-Queen's University
Press, 1986.

Hershberger, Guy F. 'Nonresistance and Industrial Conflict.' *Mennonite Quarterly Review* 13, no. 2 (April 1939): 135–54.

– *The Way of the Cross in Human Relations*. Scottdale, PA: Herald Press, 1958.

Hobsbawm, Eric. *The Age of Extremes: The Short Twentieth Century, 1914–1991*. London: Abacus, 1994.

Hofstede, Geert. 'The Cultural Relativity of Organizational Practices and Theories.' *Journal of International Business Studies* 14, no. 2 (Fall 1983): 75–89.

Huebner, Chris K. *A Precarious Peace: Yoderian Explorations on Theology, Knowledge, and Identity*. Waterloo, ON: Herald Press, 2006.

Iacovetta, Franca. *Such Hardworking People: Italian Immigrants in Postwar Toronto*. Montreal: McGill-Queen's University Press, 1992.

James, Gary E. 'Palliser purchases former LADD plant.' *Furniture/Today* (13 May 1991): 4.

John, Richard R. 'Elaborations, Revisions, Dissents: Alfred D. Chandler, Jr.'s, "The Visible Hand" after Twenty Years.' *The Business History Review* 71, no. 2 (Summer 1997): 151–200.

Johnson, Paul E. *A Shopkeeper's Millennium: Society and Revivals in Rochester, New York, 1815–1837*. New York: Hill and Wang, 1978.

Johnson, Perry L. *ISO 9000: Meeting the New International Standards*. New York: McGraw-Hill, 1993.

Joyce, Patrick. *Work, Society, and Politics: The Culture of the Factory in Later Victorian England*. New Jersey: Rutgers University Press, 1980.

Kauffman, J. Howard, and Leo Driedger. *The Mennonite Mosaic: Identity and Modernization*. Scottdale, PA: Herald Press, 1991.

Kauffman, J. Howard, and Leland Harder. *Anabaptists Four Centuries Later: A Profile of Five Mennonite and Brethren in Christ Denominations*. Scottdale, PA: Herald Press, 1975.

Kaufman, Gordon D. 'Are Traditional Mennonite Approaches Adequate?' In *Perils of Professionalism: Essays on Christian Faith and Professionalism*. Scottdale, PA: Herald Press, 1982.

Kealey, Gregory S. 'Work Control, the Labour Process, and Nineteenth-Century Canadian Printers.' In *On the Job: Confronting the Labour Process in Canada*, ed. Craig Heron and Robert Storey. Kingston and Montreal: McGill-Queen's University Press, 1986.

Kee, Kevin Bradley. *Revivalists: Marketing the Gospel in English Canada, 1884–1957*. Montreal: McGill-Queen's University Press, 2006.

Keim, Al. 'The Anabaptist Vision: The History of a New Paradigm.' *Conrad Grebel Review* 12, no. 3 (Fall 1994): 239–55.

Kelber, Harry, and Carl Schlesinger. *Union Printers and Controlled Automation.* New York: Free Press, 1967.

Kirbyson, Geoff. 'Pride in Ownership Fuels Firm.' *Winnipeg Free Press* (17 August 2002): B3.

Klaassen, Walter. '"They Were Giants on Earth in Those Days": Harold S. Bender and the Anabaptist Vision.' *Conrad Grebel Review* 12, no. 3 (Fall 1994): 233–7.

Klassen, Henry C. *A Business History of Alberta.* Calgary, AB: University of Calgary Press, 1999.

Klassen, Peter James. *The Economics of Anabaptism, 1525–1560.* The Hague: Mouton, 1964.

K'Meyer, Tracy E. '"I Just Felt Called…": Oral History and the Meaning of Faith in American Religious History.' *The Journal of American History* 86, no. 2 (September 1999): 724–33.

Knell, Michael J. 'Palliser Selling Off Eight-Unit Retail Chain.' *Furniture/ Today* (29 April 1996): 46.

Krahn, Cornelius, Melvin Gingerich, and Orlando Harms, eds. *The Mennonite Encyclopedia: A Comprehensive Reference Work on the Anabaptist-Mennonite Movement.* Vols. 1–4. Hillsboro, KS: Mennonite Brethren Publishing House, 1956.

Kraus, C. Norman. 'An Anabaptist Spirituality for the Twenty-First Century.' *Conrad Grebel Review* 13, no. 1 (Winter 1995): 23–32.

Laird, Pamela Walker. 'Introduction: Putting Social Capital to Work.' *Business History* 50, no. 6 (November 2008): 685–94.

Lazerow, Jama. *Religion and the Working Class in Antebellum America.* Washington: Smithsonian Institution Press, 1995.

Lipartito, Kenneth. 'Culture and the Practice of Business History.' *Business and Economic History* 24, no. 2 (Winter 1995): 1–41.

Livingston, James. 'The Social Analysis of Economic History and Theory: Conjectures on Late Nineteenth-Century American Development.' *American Historical Review* 92, no. 1 (February 1987): 65–95.

Loewen, Melvin J. *The Descendants of Cornelius W. Loewen (1827–1893) and Helena Bartel (1833–1876).* Steinbach, MB, and Goshen, IN: Heritage Classics, 1994.

Loewen, Royden K. 'Cars, Commerce, Church: Religious Conflict in Steinbach, Manitoba, 1905–1930.' *Journal of Mennonite Studies* 11 (1993): 111–35.

– *Diaspora in the Countryside: Two Mennonite Communities and Mid-Twentieth-Century Rural Disjuncture.* Urbana: University of Illinois Press, 2006.

- *Family, Church, and Market: A Mennonite Community in the Old and the New Worlds, 1850–1930*. Toronto: University of Toronto Press, 1993.

Long, Richard J. 'The Incidence and Nature of Employee Profit Sharing and Share Ownership in Canada.' *Relations Industrielles* 47, no. 3 (1992): 463–86.

Long, Sheila. 'DeFehr Buys Palliser Leather Divisions.' *Furniture/Today* (27 January 1995): 2.

Love, Myron. 'Major Furniture Firm Born in Barn.' *Manitoba Business* (August 1984): 30.

Lucas, Rex A. *Minetown, Milltown, Railtown: Life in Canadian Communities of Single Industry*. Toronto: University of Toronto Press, 1971.

Mandell, Nikki. *The Corporation as Family: The Gendering of Corporate Welfare, 1890–1930*. Chapel Hill: University of North Carolina Press, 2002.

Manitoba Business Journal. 'A Master Plan of Mass Production: DeFehr Furniture.' April/May 1968, 20.

Marchand, Roland. *Creating the Corporate Soul: The Rise of Public Relations and Corporate Imagery in American Big Business*. Berkeley: University of California Press, 1998.

Marks, Lynne. 'Heroes and Hallelujahs – Labour History and the Social History of Religion in English Canada: A Response to Bryan Palmer.' *Histoire Sociale/Social History* 34, no. 67 (May 2001): 169–86.

- *Revivals and Roller Rinks: Religion, Leisure, and Identity in Late Nineteenth-Century Small-Town Ontario*. Toronto: University of Toronto Press, 1996.

Marsden, George M. *Fundamentalism and American Culture: The Shaping of Twentieth-Century Evangelicalism, 1870–1925*. New York: Oxford University Press, 1980.

Marshall, David B. 'Canadian Historians, Secularization, and the Problem of the Nineteenth Century.' *Canadian Catholic Historical Association Historical Studies* 60 (1993–4): 57–81.

- *Secularizing the Faith: Canadian Protestant Clergy and the Crisis of Belief, 1850–1940*. Toronto: University of Toronto Press, 1992.

Martin, David. *A General Theory of Secularization*. Oxford: Blackwell, 1978.

Masters, D.C. *The Winnipeg General Strike*. Toronto: University of Toronto Press, 1950.

McAllister, James A. *The Government of Edward Schreyer: Democratic Socialism in Manitoba*. Kingston and Montreal: McGill-Queen's University Press, 1984.

McArthur, Keith. 'Our Father, Who Art ... at Work.' *Winnipeg Free Press* (4 September 1998): A1.

McCalla, Douglas, ed. *The Development of Canadian Capitalism: Essays in Business History*. Toronto: Copp Clark Pitman, 1990.

McDannell, Colleen. *Material Christianity: Religion and Popular Culture in America*. New Haven, CT: Yale University Press, 1995.

McGuinness, Fred. *Friesens: A Unique Company*. Altona, MB: Friesens Corporation, 2001.

McGuire, John, and Carole Swan. 'Structure of Manufacturing in Manitoba: A Comparative Analysis.' In *Manufacturing Rationalization Trends in Manitoba*. Winnipeg: Manitoba Economic Development Advisory Board, 1976.

McMurtry, John. *The Structure of Marx's World-View*. Princeton, NJ: Princeton University Press, 1978.

McNaught, Kenneth. *The Winnipeg Strike, 1919*. Don Mills, ON: Longman Canada, 1974.

McNeill, Murray. 'DeFehr Empire Has Humble Roots: Palliser Furniture Began in Founder's Home.' Canadian Manufacturers and Exporters, 21 August 2004.

Mennonite Church. *Confession of Faith in a Mennonite Perspective*. Scottdale, PA: Herald Press, 1995.

Mennonite Industry and Business Associates (MIBA). 'Report on Management/Labor Relations.' *The Marketplace* (March 1980): 9–12.

Miller, Michael B. *The Bon Marché: Bourgeois Culture and the Department Stores, 1869–1920*. Princeton, NJ: Princeton University Press, 1981.

Mills, Rachel. 'Gender, Ethnicity, and Religion in the Context of Entrepreneurship: The Loewen Lumber Businessmen of Steinbach, Manitoba, 1877–1985.' MA thesis, University of Winnipeg/University of Manitoba, 2003.

Mitchell, Tom. '"Legal Gentlemen Appointed by the Federal Government": The Canadian State, the Citizens' Committee of 1000, and Winnipeg's Seditious Conspiracy Trials of 1919–1920.' *Labour/Le Travail* 53 (Spring 2004): 9–46.

Moody, Kim. *Workers in a Lean World: Unions in the International Economy*. London: Verso, 1997.

Moore, Dorothy E. and James H. Morrison, eds. *Work, Ethnicity, and Oral History*. Issues in Ethnicity and Multiculturalism 1. Halifax, NS: International Education Centre, 1988.

Morton, Desmond. 'Some Millennial Reflections on the State of Canadian Labour History.' *Labour/Le Travail* 46 (Fall 2000): 11–36.

Murphy, Teresa Ann. *Ten Hours' Labor: Religion, Reform, and Gender in Early New England*. Ithaca, NY: Cornell University Press, 1992.

Mysyk, Avis. *Manitoba Commercial Market Gardening, 1945–1997: Class, Race, and Ethnic Relations*. Regina, SK: Canadian Plains Research Center, University of Regina, 2000.

Nafziger, Estel Wayne. 'The Mennonite Ethic and Weber's Thesis.' In *Entrepreneurship, Equity, and Economic Development*. Greenwich: JAI Press, 1986.

Nickel, J.W. 'The Canadian Conscientious Objector.' *Mennonite Life* (January 1948): 24–8.

Niebuhr, H. Richard. *The Social Sources of Denominationalism*. New York: New American Library, 1929.

Niebuhr, Reinhold. *Moral Man and Immoral Society*. New York: Charles Scribner and Sons, 1932.

– 'Must We Do Nothing?' United Church of Christ Theology. http://www.ucc.org/beliefs/theology/must-we-do-nothing.html (retrieved 8 March 2010).

Nisly, Hope. 'A Mennonite Woman in "Thanksgiving Town": Edith Swartzendruber Nisly's Work Experience 1935–1941.' *Labor's Heritage* 3, no. 1 (January 1991): 26–53.

Orsi, Robert A. 'Everyday Miracles: The Study of Lived Religion.' In *Lived Religion in America: Toward a History of Practice*, ed. David D. Hall. Princeton, NJ: Princeton University Press, 1997.

– 'Is the Study of Lived Religion Irrelevant to the World We Live In? Special Presidential Plenary Address, Society for the Scientific Study of Religion, Salt Lake City, November 2, 2002.' *Journal for the Scientific Study of Religion* 42, no. 2 (2003): 169–74.

– *The Madonna of 115th Street: Faith and Community in Italian Harlem, 1880–1950*. New Haven, CT: Yale University Press, 1985.

– *Thank You, St. Jude: Women's Devotion to the Patron Saint of Hopeless Causes*. New Haven, CT: Yale University Press, 1996.

Parr, Joy. *The Gender of Breadwinners: Women, Men, and Change in Two Industrial Towns, 1880–1950*. Toronto: University of Toronto Press, 1990.

Pasture, Patrick. 'The Role of Religion in Social and Labour History.' In *Class and Other Identities: Gender, Religion and Ethnicity in the Writing of European Labour History*, ed. Lex Heerma van Voss and Marcel van der Linden. New York: Berghahn Books, 2002.

Peachey, Urbane, ed. *Mennonite Statements on Peace and Social Concerns, 1900–1978*. Akron, PA: Mennonite Central Committee, U.S. Peace Section, 1980.

Penner, P.V. 'Unworthy Strikes.' *Red River Valley Echo* (26 April 1972): 4.

Phillips, Judy. 'Never on Sunday: Palliser Showroom Stays Dark One Day of Market,' *High Point Enterprise* (10 April 1992).

Phillips, Paul. 'Spinning a Web of Rules: Labour Legislation in Manitoba.' In *Hard Bargains: The Manitoba Labour Movement Confronts the 1990s*, ed. Errol Black and Jim Silver. Winnipeg, MB: Manitoba Labour Education Centre, n.d.

Portelli, Alessandro. *The Battle of Valle Giulia: Oral History and the Art of Dialogue*. Madison: University of Wisconsin Press, 1997.

– *The Death of Luigi Trastulli and Other Stories: Form and Meaning in Oral History*. Albany: State University of New York Press, 1991.

Quiring, David M. *The Mennonite Old Colony Vision: Under Siege in Mexico and the Canadian Connection*. Steinbach, MB: Crossway Publications, 2003.

Rea, J.E. *The Winnipeg General Strike*. Toronto: Holt, Rinehart and Winston, 1973.

Redding, Gordon. 'The Thick Description and Comparison of Societal Systems of Capitalism.' *Journal of International Business Studies* 36, no. 2 (March 2005): 123–55.

Redekop, Calvin. 'The Mennonite Identity Crisis.' *Journal of Mennonite Studies* 2 (1984): 87–103.

Redekop, Calvin, Stephen C. Ainlay, and Robert Siemens. *Mennonite Entrepreneurs*. Baltimore, MD: Johns Hopkins University Press, 1995.

Redekop, Calvin, Victor A. Krahn, and Samuel J. Steiner, eds. *Anabaptist/Mennonite Faith and Economics*. Lanham, MD: University Press of America/Institute of Anabaptist and Mennonite Studies, 1994.

Redekop, Calvin, and Benjamin W. Redekop, eds. *Entrepreneurs in the Faith Community: Profiles of Mennonites in Business*. Scottdale, PA: Herald Press, 1996.

Redekop, Calvin, and Benjamin W. Redekop, eds. *Power, Authority and the Anabaptist Tradition*. Baltimore, MD: Johns Hopkins University Press, 2001.

Redekop, Calvin, and Samuel J. Steiner, eds. *Mennonite Identity: Historical and Contemporary Perspectives*. Lanham, MD: University Press of America for the Institute for Anabaptist and Mennonite Studies, 1988.

Redekop, John. 'Decades of Transition: North American Mennonite Brethren in Politics.' In *Bridging Troubled Waters: The Mennonite Brethren at Mid-Twentieth Century*, ed. Paul Toews. Winnipeg, MB: Kindred Productions, 1995.

Regehr, T.D. 'From Agriculture to Big Business: Canadian-Mennonite Entrepreneurs after 1940.' *Journal of Mennonite Studies* 6 (1988): 60–9.

– 'The Influence of World War II on Mennonites in Canada.' *Journal of Mennonite Studies* 5 (1987): 73–89.

– *Mennonites in Canada, 1939–1970: A People Transformed.* Toronto: University of Toronto Press, 1996.

Reimer, Ellie. 'Friesen CEO Outlines Formula for Success in Global Marketplace.' *Winkler Times* (28 October 1996): 6.

Rempel-Burkholder, Byron. 'A Little United Nations on the Shop Floor.' *The Marketplace* 23, no. 5 (September/October 1993): 4.

Rempel, Elfrieda. 'An Examination of Where and How Winnipeg Mennonites Earn Their Living.' *Mennonite Mirror* 10, no. 7 (March 1981): 7–8.

– 'Mennonites and the Jobs They Take Up,' *Mennonite Mirror* 10, no. 8 (April 1981): 7–8.

– 'Mennonites Better Represented in the "Status" Jobs,' *Mennonite Mirror* 10, no. 9 (May 1981): 25–6.

Sangster, Joan. *Earning Respect: The Lives of Working Women in Small-Town Ontario, 1920–1960.* Toronto: University of Toronto Press, 1995.

– 'The Softball Solution: Female Workers, Male Managers, and the Operation of Paternalism at Westclox, 1923–60,' *Labour/Le Travail* 32 (Fall 1993): 167–99.

Sawatsky, Harry Leonard. *They Sought a Country: Mennonite Colonization in Mexico.* Berkeley: University of California Press, 1971.

Sawatsky, Rodney J., and Scott Holland, eds. *The Limits of Perfection: A Conversation with J. Lawrence Burkholder.* Waterloo, ON: Institute of Anabaptist and Mennonite Studies, 1993.

Schlabach, Theron F. 'To Focus a Mennonite Vision.' In *Kingdom, Cross and Community: Essays on Mennonite Themes in Honor of Guy F. Hershberger.* Scottdale, PA: Herald Press, 1976.

– *War, Peace, and Social Conscience: Guy F. Hershberger and Mennonite Ethics.* Waterloo, ON, and Scottdale, PA: Herald Press, 2009.

Schrag, Menno. 'H.P. Krehbiel: As I Remember Him.' *Mennonite Life* 40, no. 2 (June 1985): 7–9.

Schroeder, William. *The Bergthal Colony.* Rev. ed. Bergthal Historical Series. Winnipeg: Canadian Mennonite Bible College, 1986.

Schroeder, William, and Helmut T. Huebert. *Mennonite Historical Atlas*. Winnipeg, MB: Springfield Publishers, 1990.

Sinclair, Gordon, Jr. 'Printer's Story Real Page-Turner.' *Winnipeg Free Press* (30 March 1997): A1.

Sklar, Martin J. *The Corporate Reconstruction of American Capitalism, 1890–1916: The Market, the Law, and Politics*. Cambridge: Cambridge University Press, 1988.

Sollors, Werner. Introduction to *The Invention of Ethnicity*. New York: Oxford University Press, 1989.

Sprague, D.N. *Post-Confederation Canada: The Structure of Canadian History since Confederation*. Scarborough, ON: Prentice-Hall Canada, 1990.

Sprunger, Mary. 'Dutch Mennonites and the Golden Age Economy: The Problem of Social Disparity in the Church.' In Redekop et al., *Anabaptist/Mennonite Faith and Economics*.

– 'Rich Mennonites, Poor Mennonites: Economics and Theology in the Amsterdam Waterlander Congregation during the Golden Age.' PhD thesis, University of Illinois (Urbana-Champaign), 1993.

Stackhouse, John G. Jr. 'The Protestant Experience in Canada Since 1945.' In *The Canadian Protestant Experience, 1760–1990*, ed. George A. Rawlyk. Montreal: McGill-Queen's University Press, 1990.

Stayer, James. *Anabaptism and the Sword*. Lawrence, KA: Coronado Press, 1976.

Stayer, James M., Werner Packull, and Klaus Deppermann. 'From Monogenesis to Polygenesis: The Historical Discussion of Anabaptist Origins.' *Mennonite Quarterly Review* 49 (1975): 83–121.

Steinbach Carillon. 'Company Announces Profit-Sharing Payout.' 18 February 2002, 14A.

– 'Labor, Management, Meeting at Steinbach.' 21 January 1976, 1:1.

– 'Labor-Seminar Speaker: "Christians May Have to Pay High Price."' 4 February 1976, 1:1.

– 'Mennonites Struggle with Union Membership Issue.' 26 November 1975, 2:1.

Steinbach Carillon News. 'The Loewen Millwork Plant Is Western Canada's Largest.' 30 June 1961, 1.

– 'Serving Each New Generation: C.T. Loewen & Sons Ltd., Steinbach, Our 50th Anniversary, 1955.' Advertisement, 20 April 1955, 44–5.

– 'A Tour of the Loewen Plant.' 30 June 1961, 1.

Stinson, Lloyd. *Political Warriors: Recollections of a Social Democrat*. Winnipeg, MB: Queenston House Publishing, 1975.

Stoesz, Edgar. *Like a Mustard Seed: Mennonites in Paraguay*. Scottdale, PA: Herald Press, 2008.

Stoesz, Edgar, and Muriel T. Stackley. *Garden in the Wilderness: Mennonite Communities in the Paraguayan Chaco, 1927–1997*. Winnipeg, MB: Canadian Mennonite Bible College, 1999.

Stone, Daniel, ed. *Jewish Radicalism in Winnipeg, 1905–1960*. Winnipeg, MB: Jewish Heritage Centre of Western Canada, 2002.

Stout, Harry S., and Robert M. Taylor, Jr. 'Studies of Religion in American Society: The State of the Art.' In *New Directions in American Religious History*, ed. Harry S. Stout and D.G. Hart. New York and Oxford: Oxford University Press, 1997.

Strong-Boag, Veronica. 'Home Dreams: Women and the Suburban Experiment in Canada, 1945–1960.' In *Readings in Canadian History: Post-Confederation*, 6th ed., ed. R. Douglas Francis and Donald B. Smith. Toronto: Nelson Thomson Learning, 2002.

Taves, Ann. *Fits, Trances, and Visions: Experiencing Religion and Explaining Experience from Wesley to James*. Princeton, NJ: Princeton University Press, 1999.

Thiessen, Janis. 'Business and Labour Relations at Friesens Corporation.' *Journal of Mennonite Studies* 16 (1998): 181–202.

– 'Friesens Corporation: Printers in Mennonite Manitoba, 1951–1995.' MA thesis, University of Winnipeg/University of Manitoba, 1997.

– 'Mennonite Business in Town and City: Friesens Corporation of Altona and Palliser Furniture of Winnipeg.' *Mennonite Quarterly Review* 73, no. 3 (July 1999): 585–600.

Thompson, E.P. *The Making of the English Working Class*. London: Penguin, 1963.

Tilly, Charles. 'Citizenship, Identity and Social History.' *International Review of Social History* 40, supplement 3 (1995): 1–17.

Toews, Julius G., and Lawrence Klippenstein, eds. *Manitoba Mennonite Memories: A Century Past but Not Forgotten*. Altona: Manitoba Mennonite Centennial Committee, 1974.

Toews, Paul. *Mennonites in American Society, 1930–1970: Modernity and the Persistence of Religious Community*. Scottdale, PA: Herald Press, 1996.

Tone, Andrea. *The Business of Benevolence: Industrial Paternalism in Progressive America*. Ithaca, NY: Cornell University Press, 1997.

Tremaine, Marie, ed. *Canadian Book of Printing: How Printing Came to Canada and the Story of the Graphic Arts, Told Mainly in Pictures*. Toronto: Toronto Public Libraries, 1940.

Urry, James. *Mennonites, Politics, and Peoplehood: Europe – Russia – Canada, 1525 to 1980*. Winnipeg: University of Manitoba Press, 2006.

Visser, Jelle. 'Union Membership Statistics in 24 Countries.' *Monthly Labor Review* (January 2006): 38–49.

Vogt, Roy. 'Economic Questions and the Mennonite Conscience.' In *Call to Faithfulness: Essays in Canadian Mennonite Studies*, ed. Henry Poettcker and Rudy A. Regehr. Winnipeg, MB: Canadian Mennonite Bible College, 1972.

– 'Entrepreneurs, Labourers, Professionals, and Farmers: A Response to *Mennonites in Canada, A People Transformed.' Journal of Mennonite Studies* 15 (1997): 134–41.

– 'The Impact of Economic and Social Class on Mennonite Theology.' In *Mennonite Images: Historical, Cultural and Literary Essays Dealing with Mennonite Issues*, ed. Harry Loewen. Winnipeg, MB: Hyperion Press, 1980.

– 'Mennonite Attitudes to Property.' *Journal of Mennonite Studies* 10 (1992): 9–21.

– 'Mennonite Studies in Economics.' *Journal of Mennonite Studies* 1 (1983): 64–78.

– 'The Myth of the Anomalous Mennonite Entrepreneur: A Review of Recent Books on Economics.' *Journal of Mennonite Studies* 15 (1997): 228–33.

Vrijhof, Pieter Hendrik, and Jacques Waardenburg, eds. *Official and Popular Religion: Analysis of a Theme for Religious Studies*. The Hague: Mouton, 1979.

Walton, John K. 'New Directions in Business History: Themes, Approaches, and Opportunities.' *Business History* 52, no. 1 (February 2010): 1–16.

Weaver, J. Denny. 'The Socially Active Community: An Alternative Ecclesiology.' In *The Limits of Perfection: A Conversation with J. Lawrence Burkholder*. Waterloo, ON: Institute of Anabaptist and Mennonite Studies, 1993.

Weaver, Laura. 'A Mennonite "Hard Worker" Moves from the Working Class and the Religious/Ethnic Community to Academia: A Conflict between Two Definitions of Work.' In *Working-Class Women in the Academy: Laborers in the Knowledge Factory*, ed. Michelle Tokarczyk and Elizabeth A. Fay. Amherst: University of Massachusetts Press, 1993.

Weber, Max. *The Protestant Ethic and the Spirit of Capitalism*. Translated by Talcott Parsons. New York: Scribner, 1976.

Wells, Don. 'The Impact of the Postwar Compromise on Canadian Unionism: The Formation of an Auto Worker Local in the 1950s.' *Labour/Le Travail* 36 (Fall 1995): 147–73.

Welzer, Harold. 'Communicative Memory.' In *Cultural Memory Studies: An International and Interdisciplinary Handbook*, ed. Astrid Erll, Ansgar Nünning, and Sara B. Young. Berlin: Walter de Gruyter, 2008.

Werner, Hans. *Imagined Homes: Soviet German Immigrants in Two Cities*. Winnipeg: University of Manitoba Press, 2007.

Whittington, Richard. 'Introduction: Comparative Perspectives on the Managerial Revolution.' *Business History* 49, no. 4 (July 2007): 399–403.

Wiebe, Jeremy. 'A Different Kind of Station: Radio Southern Manitoba and the Reformulation of Mennonite Identity, 1957–1977.' MA thesis, University of Manitoba, 2008.

Williams, Peter W. *Popular Religion in America: Symbolic Change and the Modernization Process in Historical Perspective*. Englewood Cliffs, NJ: Prentice-Hall, 1980.

Winland, Daphne Naomi. 'The Quest for Mennonite Peoplehood: Ethno-Religious Identity and the Dilemma of Definitions.' *Canadian Review of Sociology & Anthropology* 30, no. 1 (February 1993): 110–38.

Winnipeg Defense Committee. *Winnipeg 1919: The Strikers' Own History of the Winnipeg General Strike*. Toronto: J. Lorimer, 1975.

Winson, Anthony, and Belinda Leach. *Contingent Work, Disrupted Lives: Labour and Community in the New Rural Economy*. Toronto: University of Toronto Press, 2002.

Wright, Gerald. *Steinbach: Is There Any Place Like It?* Steinbach: Derksen Printers, 1991.

Wuthnow, Robert. *The Restructuring of American Religion: Society and Faith Since World War II*. Princeton, NJ: Princeton University Press, 1990.

Yoder, John H. *The Politics of Jesus: Vicit Agnus Noster*. Grand Rapids, MI: Eerdmans, 1972.

Yoder, Nate. 'J. Gresham Machen: An Outside Influence on Harold S. Bender's Formulation of the Anabaptist Vision.' *Conrad Grebel Review* 12, no. 3 (Fall 1994): 257–70.

Yow, Valerie Raleigh. *Recording Oral History: A Guide for the Humanities and Social Sciences*. 2nd ed. Walnut Creek, CA: Altamira Press, 2005.

Zahavi, Gerald. *Workers, Managers, and Welfare Capitalism: The Shoeworkers and Tanners of Endicott Johnson, 1890–1950*. Urbana: University of Illinois Press, 1988.

Zunz, Oliver. *Making America Corporate, 1870-1920*. Chicago: University of Chicago Press, 1990.

Index

THE CANADIAN SOCIAL HISTORY SERIES

Terry Copp,
The Anatomy of Poverty:
The Condition of the Working Class in
Montreal, 1897–1929, 1974.
ISBN 0-7710-2252-2

Alison Prentice,
The School Promoters: Education
and Social Class in Mid-Nineteenth
Century Upper Canada, 1977.
ISBN 0-7710-7181-7

John Herd Thompson,
The Harvests of War:
The Prairie West, 1914–1918, 1978.
ISBN 0-7710-8560-5

Joy Parr, Editor,
Childhood and Family in
Canadian History, 1982.
ISBN 0-7710-6938-3

Alison Prentice and
Susan Mann-Trofimenkoff, Editors,
The Neglected Majority:
Essays in Canadian Women's History,
Volume 2, 1985.
ISBN 0-7710-8583-4

Ruth Roach Pierson,
'They're Still Women After All':
The Second World War and
Canadian Womanhood, 1986.
ISBN 0-7710-6958-8

Bryan D. Palmer,
The Character of Class Struggle:
Essays in Canadian Working Class
History, 1850–1985, 1986.
ISBN 0-7710-6946-4

Alan Metcalfe,
Canada Learns to Play:
The Emergence of Organized Sport,
1807–1914, 1987.
ISBN 0-7710-5870-5

Marta Danylewycz,
Taking the Veil: An Alternative
to Marriage, Motherhood, and
Spinsterhood in Quebec,
1840–1920, 1987.
ISBN 0-7710-2550-5

Craig Heron,
Working in Steel: The Early Years in
Canada, 1883–1935, 1988.
ISBN 0-7710-4086-5

Wendy Mitchinson and
Janice Dickin McGinnis, Editors,
Essays in the History of Canadian
Medicine, 1988.
ISBN 0-7710-6063-7

Joan Sangster,
Dreams of Equality: Women on the
Canadian Left, 1920–1950, 1989.
ISBN 0-7710-7946-X

Angus McLaren,
Our Own Master Race: Eugenics
in Canada, 1885–1945, 1990.
ISBN 0-7710-5544-7

Bruno Ramirez,
On the Move:
French-Canadian and Italian Migrants
in the North Atlantic Economy, 1860–
1914, 1991.
ISBN 0-7710-7283-X

Mariana Valverde,
'The Age of Light, Soap and Water':
Moral Reform in English Canada,
1885–1925, 1991.
ISBN 978-0-8020-9595-4

Bettina Bradbury,
Working Families: Age, Gender, and
Daily Survival in Industrializing
Montreal, 1993.
ISBN 978-0-8020-8689-1

Andrée Lévesque,
Making and Breaking the Rules:
Women in Quebec, 1919–1939, 1994.
ISBN 0-7710-5283-9

Cecilia Danysk,
Hired Hands: Labour and
the Development of Prairie
Agriculture, 1880–
1930, 1995.
ISBN 0-7710-2552-1

Kathryn McPherson,
Bedside Matters: The Transformation
of Canadian Nursing, 1900–1990,
1996.
ISBN 978-0-8020-8679-2

Edith Burley,
Servants of the Honourable Company:
Work, Discipline, and Conflict in the
Hudson's Bay Company, 1770–1870,
1997.
ISBN 0-19-541296-6

Mercedes Steedman,
Angels of the Workplace: Women and
the Construction of Gender Relations
in the Canadian Clothing Industry,
1890–1940, 1997.
ISBN 0-19-54308-3

Angus McLaren and Arlene Tigar
McLaren, *The Bedroom and the State:*
The Changing Practices and Politics
of Contraception and Abortion in
Canada, 1880–1997, 1997.
ISBN 0-19-541318-0

Kathryn McPherson, Cecilia
Morgan, and Nancy M. Forestell,
Editors, *Gendered Pasts: Historical*
Essays in Feminity and Masculinity in
Canada, 1999.
ISBN 978-0-8020-8690-7

Gillian Creese,
Contracting Masculinity: Gender,
Class, and Race in a White-Collar
Union, 1944–1994, 1999.
ISBN 0-19-541454-3

Geoffrey Reaume,
Remembrance of Patients Past: Patient
Life at the Toronto Hospital for the
Insane, 1870–1940, 2000.
ISBN 0-19-541538-8

Miriam Wright,
A Fishery for Modern Times: The State
and the Industrialization of
the Newfoundland Fishery,
1934–1968, 2001.
ISBN 0-19-541620-1

Judy Fudge and Eric Tucker, *Labour*
before the Law: The Regulation of
Workers' Collective Action in Canada,
1900–1948, 2001.
ISBN 978-0-8020-3793-0

Mark Moss,
Manliness and Militarism: Educating
Young Boys in Ontario for War, 2001.
ISBN 0-19-541594-9

Joan Sangster,
Regulating Girls and Women:
Sexuality, Family, and the Law in
Ontario, 1920–1960, 2001.
ISBN 0-19-541663-5

Reinhold Kramer and Tom Mitchell,
Walk Towards the Gallows: The
Tragedy of Hilda Blake, Hanged 1899,
2002.
ISBN 978-0-8020-9542-8

Mark Kristmanson,
Plateaus of Freedom: Nationality,
Culture, and State Security in Canada,
1940–1960, 2002.
ISBN 0-19-541866-2

Robin Jarvis Brownlie,
A Fatherly Eye: Indian Agents,
Government Power, and Aboriginal
Resistance in Ontario, 1918–1939,
2003
ISBN 0-19-541891-3 (cloth)
ISBN 0-19-541784-4 (paper)

Steve Hewitt,
Riding to the Rescue: The
Transformation of the RCMP
in Alberta and Saskatchewan,
1914–1939, 2006.
ISBN 978-0-8020-9021-8 (cloth)
ISBN 978-0-8020-4895-0 (paper)

Robert K. Kristofferson,
Craft Capitalism: Craftsworkers and
Early Industrialization in Hamilton,
Ontario, 1840–1872, 2007.
ISBN 978-0-8020-9127-7 (cloth)
ISBN 978-0-8020-9408-7 (paper)

Andrew Parnaby,
Citizen Docker: Making a New Deal
on the Vancouver Waterfront, 1919–
1939, 2007
ISBN 978-0-8020-9056-0 (cloth)
ISBN 978-0-8020-9384-4 (paper)

J.I. Little,
Loyalties in Conflict: A Canadian
Borderland in War and Rebellion,
1812–1840, 2008
ISBN 978-0-8020-9773-6 (cloth)
ISBN 978-0-8020-9825-1 (paper)

Pauline Greenhill,
Make the Night Hideous:
Four English Canadian Charivaris,
1881–1940, 2010
ISBN 978-1-4426-4077-1 (cloth)
ISBN 978-1-4426-1015-6 (paper)

Rhonda L. Hinther and
Jim Mochoruk,
Re-imagining Ukrainian Canadians:
History, Politics, and Identity, 2010
ISBN 978-1-4426-4134-1 (cloth)
ISBN 978-1-4426-1062-0 (paper)

Lara Campbell, Dominique Clément,
and Gregory S. Kealey,
Debating Dissent: Canada and the
Sixties
ISBN 978-1-4426-4164-8 (cloth)
ISBN 978-1-4426-1078-1 (paper)

Janis Thiessen,
Manufacturing Mennonites:
Work and Religion in Post-War Manitoba
ISBN 978-1-4426-4213-3 (cloth)
ISBN 978-1-4426-1113-9 (paper)